D1542284

HM1 D. J. MORANO USNR-R TAR
Medical Department Representative

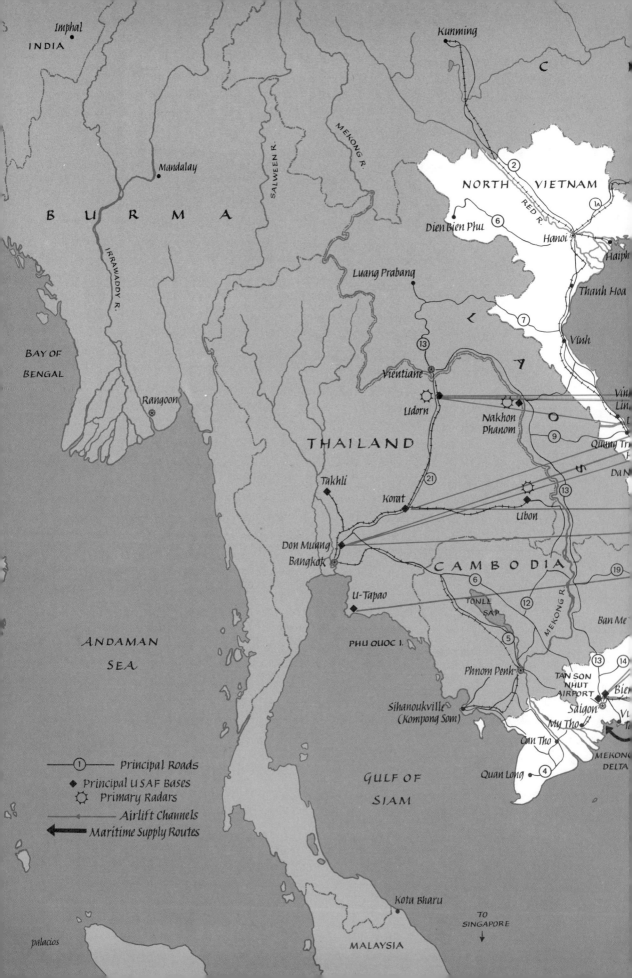

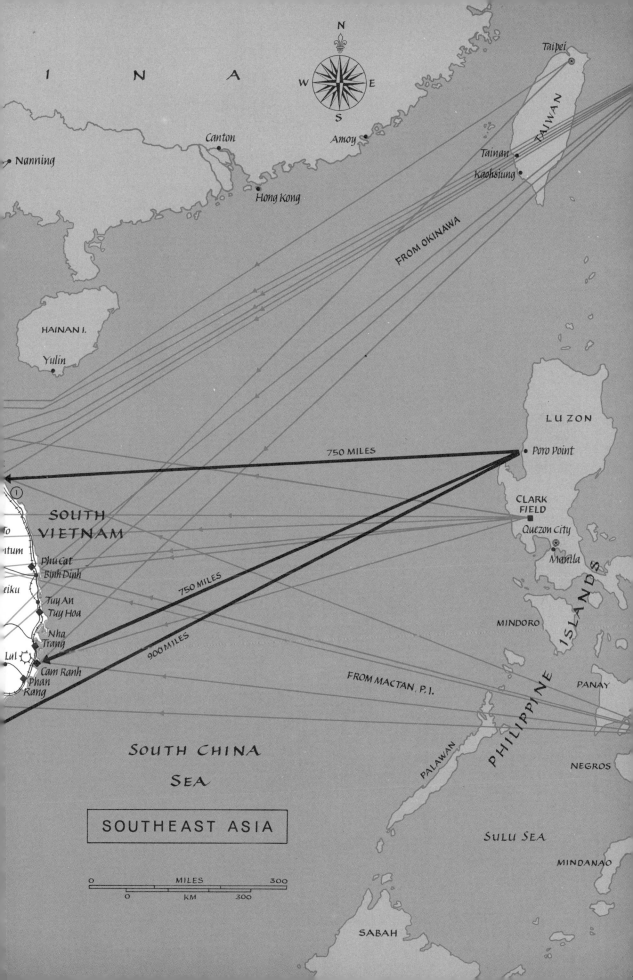

I CORPS

Province Number	Name	Capital
1	Quang Tri	Quang Tri
2	Thua Thien	Hue
3	Quang Nam	Da Nang
4	Quang Tin	Tam Ky
5	Quang Ngai	Quang Ngai

III CORPS

Province Number	Name	Capital
18	Phuoc Long	Phuoc Binh (Song Be)
19	Long Khanh	Xuan Loc
20	Binh Tuy	Ham Tan
21	Tay Ninh	Tay Ninh
22	Binh Long	An Loc
23	Binh Duong	Phu Cuong
24	Bien Hoa	Bien Hoa
25	Phuoc Tuy	Phuoc Le (Ba Ria)
26	Hau Nghia	Khiem Quong
27	Long An	Tan An
Saigon	SEPARATE DISTRICT	
28	Gia Dinh	Gia Dinh

II CORPS

Province Number	Name	Capital
6	Kontum	Kontum
7	Binh Dinh	Qui Nhon
8	Pleiku	Pleiku
9	Phu Bon	Hau Bon
10	Phu Yen	Tuy Hoa
11	Darlac	Ban Me Thuot
12	Khanh Hoa	Nha Trang
13	Quang Duc	Gia Nghia
14	Tuyen Duc	Tung Nghia
15	Ninh Thuan	Phan Rang
X	Cam Ranh Bay	Separate enclave between Provinces 12 and 15
16	Lam Dong	Bao Loc
17	Binh Thuan	Phan Thiet

IV CORPS

Province Number	Name	Capital
29	Chau Doc	Chau Doc (Chau Phu)
30	Kien Phong	Cao Lanh
31	Kien Tuong	Moc Hoa
32	Kien Giang	Rach Gia
33	An Giang	Long Xuyen
34	Sa Dec	Sa Dec
35	Dinh Tuong	My Tho
36	Go Cong	Go Cong
37	Phong Dinh	Can Tho
38	Vinh Long	Vinh Long
39	Kien Hoa	Truc Giang (Ben Tre)
40	Chuong Tien	Vi Thanh
41	Ba Xuyen	Soc Trang (Khanh Hung)
42	Vinh Binh	Phu Vinh
43	Bac Lieu	Bac Lieu
44	An Xuyen	Quan Long

An Thoi
PHU QUO
I.

GUL
OF
SIA

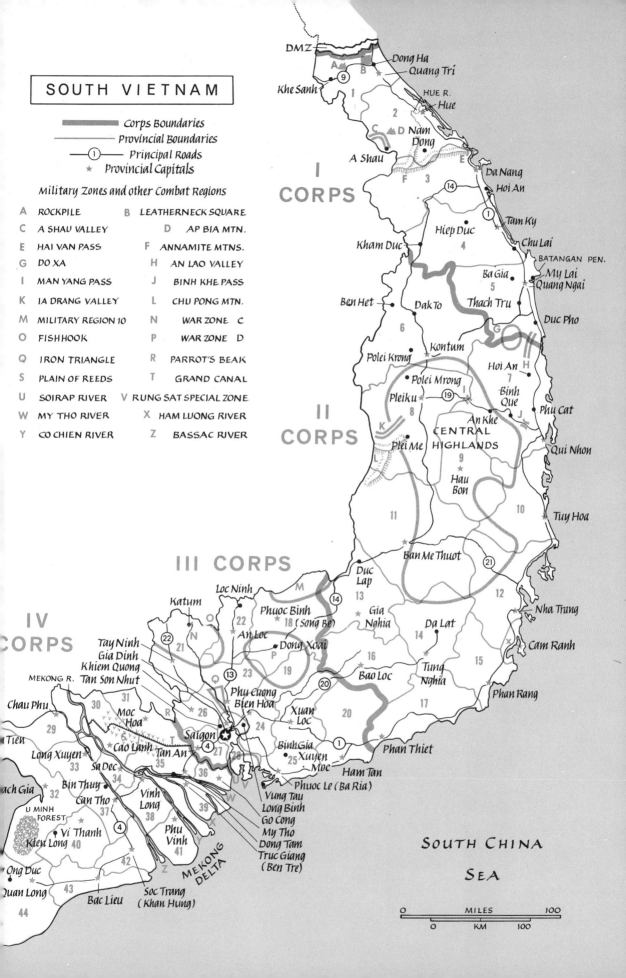

SOUTH VIETNAM

Corps Boundaries
Provincial Boundaries
1 Principal Roads
★ Provincial Capitals

Military Zones and other Combat Regions

A	ROCKPILE	B	LEATHERNECK SQUARE
C	A SHAU VALLEY	D	AP BIA MTN.
E	HAI VAN PASS	F	ANNAMITE MTNS.
G	DO XA	H	AN LAO VALLEY
I	MAN YANG PASS	J	BINH KHE PASS
K	IA DRANG VALLEY	L	CHU PONG MTN.
M	MILITARY REGION 10	N	WAR ZONE C
O	FISHHOOK	P	WAR ZONE D
Q	IRON TRIANGLE	R	PARROT'S BEAK
S	PLAIN OF REEDS	T	GRAND CANAL
U	SOIRAP RIVER	V	RUNG SAT SPECIAL ZONE
W	MY THO RIVER	X	HAM LUONG RIVER
Y	CO CHIEN RIVER	Z	BASSAC RIVER

DMZ

Dong Ha
Quang Tri
Khe Sanh
A B
9
1
HUE R.
2 Hue
C D Nam
Dong
A Shau
E
F
3
Da Nang
Hoi An
14
I
CORPS
1 Tam Ky
Hiep Duc
Chu Lai
Kham Duc
4
BATANGAN PEN.
Ba Gia My Lai
Quang Ngai
Ben Het
Dak To
Thach Tru
5
Duc Pho
6
Kontum
G
Polei Krong
Hoi An
H
7
Polei Mrong
Binh
Pleiku
I
Que
19
Phu Cat
II
K
8
An Khe
J
CORPS
CENTRAL
Plei Me
HIGHLANDS
Qui Nhon
L
9
Hau
Bon
11
10
Ban Me Thuot
Tuy Hoa
III CORPS
21
Duc
Lap
12
M
13
Nha Trang
Katum
Loc Ninh
14
Phuoc Binh
Gia
22
18 (Song Be)
Nghia
Da Lat
Cam Ranh
IV
An Loc
14
CORPS
O
21
P
Dong Xoai
15
Tay Ninh
22
19
16
Tung
Gia Dinh
23
Bao Loc
Nghia
Khiem Quong
13
20
MEKONG R. Tan Son Nhut
Q
Phu Cuong
Phan Rang
31
26
Bien Hoa
17
Chau Phu
30
Moc
R
24
Xuan
20
Hoa
Loc
Tien
29
Saigon
T
Phan Thiet
Long Xuyen
Cao Lanh
4 27
Binh Gia
33
Tan An
25 Xuyen
Sa Dec
35
36
Moc
ach Gia
34
28
Ham Tan
Bin Thuy
32 Can Tho
Vinh
Phuoc Le (Ba Ria)
U MINH
37
Long
Vung Tau
FOREST
38
39
Long Binh
Vi Thanh
4
Go Cong
Kien Long 40
Phu
My Tho
Vinh
Dong Tam
42
41
Truc Giang
Ong Duc
(Ben Tre)
SOUTH CHINA
43
MEKONG
uan Long
Bac Lieu
DELTA
SEA
44
Soc Trang
(Khan Hung)

0 MILES 100
0 KM 100

A PICTORIAL HISTORY OF
THE VIETNAM WAR

A PICTORIAL HISTORY OF

—— THE ——

VIETNAM WAR

RICHARD F. NEWCOMB

Maps by Rafael Palacios

DOUBLEDAY & COMPANY, INC.
Garden City, New York

Library of Congress Cataloging-in-Publication Data

Newcomb, Richard F.
  A pictorial history of the Vietnam War.

  Bibliography: p. 283
  Includes index.
  1. Vietnamese Conflict, 1961–1975—Campaigns.
2. Vietnamese Conflict, 1961–1975—Campaigns—
Pictorial works.   I. Title.
DS557.7.N38   1987   959.704'3   86–29381
ISBN 0-385-18540-5
Printed in the United States of America

Contents

LIST OF MAPS

Parenthetical references in the text, such as (III 21), denote the location of a particular Vietnamese province on the map appearing on pages iv–v. (III 21) would refer to III Corps, Province 21—Tay Ninh.

Part I

PRELUDE TO DOOM

1

From Hanoi to Geneva
1944–54

AUGUST OF 1945 was a month that changed the world. Two entire cities were destroyed, each with a single bomb dropped from the skies. World War II came to an end and the world stood back to contemplate the work it had accomplished—the greatest human slaughter in history.

But the war had not really ended. Embers still burned in small, far-off places, and there were people to fan them, keep them alive. One such place was Vietnam. The embers smoldering there would burn fitfully for twenty years, until finally they would burst into the full flame of war, a war that would test the fabric of the United States of America. In 1945 hardly anyone in America had heard of a place called Vietnam.

On August 6, 1945, the news of Hiroshima came to Vietnam, and three days later the news of Nagasaki. It clearly meant the end of World War II, but it also meant the beginning of other wars. Native leaders were ready all over Asia; it was time to close out the white man's empires, for that had been promised to them four years ago this very month, in the Atlantic Charter.

Within a few years the great colonial empires of the Orient were destined to oblivion. The United States kept its wartime promise and granted independence to the Philippines. Britain, Portugal, and the Netherlands gradually surrendered their vast holdings in the Orient and on the Indian subcontinent. Only France attempted to hold back the tide of history; it would not surrender French Indochina to any native leadership, and certainly not to Communist leaders.

On August 16, 1945, a frail man, then using the name Ho Chi Minh, arose before the People's National Congress meeting at Tan Tras, outside Hanoi, and recited from memory those words from the Atlantic Charter that said the signatories would ". . . respect the right of all people to choose the form of government under which they will live . . ." Surely those words must apply to Vietnam, and surely the time had come. Those words had been written by President Franklin D. Roose-

3

velt of the United States and Prime Minister Winston S. Churchill of Britain, and already they formed the foundation stone of the Declaration of the United Nations.

On the following day, the People's National Congress chose Ho Chi Minh as president of the Democratic Republic of Vietnam (DRV). The fifty-five-year-old Ho was head of the Viet Minh, a coalition of many Vietnamese parties and factions. He was also a Communist, and the Indochinese Communist party he headed was the dominant force in the Viet Minh.

The Viet Minh did not represent all Vietnamese people, but it was the largest and most powerful group in the north, and carried considerable weight in the south. More importantly, it spoke not as the voice of Communism but as the voice of nationalism. This was standard Communist doctrine, which Ho had learned well. The Viet Minh called for the end of French rule and the independence of Vietnam, and nearly all Vietnamese could embrace that goal. They did, in mass demonstrations in both Hanoi and Saigon. The French had been driven out; they must never be let back in.

Indochina had known foreign subjugation for centuries. As the name implied, India and China had been the dominant powers in Southeast Asia from earliest times. The Chinese were the first occupiers of Indochina, and they stayed nearly two thousand years, approximately 200 B.C.–1425 A.D. The Europeans began arriving in the sixteenth century, as traders and conquerors, staking out colonial empires for Portugal, Holland, Britain, and France. They came for the riches of the Orient, silk, rice, tea, and spices at first; later for the wealth of oil, rubber, tin, and gold.

By the late nineteenth century, France had consolidated the areas known as Cambodia, Laos, and Vietnam into what the world came to call French Indochina, a large and ill-defined area consisting mostly of mountains and heavy jungle. Only Vietnam, stretching for a thousand miles along the coast of the South China Sea, offered access to the world, mainly through the trading centers of Hanoi in the north and Saigon in the south.

Vietnam itself was an artificial amalgam of three ancient regions and peoples— Tonkin in the north, with its capital at Hanoi; Annam, centering on Hue; and Cochin China, with its capital at Saigon. The peoples of the three regions had more differences than similarities, and Vietnam had no tradition of central government or nationhood. Vietnam's economy rested mainly on rice; it was one of the great rice-producing areas of the Orient. As World War II came on, the French had established a few basic industries—steel, cement, manufacturing—most of them in the north. Trade with the world was rich and growing, but late in 1941 the Japanese military hordes poured out of southern China and quickly conquered all Southeast Asia, Indochina included. Vietnam was overrun. The French military were killed or imprisoned, the French business community was granted parole; it was free to run the economy under Japanese rule, and for the benefit of the Japanese. The French bided their time, believing that at the end of the war they would resume their rule. But others, especially in Hanoi, had different ideas.

On Sunday afternoon, September 2, 1945, a great crowd assembled in Hanoi, jamming Ba Dinh Square, to hear the words they had waited so long for. Once

Ho Chi Minh, shown here in 1946, emerges from the radical underground to claim all of Indochina for the Vietnamese people.

again Ho Chi Minh arose. He raised his arms for attention, and began: "All men are created equal. The Creator has given us certain inviolable rights; the right to life, the right to be free, and the right to achieve happiness. These immortal words are taken from the Declaration of Independence of the United States of America in 1776." He spoke for more than an hour, detailing the long history of Vietnam, and concluded:

"The French have fled, the Japanese have capitulated, Emperor Bao Dai has abdicated. Our people have broken the chains which for nearly a century have fettered them and have won independence for the nation . . . We are convinced that the Allied nations which at Teheran and San Francisco acknowledged the principles of self-determination and equality of nations, will not refuse to acknowledge the independence of Vietnam."

Ho's speech was a triumph. He had made masterful use of nationalism to mark his true aim—a brutal Communist dictatorship for all of Indochina. Throughout the throng the red flag with the yellow star, the flag of the Viet Minh, waved. No French tricolor could be seen, nor any Frenchmen; only Vietnamese, workers, peasants, Buddhist monks in orange robes, Cao Dai priests in white, Catholic priests, soldiers of the Vietnamese Army of Liberation. There was no disorder, just a day of celebration.

5

That same day things had not gone as well in Saigon. Dozens of religious and political factions, the Viet Minh among them, paraded down the Rue Catinat, some two hundred thousand strong. Gunfire broke out and a Catholic priest lay dying on the steps of the cathedral. Crowds fled in terror, and the day of celebration was lost in chaos. First reports reaching Hanoi spoke of "massacres" and "Black Sunday." Next day the toll was reckoned at four Frenchmen, fourteen Vietnamese. But the eyes of the world that day were on Tokyo Bay, where the Japanese were signing the surrender before General Douglas MacArthur on the deck of the battleship *Missouri.*

Ho was not discouraged. He was a case-hardened zealot, and he possessed unlimited patience. He had been working for years to catch American attention; he would continue that quest for as long as it took. The OSS (Office of Strategic Services) had first noticed Ho in 1944, not for his political activities but because he had something they wanted. The OSS station in Kunming, China, only three hundred miles from Vietnam, needed intelligence on the Japanese army in Indochina. Ho was already at work north of Hanoi, getting ready to fill the power vacuum when the Japanese were driven out. His guerrillas and a shadow government already controlled some northern provinces of Vietnam and were preparing to move into Hanoi.

Ho was quite willing to help the OSS, hoping that in return they would open his way to get a hearing in Washington. He believed the United States, itself a product of revolution, would certainly understand the aspirations of the Vietnamese. But the OSS had no interest in Ho's politics and explained this to him many times. Ho kept pressing his case, and also produced what the Americans wanted—intelligence on the Japanese military and help in preparing a special mercy mission to rescue Allied prisoners of war in Indochina.

Two weeks earlier, on August 22, 1945, an OSS mission, headed by American Army Major Archimedes L. A. Patti, had flown into Hanoi. The party of twelve, including two lieutenants and four sergeants, had two assignments: Arrange the rescue of thousands of Allied POWs and arrange for the surrender of the Japanese. The Allied victors had just decided at the Potsdam conference (July 17–August 2) that Vietnam would be cut in half at the 16th parallel (Da Nang). The partition had no political significance; it was regarded as temporary and only for operational convenience. Since France was still prostrate from the war, and the United States was overburdened with worldwide problems, the Potsdam conferees decided that British forces would take the Japanese surrender at Saigon for the southern half of Vietnam, and the Chinese would take it at Hanoi for Japanese forces in northern Vietnam. Both Britain and China were simply to protect French interests until France could rally enough to send its own troops.

Ho was greatly concerned by the Chinese occupation of the north. History told him that the last time the Chinese had come they had stayed a thousand years. As for the British, they were another hated colonial power and had no rights whatever in Vietnam, even as custodians. The French, of course, at least in Ho's view, had forfeited all rights when they began surrendering Vietnam to the Japanese in 1940; since then they had conspired with the Japanese occupiers merely to protect their

6

colonial riches. These resources belonged to the Vietnamese people, Ho believed, and now was the time to strike, before the French attempted to return to the Orient.

Major Patti, then just twenty-four, had met Ho several times in China, and each time Ho had attempted to subvert him to Communist purposes. Each time, Patti explained that the OSS had no authority in the political realm; any American decisions about Vietnam's future would be made in Washington. Ho never gave up trying. Patti sent reports of these meetings to his superiors at Kunming, for transmission to Chinese headquarters at Chungking and on to Washington.

There was no hope for Ho's cause. The American command in China, both military and diplomatic, could hardly keep Ho's name straight. Some records reaching the Department of State in Washington referred to him as Hoo, Ho Chin Chin, Ho Chu Chan, and other approximations. All references to him made clear, first and foremost, that he was a Communist, and that was enough to doom his cause. Chiang Kai-shek, leader of the Nationalist regime at Chungking, was already having trouble with the Communists in his own country, and the United States was beginning to see Communist offensives on a half dozen fronts around the world. It was out of the question to expect the United States to turn over Indochina to a Communist regime.

When Major Patti's plane landed at Gia Lam airport, outside Hanoi, on August 22, the Americans were received correctly, if not cordially, by armed Japanese. But there was a surprise package aboard. By Allied military order, Patti had brought with him Major Jean R. Sainteny, chief of French Intelligence at Kunming, three French lieutenants, and a civilian agent. This angered Ho and the Vietnamese, and presented problems for the Japanese, who were under Allied orders to maintain peace and order in Indochina until the Allies could arrive and take the surrender.

Sainteny's party, hoping for a triumphant French return to Indochina, found instead that the Vietnamese people were outraged. Earlier the streets had been full of happy Vietnamese, waving the Viet Minh flag and welcoming the American "liberators," but when they discovered the French party their mood turned angry. Finally the Japanese sequestered Sainteny and his party in the Governor-General's Palace, in "protective custody." Sainteny asked in vain to use Radio Hanoi to announce the glad tidings to the Vietnamese that the French were back. The Japanese suggested that he get back on the plane and return to China. Sainteny stayed in Hanoi, but his mission was sterile.

Major Patti set up headquarters at the Hotel Metropole, established radio communications with Kunming, and opened negotiations with General Yuitsui Tsuchihashi, commander of the fifty thousand Japanese troops in Indochina. Patti reestablished relations with Ho Chi Minh, and once again received Vietnamese intelligence and constant political pressure. Was not Vietnam a mirror image of America's very own revolution? Ho asked. Why couldn't President Truman and the American people see this, and offer the Vietnamese people at least moral support? Had not France come to the aid of the American colonies against the British? Wasn't it time for the Americans to help Vietnam against the French?

Ho asked that Patti transmit this message to President Truman and Secretary of

State James F. Byrnes. Major Patti put it all in his dispatches to Kunming, and these reports were never heard of again, just as Patti had told Ho.

Small advance parties of British and French troops arrived in Saigon by air four days after Black Sunday, and three days later, on September 9, the first Chinese troops, representing Lieutenant General Lu Han, arrived on foot in Hanoi, marching overland from China. One of their first acts was to expel Major Sainteny and his French party from the Governor-General's Palace, their so-called "golden cage." The French, now emerging from internment to reclaim the banks and businesses of Indochina, were humiliated. They plotted revenge.

Ho's star seemed to be ascending, and he gave Patti yet another letter for Truman. But events were outrunning the Viet Minh. The Chinese took firm control over the north. In the south, the British assumed command in the person of Major General Douglas D. Gracey, a colonial type still living in the nineteenth century. Riots and bloodshed broke out, and the United States suffered its first official casualty of the Indochinese revolution.

On September 26, 1945, Major A. Peter Dewey, twenty-eight, chief of the OSS mission in Saigon, drove toward OSS headquarters shortly after noon, with Captain Herbert J. Bluechel as a passenger in his jeep. They were to lunch at headquarters, then jeep to Tan Son Nhut to catch a plane for China; now that the British were in control, the United States mission in southern Vietnam was finished.

As Dewey slowed to maneuver around a street barricade, a hidden machine gun opened fire. Dewey was struck in the head and died instantly. A hot gun battle around OSS headquarters lasted until 3 P.M. When it was over, Major Dewey's jeep was gone, and so was his body; neither was ever found. Dewey's last report from Saigon had said: "Cochin China is burning, the French and the British are finished here, and we ought to clear out of Southeast Asia."

The final acts of World War II in Vietnam were soon over. The formal surrender of Japanese forces in Indochina took place in Hanoi on Friday, September 28. Major Patti met Ho Chi Minh on the thirtieth for the last time, and the next day took his party back to China. The French command returned to Saigon on October 5, in the person of General Jacques Philippe Leclerc. The Viet Minh openly attacked Tan Son Nhut airport on October 10, made a futile last stand in Saigon on the sixteenth, and retired into the jungle to resume guerrilla warfare.

In the north, Ho Chi Minh adopted a new strategy. He considered his bid for Vietnamese independence not as lost, only delayed. He decided to fight on. But who was Ho, really? There is much legend about Ho, but he appears to have been born May 19, 1890, in a village of Nghe An Province, not far north of Hue. His name was Nguyen That Thanh and his father was a one-time teacher and civil servant at the imperial court in Hue, fired by the French for anticolonial activities.

Ho left Vietnam about 1912, shipping out for Europe as a cabin boy on a steamer. His travels, under many aliases, took him to London, Paris, Moscow, and even the United States, and finally, about 1925, to China. It was there that World War II found him, now working for Vietnamese independence under the name of Ho Chi Minh, "He Who Enlightens."

Ho had built around himself a close circle of dedicated Communists, whose names would one day be known throughout the world. They were younger than Ho; Pham Van Dong, born in 1908, would lead the Viet Minh delegation to Geneva in 1954, and later become the first prime minister of the Democratic Republic of Vietnam; Le Duc Tho, born in 1912, a director of the revolt in the south, would later be chief negotiator for the Communists in the torturous peace negotiations with the United States.

And there was Vo Nguyen Giap, also born in 1912, who chose the military as a career, and held Napoleon as his idol. A Communist from the early days, Giap held center stage as commander of Ho Chi Minh's forces in the underground war against the French.

In the waning months of 1945 and into the spring of 1946, Ho Chi Minh was still pressing the United States to intervene on his side in Vietnam, in the spirit of the Atlantic Charter and the United Nations. He also continued talking with the French, hoping for some accommodation, and sending telegrams, letters, and hand-delivered missives to the leaders of Britain, the Soviet Union, China, and the United States. There was no hint of recognition for Vietnam from anyone.

The talks with France finally seemed to bear some fruit in March 1946, when France and the Viet Minh agreed that French troops could return to the north as the Chinese withdrew but would themselves be withdrawn by 1952. France agreed to recognize Vietnam as a "free state within the French Union." Ho even went to France in the summer for further talks, but relations grew worse rather than better, and in November fighting broke out in Vietnam.

On November 20, 1946, a French patrol boat was fired on while seizing a junk in Haiphong harbor. Three days later a mob moved toward the French airfield at Cat Bi, near the city of Haiphong. The French cruiser *Suffren* opened fire, and thousands of Vietnamese died in the ensuing shelling and panic. On December 19, Viet Minh agents destroyed the Hanoi power plant. The Vietnamese war against the French had begun.

Ho Chi Minh and his government went into hiding in the mountains of Tonkin, and General Giap's forces launched a war of attrition that was to last eight years. As the conflict wore on, the French grip on its Asian colonies would slowly ebb.

Giving ground on the political front, France resurrected Bao Dai in 1947 and granted Vietnam a limited independence. Bao Dai, then thirty-four, had a certain legitimacy; he was the son of Emperor Khai Din of Annam and actually occupied the throne at Hue from 1932 to 1945, cooperating with the French and then the Japanese occupation. He resigned when Ho and the Viet Minh came to the fore in the early days following Japan's surrender.

Bao Dai was well intentioned but favored the fleshpots of Europe over the throne at Hue. When the French recalled him they gave him limited powers over the states of Annam, Tonkin, and Cochin China—the modern Vietnam. Unfortunately, much of the world remembered Bao Dai as "the playboy of Paris," fond of women, drink, gambling, and tennis. The Soviet Union and China immediately denounced him as the puppet ruler of Vietnam.

9

But the United States had little time for Vietnam in the "peace" years of 1945–50. The Truman administration had some sympathy for the Vietnamese aspirations, and did try to cajole the French into granting more autonomy to the colonies. However, great events were transpiring in the larger world of Europe and Asia. For the United States it was the era of the "containment" policy, the Truman Doctrine, the Berlin airlift, the Marshall Plan, and the civil war in China. President Truman, with the support of Congress, sent economic and military aid to Greece and Turkey to contain Communist pressure on that front. He broke the Communist blockade of Berlin with a massive eighteen-month airlift of food and fuel into the city. The Marshall Plan pumped blood back into the life of America's European allies.

By 1949, NATO (North Atlantic Treaty Organization) was in place and the United States seemed to have won checkmate with the Communists in Europe. Not so in Asia. China had been in the grip of civil war since the end of World War II, the Nationalist forces of Chiang Kai-shek gradually losing ground to the Communist armies of Mao Zedong. Peking fell to the Communists in early 1949, and on October 1 Mao proclaimed the People's Republic of China. This was a great blow to American hopes.

The United States now saw itself as arrayed against not only the Communist hordes of China, but a China that had the full backing of the Soviet Union. Thus began the concept of Communism as a worldwide "monolith," a concept that was to shape American thought and action for the next thirty years. One of the first casualties was Ho Chi Minh; the United States could have no sympathy for a Communist regime in Indochina.

This became apparent as 1950 opened. On January 18, the Communist China regime formally recognized Ho Chi Minh's Democratic Republic of Vietnam, the first powerful nation to do so, and twelve days later the Soviet Union followed suit. The next day Secretary of State Dean Acheson left no doubt as to where the United States stood. He denounced Ho and said the Soviet recognition "should remove any illusions as to the 'nationalist' nature of Ho Chi Minh's aims and reveals Ho in his true colors as the mortal enemy of native independence in Indochina."

Ho noted wryly that, even though he had long been an avowed Communist, it had taken the Russians nearly five years to recognize his government, and in that period the Soviets had given him no aid, moral or material. Ho recalled that he had worked with the Americans in China and Hanoi from 1944 on, hoping for American recognition of his forces in Vietnam. He realized that dream was now gone.

On February 3, 1950, President Truman recognized Bao Dai as head of the Associated States of Indochina, as the French now called their colonies. Two weeks later the French Foreign Office in Paris called in American Ambassador Jefferson Caffrey and told him the situation in Indochina was grave; if Communist Chinese military aid began to flow to Hanoi, France was not strong enough to stand alone and might have to withdraw from Indochina.

Acheson hurried to Paris to confer with the French, and in early May the American stance became clear. President Truman approved $10 million for military aid, the first tangible American contribution toward saving Vietnam for the West.

President Truman, beset with post–World War II problems, talks with Secretary of State Dean Acheson in 1949 as American policy on Vietnam firms up on supporting the French against Ho Chi Minh's Communists.

Within days, the administration had found a "modest $60 million" more in the budget to help the French in Indochina. The aid would be administered by the Departments of Defense and State, Washington said, and "the details will not be made public for security reasons."

On July 6, 1950, Donald R. Heath became United States minister to the Associated States of Indochina. The event was hardly noticed in the United States because ten days earlier, on June 26, the North Koreans had opened the Korean war by invading South Korea. President Truman immediately committed American troops to Korea and also moved quickly on the Indochina "front" by creating the U.S. Military Assistance Advisory Group (MAAG), with headquarters in Saigon. Brigadier General Francis G. Brink, United States Army, assumed command of MAAG on October 10. On November 8 Colonel Joseph B. Wells opened the Air Force Section of MAAG. The American military structure in Vietnam had begun.

American military goods began to flow to the French in October, when a French aircraft carrier arrived in Saigon with forty United States Navy F-6F Hellcats. (The French had wanted F-63 Kingcobras, because of their 37-mm cannon, but the United States no longer had spare parts or ammunition for this plane.)

The hour was already late. By October, General Giap had driven the French out of the Chinese border strongholds of Lao Cai, Cao Bang, and Lang Son. All main highways and railroads were now open for Chinese military equipment to flow

11

south to Ho's army. In an attempt to stop the rebels, France sent out a new high commissioner and military commander, General Jean de Lattre de Tassigny, a military hero of great dash and éclat. The French forces in Vietnam were heartened, but the upsurge of hope soon vanished. The French offensive bogged down and the general's only son, Bernard, died in battle. (The general himself died of cancer in January 1951.)

The French, with many problems at home and in their African colonies, were steadily losing interest in Vietnam. The war never seemed to end, and it was costing much in French money and lives. Giap and his irregulars kept up steady pressure, never seeming to flag, and gradually forced the French back to the cities of Hanoi and Haiphong.

The United States' position on Southeast Asia had been set forth in a National Security Council paper approved by President Truman on March 27, 1950. It said that "Thailand and Burma could be expected to fall under Communist domination if Indochina were controlled by a Communist-dominated government" and that "the balance of Southeast Asia would then be in grave hazard." The United States, the paper made clear, did not intend to let that happen.

A second shipment of American planes, ninety F-8F Bearcats, arrived in Saigon in February and March 1951. In the same year, the French received five American RB-26 reconnaissance planes and twenty-four B-26 bombers, all flown into Da Nang, completing the first aviation schedules under the United States Mutual De-

French troops, now receiving American equipment, fight to hold back Ho's Communist rebels but by 1950 are being driven south from the Chinese border. Both Russia and China are backing Ho; the United States is committed to help France.

fense Assistance Program. The planes jumped the French sortie rate from 450 weekly to 930 in 1951. General de Lattre de Tassigny was grateful, saying the air help, "especially napalm bombs, arrived in the nick of time."

During 1952, Truman's final year in office, more planes went to Indochina, in spite of the heavy American commitments in Korea. The United States could not spare more fighters or bombers, but sent the first ten C-47 transport planes in the spring, ten more in early fall, and yet another twenty-one by year's end, in response to urgent French pleas. The C-47s stopped at Clark Air Force Base in the Philippines, where all American markings were removed and paradrop equipment was installed. The Americans delivered the planes to Nha Trang in 1952, and sent along USAF technicians to service and maintain them. These servicemen, the first USAF contingent to see active duty in Vietnam, remained until the French relieved them in August 1953.

French hopes had rallied briefly early in 1951 when Giap mounted three heavy offensives in succession north of Hanoi and was beaten back in all three. But Giap learned a lesson he would remember—avoid direct assault against the enemy if he is stronger. From then on, the Vietnamese struck only when the odds favored them.

In the fall of 1951 the United States signed economic cooperation agreements with Vietnam, Laos, and Cambodia. The signing took place in Saigon, which soon had an American visitor, Senator John F. Kennedy. The young senator, grooming himself for a larger role in American politics, had decided to look at Southeast Asia for himself. He returned home to report in speeches in his home state of Massachusetts that "in Indochina we have allied ourselves to the desperate effort of the French regime to hang on to the remnants of an empire."

Giap increased his guerrilla pressure in 1952 and gradually drove the French from large areas of northern Vietnam. The United States continued financial aid to Indochina, through the French, and raised its legation in Saigon to embassy status. In return, the Bao Dai regime opened a Vietnamese embassy in Washington.

A month after the inauguration of Dwight D. Eisenhower in 1953, he sent his Vice-President, Richard M. Nixon, to the Far East. Nixon made stops in New Zealand and Australia, Indonesia and Malaya, and then spent six days in Cambodia, Laos, and Vietnam. The French were cordial, took him wherever he wanted to go, including the battlefronts. (Nixon was to recall later that he visited Son Tay, never imagining that in 1972, as President of the United States, he would order a parachute raid on the torture camp there in a spectacular attempt to rescue American prisoners.) Nixon was amazed by the French attitude toward the Vietnamese people; after a hundred years of occupation the French were still treating them as nineteenth-century subjects.

The Eisenhower administration was quickly drawn into Vietnam decisions. Soon after Nixon's return from the war front, Secretary of State John Foster Dulles told the French that American money would continue to flow through Paris if France had a plan for winning the Indochina war. General Giap's forces were even then heading toward Laos, and the French were sending yet another new commander to Hanoi, General Henri Navarre.

13

A young U.S. Senator, John F. Kennedy, visits Indochina in late 1951 and returns with qualms about French efforts "to hang on to the remnants of an empire."

The French asked for the loan of some C-119s to lift tanks, artillery, and other heavy equipment into Laos to cut off Giap. In May 1953, the United States delivered six C-119s to Nha Trang, where private contract pilots (mostly Americans) picked them up and flew them to Haiphong. The USAF sent along a maintenance and supply detachment from its 24th Air Depot Wing to keep the planes in shape at Cat Bi airfield, near Haiphong, and Gia Lam airfield, outside Hanoi. This was the

14

Bao Dai, recognized by France and the United States as the legitimate ruler of Vietnam, reviews loyal Vietnamese troops in December 1951, at the fortress town of Hoa Binh, 50 miles southwest of Hanoi. The town is now menaced by Ho's Viet Minh troops.

nearest that American servicemen had yet come to the battle lines in the north. The French returned both the planes and the United States airmen in July.

Navarre, meantime, had shaped up a plan to bring the Communist rebels to battle and smash their main forces. To help Navarre, and to get a look at conditions in the field, the United States sent a military mission to Saigon in June 1953, under Army Lieutenant General John W. O'Daniel, with the Air Force side headed up by Major General Chester E. McCarty, a specialist in combat cargo.

The United States finally achieved armistice in Korea on July 27, 1953, and by autumn could offer France more aid in Indochina, provided France would guarantee eventual independence for Vietnam.

The French gave these assurances in September, and General Navarre disclosed his grand plan. He would lure the Communists to battle at Dien Bien Phu, an old town 175 miles west of Hanoi. If Navarre took a strong position there, General Giap would have to respond and the French would then defeat him, once and for all. From a military standpoint, the plan was a bad one; Dien Bien Phu was in a valley, closed in by mountains, and if the roads were cut, the French could be supplied only by air. Navarre said he realized this but Dien Bien Phu would be the bait, and he was sure his forces could destroy the enemy.

As 1952 ends, French paratroopers (above) and loyal Vietnamese troops counterattack against Communists on hill near Na San, 100 miles west of Hanoi, and later aid the wounded and guard Viet Minh prisoners (below).

A month after President Eisenhower's inauguration in January 1953, Vice-President Richard Nixon tours Vietnam, inspects both French and native forces, and assesses Allied position for Ike.

In late November, the French force of some fifteen thousand paratroopers, using fifty C-47s put at Navarre's disposal by the United States, parachuted into Dien Bien Phu. The French troops immediately began to build bunkers, enlarge the airstrip, and set up artillery positions. Giap welcomed the bait and began one of those military miracles akin to Hannibal's transit of the Alps.

From every section of Vietnam he rallied men, women, and children to help build an iron ring around Dien Bien Phu. Using their backs, bicycles, carts, and five hundred new trucks supplied by the Soviet Union, a motley army began dragging heavy equipment over mountains and through jungles, subsisting on bags of rice carried all the way from the coastal lowlands. The Chinese contributed much armament, including American 75-mm and 105-mm artillery they had captured in Korea.

By December 1953 the roads to Dien Bien Phu were cut. Navarre was surrounded, and he was having second thoughts about his strategy. The United States

Through the summer of 1953, loyal Vietnamese (above) fight to hold and pacify the country west of Hanoi; but by November the tide was turning and the French dropped in paratroopers (below) to strengthen and hold a town called Dien Bien Phu, already threatened by advancing Viet Minh forces.

A wounded Vietnamese paratrooper fighting for France is carried to the rear by his comrade after a fierce jungle clash with the Viet Minh late in January 1954.

was supplying and maintaining from twelve to twenty-two C-119s at Cat Bi and, at French urging, was also moving in more B-26s and C-47s. The Americans watched one B-26 crash-land at Cat Bi, and a C-119 crash on takeoff with a load of napalm drums headed for Dien Bien Phu. USAF experts flew to Dien Bien Phu to advise the defenders. This was getting pretty close to overt American involvement, and news leaks were developing. Eisenhower opined that "some aircraft mechanics" had been sent to Vietnam, but he said they "would not get touched by combat."

As the battle shaped up, the major powers became more nervous, and in January

19

1954 the Soviet Union, France, Britain, and the United States agreed they should meet in Geneva and attempt to resolve the Indochinese conflict. But events would not wait; the French position at Dien Bien Phu steadily worsened.

The French, desperate for reinforcements, asked the United States to fly French troops from Paris to Da Nang. The United States agreed, and the first flight of six C-124s left Paris on April 15 with 514 French soldiers, unarmed and in civilian clothes to allay protests. The flight was made by a circuitous route, with refueling stops in six countries, but not in India: Prime Minister Jawaharlal Nehru had forbidden the use of Indian airspace for colonial wars.

A second flight of five U.S. C-124s made the trip from Paris to Da Nang early in May with 452 more French paratroopers.

Navarre had paid his last visit to Dien Bien Phu in early March, rallying the troops and embracing their commander, Colonel Christian de Castries. Both knew the odds against the French were bad. Giap had some four divisions of regulars in the circling mountains, nearly fifty thousand men, against fifteen thousand defenders, about half of whom were French. The rest were Foreign Legionnaires, Vietnamese, and Algerians. Morale ran high in the mountains; Giap's troops saw themselves

General Henri Navarre (left), commander in chief of French forces in Indochina, has a last look around the Dien Bien Phu fortress in February 1954, accompanied by Gen. René Cogny (right), commander of French forces in North Vietnam, and Colonel Christian de Castries (center), commander of the garrison.

as nationalist patriots, about to clear the homeland of the hated foreigner. In the valley, the French forces prepared to do what had to be done, even to die.

The Vietnamese offensive opened on March 13, 1954, and Giap, as he had planned, applied his strength slowly. By the end of March, the French could no longer use their airstrip, and even airdrops of food and munitions were precarious. The free world watched in horror and sorrow, each day's newspapers bringing word of the hopelessness and helplessness inside Dien Bien Phu. The dead unburied, the wounded untended, ammunition shortages, food declining, but courage, heroism, and gallantry unbounded.

These were grim days in Washington. The Joint Chiefs of Staff and the National Security Council met often, discussing options, drafting reports, briefing President Eisenhower. The president, with no serious opposition in Congress, had already sent American planes, and Army mechanics to service them. In the present crisis, how far should the United States go to save Dien Bien Phu? Should the United States send more arms and men? Should it use the atom bomb as a tactical weapon?

When the French requested air strikes by United States Navy carrier pilots, and the loan of up to twenty B-29s, the United States hesitated. President Eisenhower was deeply concerned at the prospect of losing Vietnam to the Communists. He talked with the press on April 7, 1954, and first used a figure of speech that was to become historic: "You have a row of dominos set up, you knock over the first one, and what will happen to the last one is the certainty it will go over very quickly." After Vietnam there went Cambodia, Laos, the whole of Southeast Asia.

For John Foster Dulles, the Chinese were the real devils. All through the spring of 1954 the Secretary of State spoke out at every opportunity about what he saw as the threat of Chinese aggression against Vietnam. He hammered away at the theme almost as though obsessed, and on April 5 he told the House Foreign Affairs Committee that the Chinese were "coming awfully close" to overt military intervention. He seemed not to know that Ho Chi Minh would have considered this as great a disaster as Dulles. Ho was a Communist first, a nationalist second. His whole adult life was dedicated to conquering all of Indochina and installing a ruthless Communist regime patterned after that of Joseph Stalin.

The United States declined the French request to loan them B-29s. The generals concluded there were no proper targets for the Superfortress bombers, and the French could neither maintain nor fly the big planes. In any event, time was running out.

Nixon would recall in his *Memoirs* (see Bibliography) that the British were approached about joint efforts to help France, and he was "astonished" when Churchill replied, with asperity (and a little profanity) that the British would have nothing to do with any military action in Southeast Asia. The atom bomb? Nixon said its use had been discussed several times by the Joint Chiefs of Staff, and some believed that three small bombs, well placed, might save the French at Dien Bien Phu. The use of atomic weapons had been thoroughly discussed by the Joint Chiefs of Staff during the Korean war; MacArthur had enthusiastically supported atomic bombing to keep the Chinese hordes out of Korea, even suggesting that he plant atomic materials along the Yalu River boundary as an impassable corridor for decades to come.

But the hour was too late for atomic warfare—the Russians and the Chinese might reply in kind, leading to a world holocaust. And the hour was too late to save Dien Bien Phu and the French. In addition, the time was not right for American intervention. House Majority Leader Lyndon B. Johnson opposed it. Senator John F. Kennedy opined: "No amount of American military assistance in Indochina can conquer an enemy which is everywhere and at the same time nowhere . . ." The Joint Chiefs of Staff saw no military advantage for the United States in ground warfare in Asia. General Matthew B. Ridgway, the Army Chief of Staff, remembered his command in Korea. He estimated it would take seven, perhaps twelve, American divisions to capture Vietnam and he wanted no more war on the Asian land mass. The United States had military commitments elsewhere of greater importance—in Europe, for example. Vietnam would be the wrong war, in the wrong place, at the wrong time.

Giap's forces drew the noose tighter around Dien Bien Phu, and by early May were digging trenches within five hundred yards of the French lines. The American "civilian" pilots parachuted 196 tons of vital supplies down to Dien Bien Phu on May 6, the last day it could do any good. And as one of the C-119s went down to Giap's guns, there went pilot James B. McGovern, who had been a Fourteenth Air Force pilot in World War II. He was a huge man with a heavy black beard, and went into the history books as "Earthquake McGoon," a comic strip hero.

The French, out of nearly everything but courage, could only wait for the final enemy assault. Defeat for France finally came, as officially recorded, at "1750 hours, 7 May 1954," fifty-five days almost to the minute from Giap's opening assault. The Viet Minh simply swarmed over the last bunkers. Eight thousand

The battle at Dien Bien Phu is on, as the French and loyal colonial troops are surrounded and decimated by incoming Viet Minh fire from the surrounding hills. The fortress fell to rebel forces of General Vo Nguyen Giap on May 7, 1954, and the French were finished in Indochina.

As decreed by the Geneva Conference in July 1954, Vietnam is split into north and south spheres at the 17th Parallel. In November the last French forces march out of Hanoi (above) and the Communist Viet Minh forces take over right behind them (below). The north now belongs to Ho Chi Minh.

survivors of Dien Bien Phu on the French side were marched into prison camps. The Viet Minh had lost perhaps eight thousand men. The French had lost Indochina; the colonial era in Asia had ended. And the United States? The United States had never been fighting for France or colonialism. It had been fighting against world Communism, and it kept right on. The next battleground, Geneva.

In early April 1954, even before the final act at Dien Bien Phu, the great powers had convened on the beautiful lakefront at Geneva. The conference seemed to go badly from the start. No two parties had similar aims. Anthony Eden of Great Britain, conference cochairman, said he had never seen another international conference like it. The Chinese delegation, headed by Chou En-lai, cochairman with Eden, worked for disruption, hoping to capitalize on it with further influence in Indochina. Pham Van Dong, heading the Viet Minh delegation, hoped to bring all of Indochina into Ho Chi Minh's circle and, surprisingly, found the French on his side. The Soviet Union made coarse remarks about China and sought ways to foil the Chinese.

The French, beleaguered with home problems and in serious troubles in Algeria, wanted nothing more than to give the whole package to Ho and forget Indochina. The United States went to the meeting in a sullen mood (Secretary of State John Foster Dulles refused to shake hands with Chou En-lai, and reportedly said the only way they'd ever meet was if their cars collided), withdrew early, and refused to sign the final document. Actually, none of the parties signed, each instead submitting a document saying it would live up to the agreement, more or less.

Actually, the United States (from its viewpoint) made out quite well at Geneva, though the American delegation exhibited dejection. The French and Pham Van Dong pressed for a simple and immediate turnover of sovereignty, from France to Ho's Viet Minh. France still had a vast industrial stake in Vietnam, with thousands of French businessmen there. It looked as though Ho Chi Minh might not disturb that pattern (for his own reasons) for years to come. The Russians and the Chinese stood each other off, exposing fractures in the so-called Communist monolith. The conference stumbled to a close on July 21, 1954.

The Geneva Accords, as they were called, decreed a partition of Vietnam at the seventeenth parallel, commencing October 11, 1954, and called for elections for reunification of North and South Vietnam to be held within two years after that date. France was to remove all its troops within one year, and the Vietnamese could migrate freely, north or south, until October 11, 1954. There were other provisions (for example, the United States could not increase the number of Americans in Vietnam above the current total of 342), but it really did not matter. None of the Geneva Accords was obeyed. Elections were never held and the partition ended only after years of bloody warfare and the expulsion of all Americans from Vietnam in 1975.

What the United States did gain at Geneva was time—time, it hoped, to save a place for some brand of American democracy in an Asian sea of communism.

2

The Eisenhower Years
1954–60

THE GENEVA agreements made a fundamental change in the balance of power in Asia, though this was not clearly seen at the time. They created two small, weak nations, each supported by strong world powers: North Vietnam, backed by China and the Soviet Union; South Vietnam, backed by the United States.

Physically the two Vietnams were about the same size (each 65,000 square miles, a little larger than Florida), and about equal in population, with some twelve million people in each half. Each nation was built around a major river system, the Red River in the north and the Mekong River in the south. South Vietnam was mainly agricultural and rural. North Vietnam was more industrialized, with considerable agriculture along the seaboard.

Ethnically and socially, North Vietnam was more homogenized and organized, with a well-developed sense of nationhood and a predominant party, the Viet Minh. Most of the people were Tonkinese, recognized Ho Chi Minh as the national leader, and had a sense of national loyalty and patriotism.

South Vietnam had no such traditions. The peasants and farmers, mostly Annamese, knew little of any government farther away than their district town, and what they did know of Saigon meant corruption, taxes, and upheaval. In the central highlands, aboriginal tribes like the Hmongs gave allegiance to no government. In Saigon, the Chinese population controlled much of the mercantile trade, while military officers, politicians, religious sects, and bands of brigands struggled endlessly for political power. No one had ever ruled southern Vietnam with much success, and one of the few unifying forces was the Viet Minh, later to be known in South Vietnam as the Viet Cong.

What the United States needed for South Vietnam after the Geneva partition was a ruler. One appeared, as if by a miracle, in the person of Ngo Dinh Diem. Diem burst upon the world scene between the fall of Dien Bien Phu and the Geneva conference. By more than a little coincidence he was in France, and so was Bao Dai, the on-and-off emperor of Vietnam. With the fall of Dien Bien Phu, Bao Dai thought it time to reassert himself; he summoned Diem to his château near Cannes, and on June 18, 1954, appointed him prime minister of Vietnam, an entity that existed only in Bao Dai's mind.

To the Americans, Diem seemed heaven-sent. He was a true Vietnamese, fifty-four years old, anti-French, anti-Communist, with some experience in the colonial bureaucracy, and a Catholic. (Never mind that South Vietnam was 85 percent Buddhist.) Furthermore, he had powerful American friends, among them Francis Cardinal Spellman of New York; William O. Douglas, an associate justice of the Supreme Court of the United States; and a young senator named John Fitzgerald Kennedy.

Diem had fled Vietnam in 1950 (the Communists hated him, and the French had condemned him to death in absentia) and lived for two years in the Maryknoll Seminary in Lakewood, New Jersey. He had made American friends during that hegira, and then had gone to Europe, placing himself in readiness for the call that came in 1954.

Soon after the Geneva partition, Diem returned to Saigon, ready to function as Bao Dai's prime minister. He was a short man, barely five feet tall, and rotund, and when he sat in the ruler's chair his feet just touched the ground. But he was not a figure of fun; he dressed impeccably and took life very seriously. He was intelligent, honest, dedicated to fashioning a reputable government, but not above a little nepotism. He named a younger brother, Ngo Dinh Nhu, as his chief adviser, and two other brothers to regional posts. Yet another brother was Catholic archbishop of Hue, and other relatives held numerous lesser posts.

The real trouble was Nhu and Nhu's wife, a beautiful and imperious woman who had opinions on all subjects and stated them with stridency. Nhu was one of the few people Diem trusted, and thus the Nhus came to be seen as alter egos of the ruler. Diem was Catholic, and very intransigent. He could not be moved from his opinions or his contemplated actions, nor would he delegate even slight amounts of power. He never married, his only sin was incessant smoking, and he did not mix well; he could not relate to the people he ruled, being a true mandarin at heart.

Within weeks after the Geneva partition, Vietnam's first Great Migration began. By land and sea Vietnamese men, women, and children began streaming south from the Hanoi-Haiphong area, desperate to escape what many feared would be a Communist bloodbath. Most refugees were Catholics, as was Diem, who abetted the migration with a slogan, "God has gone south." An armada of boats, including many United States Navy craft, carried the human waves south amid near panic. No one knows how many made the exodus, but accepted estimates put the number at about nine hundred thousand. At the same time, about ninety thousand Vietnamese went north. According to popular belief, the tide each way contained Communist agents, some moving south to infiltrate that area, others moving north to join Ho's forces for a later return south, as military conquerors.

August 1954 was an extremely busy month in Washington, where the Geneva

Accords were looked upon as a major disaster. As the National Security Council put it, the events of summer "completed a major forward stride of Communism, which may lead to the loss of Southeast Asia." President Eisenhower was determined that was not going to happen. He set the National Security Council (NSC) and the Joint Chiefs of Staff (JCS) to work on the problem of filling the French vacuum.

The Joint Chiefs of Staff quickly told Secretary of Defense Charles E. Wilson that certain things were necessary: (1) The French should withdraw entirely from Indochina; (2) if Diem was to receive American military aid "it [was] absolutely essential that there be a reasonably strong, stable government in control" in South Vietnam; and (3) a way must be found around the Geneva limitation of 342 Americans in the country.

By August 20, Eisenhower had approved an NSC paper stating that the United States would give economic aid directly to South Vietnam, not through France. This was confirmed officially on October 24 when Eisenhower wrote directly to Diem:

"I am, accordingly, instructing the American ambassador to Vietnam to examine with you in your capacity as chief of government how an intelligent program of American aid given directly to your government can serve to assist Vietnam in its present hour of trial."

Meantime, U.S. Army Colonel Edward G. Lansdale was gearing up the Saigon Military Mission (SMM), which had been planned in Washington even before Dien Bien Phu. On Eisenhower's orders he arrived in Saigon in June, flying in from Clark Air Force Base with only a box of files, a change of clothes, and a borrowed typewriter, ostensibly as Assistant Air Attaché. His real assignment was to set up a full range of CIA activities—espionage, sabotage, propaganda—in North Vietnam and keep Washington informed via secret communications through the Saigon CIA station.

By July, Lansdale had been joined by Major Lucien Conein, an OSS veteran who had worked underground with American forces in China and Indochina during World War II. A month later Conein moved into North Vietnam, ostensibly working to ease the problems of the Great Migration. Concin set up a network of Vietnamese agents in Hanoi and Haiphong. The United States Navy smuggled out trusted Vietnamese through Haiphong and flew them to the Philippines for training in underground warfare in a hidden valley near Clark Air Force Base. Lansdale had worked there for years just after World War II, training agents for the new Philippine government in its war against the Communist rebels, the Huks, in the Philippines.

October 9, 1954, was the last day for French forces in Hanoi and, a month later, U.S. Army General J. Lawton ("Lightning Joe") Collins arrived in Saigon to evaluate the situation in South Vietnam for President Eisenhower, his old boss in the European theater during World War II.

On the diplomatic front, Dulles had put together SEATO (the Southeast Asia Treaty Organization) as an Asian counterpart to NATO (the North Atlantic Treaty

27

Secretary of State John Foster Dulles signs the SEATO agreement in Manila for the United States, hailing it as an "Asiatic Monroe Doctrine" to halt the advance of communism.

Organization). On September 8, 1954, eight nations had signed the SEATO charter, agreeing to work together "to oppose further Communist gains in Southeast Asia." SEATO never functioned as well as NATO, but did provide the United States with some backing, politically and militarily. The Allied nations—Australia, Britain, France, New Zealand, Pakistan, the Philippines, Thailand and the United States—could now make common cause in what the United States looked upon as a world-wide struggle of the democracies against the Communist monolith.

From the first, "Lightning Joe" believed Diem lacked the leadership qualities needed to rule South Vietnam. General Collins felt so strongly on this point that he recommended Diem either be removed or "I recommend re-evaluation of our plans for assisting Southeast Asia." Dulles overruled Collins, asserting that "we have no other choice but to continue our aid to Vietnam and support Diem." In April 1955,

Saigon becomes the battleground in 1955, as rival sects and military cliques struggle for power (above), and civilians, caught in the middle, flee for safety during the constant gun battles (below).

Collins flew to Washington to plead his case, and Dulles softened; Diem would be ousted.

At the last minute, however, Diem stiffened and executed a series of bold moves, with strong aid from Lansdale and the CIA. At that time, Saigon was "governed" by a bizarre coalition of bandit gangs and weird religious sects. Bao Dai had never dared oppose them, nor had Diem, until at last he realized a showdown was at hand. The Binh Xuyen, a band of brigands with its own armed forces and fleet of river boats, controlled gambling, the opium trade, much legitimate commerce, and even the Saigon police force. The religious sects—Hoa Hao, Cao Dai, and many smaller groups—flourished with little regard to any authority.

Diem, working through his family, friends, and political associates, began by curbing the sects and by the end of April 1955 was ready to take on the Binh Xuyen. He assaulted and captured the Saigon police headquarters and divided and scattered the bandits. Bao Dai, still at the gambling tables in Monte Carlo, cabled his prime minister to desist, and Diem hesitated. What should he do? General Collins and Colonel Lansdale counseled Diem to take full power by legal means. Diem did, with a plebiscite October 23. Lansdale had warned him not to win it by

Ngo Dinh Diem, considered by many an aristocratic dilettante or "mandarin," consolidates his power, engineers a 98% victory in an October plebiscite, and in November is proclaimed the first President of the Republic of Vietnam. The United States recognizes him; Ho and the Communist world denounce him as an American puppet.

99.9 percent, and he didn't. Diem's count was 98 percent. The United States reluctantly termed the results a mandate. On October 26 Diem proclaimed the birth of the Republic of Vietnam, with himself as president.

As early as May 1955, Diem had asked the United States to send military instructors for his armed forces. In the same month, Ho Chi Minh's forces took control of Haiphong, the best harbor in all of Vietnam. In January, General Collins had put Colonel Lansdale in charge of coordinating all United States civil and military programs, and things had begun to happen. Colonel Napoleon Valeriano and three junior officers had flown in from the Philippines to help train Diem's agents to infiltrate Communist guerrilla forces working underground in South Vietnam. The United States supplied these agents with radios, carbines, pistols, ammunition, and explosives, flown in by the U.S. Air Force from the Philippines.

In addition, special South Vietnamese infiltration teams were trained in the Philippines and put ashore at night in North Vietnam from U.S. Navy vessels. Their mission was sabotage and subversion among Ho Chi Minh's supporters, but the agents had little success. Most of them simply faded from sight—captured or killed, or as defectors to the Communist side. And by July 1955, Ho Chi Minh's diplomatic efforts began to bear fruit: both Communist China and the Soviet Union announced agreements to supply North Vietnam with military and economic aid.

But the late 1950s, the years just after the Geneva partition, brought serious internal problems for both North Vietnam and South Vietnam. Millions of Vietnamese were uprooted from their homes by the Great Migration, and the French were slow and troublesome in surrendering power in Indochina. In addition, "land reform" became the battle cry in both North Vietnam and South Vietnam. Ho Chi Minh used the ritual Communist methods in the north, seizing land and "reeducating" the peasants to work for the state. In South Vietnam, Diem seized the land by autocratic methods to benefit the mandarin ruling class.

Both rulers turned to terrorism, torture, and murder, and hundreds of thousands of peasants were slaughtered in the name of "reeducation." But both Ho and Diem had to pull back within a few years—the "land reform" terror was too costly and obscured the real goal—pacification of the countryside and the building of national strength. Diem would have been satisfied with a secure South Vietnam, but not Ho. His goal was all of Indochina—the other half of Vietnam, plus all of Laos and Cambodia.

The United States had its goals, too. In May 1956, President Eisenhower sent 350 more Americans to South Vietnam under the guise of TERM (Temporary Equipment Recovery Mission). TERM's mission ostensibly was to help the Vietnamese recover and re-use military equipment the French had left behind. Actually these men would stay on, doubling the strength of MAAG. Meanwhile, the eyes of the world were on Europe, where tank-led Soviet forces put down an uprising of patriots in Hungary in October, and on the Middle East, where Israel smashed the Egyptians at the Suez Canal in the Sinai War. These crises diverted attention from a steady growth in American interests in Southeast Asia.

The United States scored one point on the diplomatic front in 1956: It prodded

Diem into promulgating South Vietnam's first constitution, a high-sounding document patterned after the American model. This event, on October 26, had little real effect in Vietnam, but it made the United States feel better, and did help the Eisenhower administration keep the Congressional purse strings open for aid to Diem.

Eisenhower was, on the whole, encouraged by events in Southeast Asia. Cambodia, with military aid from the United States, had declared its independence in late 1955, and there were signs that Laos might follow that lead. In early 1956, the U.S. Navy opened a small office in Bangkok, Thailand, to supervise all American military construction in Southeast Asia.

With little notice by the world, Thailand was becoming America's strongest ally in Southeast Asia. Within a few years in the early 1960s, thousands of native laborers, directed by American engineers, would transform Thailand, building six jet airfields with runways of ten thousand feet or more; a major port city, Sattahip, on the Gulf of Siam; highways, railroads, fuel pipelines, power plants, and cantonments. The cost was a half billion dollars, which included U-Tapao, near Sattahip, the largest airfield in Southeast Asia. When the Thailand bases were needed, they were ready.

By 1957, President Diem's regime seems to be progressing so well that he is invited to Washington and officially welcomed by President Eisenhower and Secretary of State Dulles.

By 1957, the United States was beginning to feel some confidence in the Diem regime, and in a spirit of euphoria invited President Diem to visit the United States. He came in May, conferred with Eisenhower, addressed a joint session of Congress, received the ritual ticker-tape parade up Broadway, and left for home in ten days.

During his visit, he outlined his plans for building a Vietnamese army of 170,000 men, some seven divisions, and the Vietnamese air force. The United States encouraged these developments. As of June 1, the U.S. Air Force was officially charged with the complete training of the Vietnamese Air Force. A 7,200-foot runway had been completed at Tan Son Nhut, and a 10,000-foot concrete runway was under construction. Optimism abounded.

In the fall of 1957, the U.S. Army's Special Forces, destined to fame as the Green Berets, came to Vietnam. A team from the First Special Forces Group in Okinawa flew into the Vietnamese Commando Center at Nha Trang and began training the first cadre for the Vietnamese Special Forces. The first class of fifty-eight men became instructors for their fellow Vietnamese, and in May 1960 the United States sent thirty more instructors from Fort Bragg. They brought with them the traditions of the First Special Service Force of World War II, the "Devil's Brigade," which had served with distinction in the Aleutians, North Africa, Italy, and southern France.

But Ho Chi Minh was not to be cheated of the southern half of "our territories." He gave the word, and Viet Minh supporters inside South Vietnam began a campaign of assassination of local leaders. In the last half of 1957, hundreds of village chiefs, rural police, school teachers, and district officials were murdered.

As the terror spread south early in 1958, Diem coined the phrase Viet Cong, short for Vietnamese Communist. The phrase and its shortened form, VC, entered the American lexicon as an epithet. By mid-year, the VC were attacking plantations near Saigon and had set up a coordinated command in the Mekong Delta. Ho's major concern was that the Viet Cong were proceeding too fast; he needed more time to build his military strength in the north.

By early 1959, Ho was ready. He authorized the VC in South Vietnam, now organizing in groups of one hundred or more, to defend themselves if attacked, and soon they were taking over whole areas of the countryside. The North Vietnamese Army began serious work on the Ho Chi Minh trail that spring. It had long been a foot trail winding down through Laos and Cambodia, west of the Vietnam border.

The southern exit was in Tay Ninh Province (III 21), fifty miles northwest of Saigon, in an area that became known as War Zone C, a bloody battlefield during the second half of the 1960s. With military supplies soon coming down the trail, the VC claimed its first American lives. On the night of July 8, 1959, six American advisers were watching a movie (Jeanne Crain in *The Tattered Dress)* in a barracks at their camp near Bien Hoa, twenty miles northeast of Saigon. Guerrillas opened fire through the windows and two Americans fell dead. Their names—Major Dale R. Buis and Master Sergeant Chester M. Ovnand—now stand at the head of the Vietnam War's stunning black granite monument on the Mall in Washington, not far from the Lincoln Memorial.

Photos such as this amused American readers in 1958 but obscured the grim facts: Ho Chi Minh's forces in the south, made up of the native Communists, or Viet Cong, and the infiltrating Viet Minh moving down from Hanoi, now outnumber President Diem's forces and are growing steadily in numbers and equipment.

During the fall of 1959, the Viet Cong opened real warfare in the Mekong Delta, with two bloody ambushes in the Plain of Reeds in September, and attacks in Kien Phong Province (IV 30), on the Cambodian border. Diem preferred not to draw attention to these offensives, instead pointing to his program of building "agrovilles," which now consisted of some twenty-eight armed outposts, mostly in the central highlands around Pleiku, Kontum, and Ban Me Thuot. In fact, he announced in July that the program was eminently successful and would be expanded.

In North Vietnam, the Communist Party (then called Lao Dong) resolved in May 1959 "to continue the national democratic revolution in South Vietnam" and "to use force to overthrow the feudalist imperialist regime . . . and create the conditions for the peaceful reunification of the fatherland."

The Lao Dong announced in September 1960 that it had formed in the south a "broad national united front" of workers, peasants, and soldiers dedicated to over-

U.S. TROOPS IN VIETNAM

Administration	Role		Year	Added (or subtracted) During Year	Year-end Totals
Dwight D. Eisenhower	A D V I S		1960	+327	700
John F. Kennedy	O R Y		1961 1962 1963	+2,500 +8,800 +4,500	3,200 12,000 16,500
Lyndon B. Johnson	C O M B A T		1964 1965 1966 1967 1968	+6,500 +158,000 +204,000 +101,000 +50,100	23,000 181,000 385,000 486,000 536,100
Richard M. Nixon	C O M B A T and	W I T H D R A W A L	1969 1970 1971 1972 1973	−62,100 −138,200 −195,800 −116,000 March 29: Last troops leave	474,000 335,800 140,000 24,000

Note: With rotations, a total of 2,594,000 Americans served in Vietnam.

throwing Diem, and on December 20, 1960, as President Eisenhower's administration drew to a close, Ho Chi Minh officially announced to the world the National Front for Liberation of South Vietnam. The South Vietnamese continued to call it the Viet Cong.

Diem's power outside the Saigon area was clearly slipping. America's answer was to double the number of advisers, from 327 to 685. This decision was taken in the fall of 1959, to be implemented early in 1960. At the same time, the Joint Chiefs of Staff urged Diem to set up a unified military command, enlarge his army and augment his air force. In September 1960, Eisenhower shipped Diem the first of twenty-five U.S. Navy AD-6 planes and eleven H-34 helicopters, but the Vietnamese could neither use them nor maintain them effectively.

On November 8, 1960, John Fitzgerald Kennedy narrowly defeated Richard Milhous Nixon and was elected the youngest president in American history. At Kennedy's side as vice president stood Washington's master politician, Lyndon Baines Johnson, and they made an odd couple. Johnson had wanted the presidency himself, but the Kennedy juggernaut rolled him under. When the Democratic convention had given Kennedy the top spot on the first ballot, he had firmly rejected Johnson as his running mate. (He may have heard that Johnson had told friends he didn't like "to be pushed around by a forty-two-year-old-kid," or a reference to "a little scrawny fellow with rickets.") But finally the political wise men prevailed: Johnson would balance the ticket—South and North, maturity with youth, Bible-belt Protestant with Irish Catholic. For Johnson, vice president was better than nothing, and he accepted. No one could have foreseen the consequences, for the two men, for the nation, and for the world.

Three days after the American election, dissident Vietnamese Army paratroopers fluttered to earth in Saigon at 5 A.M. and quickly surrounded important spots, including the presidential palace. It was the first internal revolt against Diem, but the plotters were amateurs; what they wanted was more action from Diem against the Viet Cong, and less interference in Army affairs. Diem stalled for time, and in thirty-six hours troops loyal to him put down the revolt in a brief burst of violence. Some four hundred people were killed, many of them curious civilians who had come to watch the final confrontation at the palace. Diem was unscathed, this time.

In Washington, Eisenhower took no substantive actions during the final months of his administration; he would leave those to his young successor, John F. Kennedy. However, Eisenhower did warn Kennedy of a clandestine operation soon to be ready, an action that came to be known as the Bay of Pigs, and he counseled Kennedy on Southeast Asia. Laos was the most dangerous place, Eisenhower said, and it must be defended. If Kennedy had to send troops to Laos, Eisenhower said, he would "come up here and stand beside you."

Then Eisenhower left office. During the eight years of his presidency he had committed only a few hundred Americans to Vietnam, and when he left the total was only seven hundred.

3

THE YEAR 1961 looked as though it might be a good one for the American military, and it was. John F. Kennedy knew something about war in the Pacific (everyone knew his exploits in PT 109); he knew a good deal about Southeast Asia (he'd visited there twice in recent years); and he had some pretty firm ideas on what America's role in any 1960s warfare should be. Even before his inauguration, Kennedy had asked each of the armed services to give thought to what role it might play in counterinsurgency, specifically guerrilla warfare.

John Fitzgerald Kennedy took the oath of office January 20, 1961, a bitterly cold day in Washington, and charmed a nation with his calmness and resolution, his hopes, and above all the vigor of his youth. Millions watching on television saw him standing bareheaded in the wind, his words catching fire even as the audience did . . . "the torch has been passed to a new generation of Americans . . ."

Indeed it had, for if any one word described the Kennedy regime, it was youth. Truman and Eisenhower had been in their sixties as presidents; most of the Kennedy team were in their forties, and the president's brother Robert was only thirty-six. Many were Harvard graduates and veterans of World War II, untried in government but brilliant in their own careers. Robert Strange McNamara, forty-five, business teacher at Harvard, first president of the Ford Motor Company who was not a Ford, was the "whiz kid" with a "mind like a computer." Arthur Schlesinger, Jr., prize-winning Harvard historian, had worked in the Office of War Intelligence (OWI) and Office of Strategic Services (OSS) in World War II. McGeorge Bundy was a Harvard graduate and had served in Army intelligence.

One stood out as a bit of a maverick: the Vice President, Lyndon Baines Johnson. He was already in his fifties, a Texan, and not entirely comfortable with all those Eastern intellectuals. Above all, he was a political accident, a last-minute compromise choice, a political veteran ten years older than his "boss." Nonetheless, John-

When John F. Kennedy took the oath of the presidency in January, 1961, he rallied "a new generation of Americans" to his side. None could foresee the decade of tragedy that lay ahead, for Kennedy and the two men at his left, Lyndon Johnson and Richard Nixon.

son had proved himself a good soldier, campaigning hard for Kennedy and carrying enough critical southern states to give Kennedy the narrow victory over Nixon.

The day after Kennedy's inauguration, Radio Hanoi broadcast a paean of praise for the National Front for Liberation of South Vietnam—the Viet Cong, its own creation—and vowed to "overthrow the United States–Diem clique." But Vietnam was not high on Washington's list. Kennedy already had in mind a firm policy for Southeast Asia, dating back ten years to his visits to that area. He could see that French policy had been fatally flawed, and any hope of success must rest with the allegiance of the people, not "the legions of General de Lattre." To attempt to hold this part of the world "in defiance of innately nationalistic aims spells foredoomed failure."

38

Barely two months into the Kennedy regime, the Russians test him by sending arms to the Laotians and backing their prodding offensive in Indochina. President Kennedy moves the U.S. Seventh Fleet into position, helicopters 500 U.S. Marines into Thailand, and alerts the U.S. Army. On March 23, Kennedy warned the world that Laos must remain independent. The Russians backed down.

Two weeks after Kennedy took office Walt Whitman Rostow brought him a pessimistic report from Vietnam written by Colonel Lansdale—graft, corruption, poor leadership. After reading it, the President said to Rostow, "This is the worst yet. You know, Ike never briefed me about Vietnam." Ike's timing was right; trouble came first in Laos, a bewildering little country about the size of Wyoming. But, by accident of geography, Laos was a cockpit for the world's most powerful adversaries, the United States and the Soviet Union. Laos was landlocked, mountainous, and almost roadless, but it could serve as a corridor between north and south Vietnam. It also had a border with Communist China, and the northern part of Laos overhung Thailand in a menacing fashion, with Burma, Malaya, and India beyond.

Laos had only two or three million people (nobody knew for sure), but by the time Kennedy came to office the United States had already poured $300 million of "aid" money, mostly military, into the country to support the Royal Laotian Army, in the hope that it would one day repay American kindness. The Soviet Union had likewise been supporting its own interests through the Pathet Lao, a pro-Communist faction.

Early in March 1961, the Pathet Lao, armed by a massive Soviet airlift, opened an offensive. The Royal Laotian Army immediately began a retreat. On March 23, President Kennedy went on national television to make clear the American objective for Laos: "A peaceful country, an independent country, not dominated by either side." The Russians had flown over one thousand sorties into Laos since December, and Kennedy felt that now was the time to warn Soviet Premier Nikita Khrushchev. "The security of all Southeast Asia will be endangered if Laos loses its neutral independence," the President said. "Its own safety runs with the safety of us all—in neutrality observed by all."

Kennedy then ordered the U.S. Seventh Fleet into the Gulf of Siam, helicoptered five hundred Marines into Thailand, and alerted Army troops on Okinawa. On April 1, Khrushchev signaled a hold through diplomatic channels, and three weeks later the Russians agreed to a cease-fire in Laos.

At the same time, Kennedy was facing another test of fire—the invasion of Cuba on April 17 at the Bahia de Cochinos, or Bay of Pigs. The plan had been for eight hundred Cuban exiles to train in Guatemala with CIA support, assault their homeland, and overthrow the Communist regime of Fidel Castro.

The whole operation was a poorly kept secret, and it failed quickly; most of the invaders were captured, and the United States was exposed. The important thing was President Kennedy's reaction; he remained calm, accepted complete responsibility, and demonstrated an inner strength that would be needed in the days ahead. For now, he quickly closed the door on the Bay of Pigs, finessed the Russians in Laos, and dispatched his vice president on a tour of Southeast Asia. The main purpose was to assure friends there—Chiang Kai-shek in Taiwan, Diem in South Vietnam, and Thanarat Sarit in Thailand—of the Kennedy administration's interest in that part of the world.

On May 5, President Kennedy told a news conference he would consider the use of United States forces "to help South Vietnam resist Communist pressures." This did not mean the sending of combat troops; that was never Kennedy's policy. His policy was clear and firm: Whatever had to be done in South Vietnam would be done by Vietnamese troops. The United States would provide arms and training, implemented mainly by the Army Special Forces, the Green Berets.

Lyndon Johnson flew into Saigon May 13 with typical Texas ebullience, addressed South Vietnam's national assembly, talked privately with Diem on economic matters and social and government reforms, and somehow gave the impression that Diem was a combination George Washington and Winston Churchill of Southeast Asia. Actually Diem was becoming more rigid, more remote from his people, and more fearful of American influence. He did promise social reforms, but he did not want American troops; somehow the reforms never materialized.

In his report to Kennedy, Johnson said: "The battle against Communism must be joined in Southeast Asia with strength and determination to achieve success there— or the United States inevitably must surrender the Pacific and take up our defenses on our own shores . . . Without this inhibitory influence, the island outposts— Philippines, Japan, Taiwan—have no security and the vast Pacific becomes a Red sea . . . The basic decision in Southeast Asia is here. We must decide whether to help these countries to the best of our ability or throw in the towel in the area and pull back our defenses to San Francisco and a 'Fortress America' concept."

It was on this trip that the vast Mekong River seized Johnson's imagination. He saw it in terms of what the United States had done with the Tennessee Valley Authority. The Mekong was a river that flowed twenty-five hundred miles from China through Thailand, Laos, Cambodia, and Vietnam, with twenty million people living along the river in poverty, hunger, and illiteracy. Imagine what could be done for these people if this mighty river could be harnessed! He would return to this theme during his own presidency. Johnson concluded his report: "I recommend that we move forward promptly with a major effort to help these countries defend themselves."

At the same time, Kennedy was receiving reports on the status of the American military establishment. He did not find them encouraging. The Army, in particular, seemed to be directing most of its money toward preparing for warfare of huge armies on the great land masses of the world. Kennedy believed that kind of war was gone forever, buried in the atomic rubble of Hiroshima. The wars of the future, he felt, could only be small, "brush-fire" operations, to be quickly controlled and smothered by specialized elite troops.

The President was encouraged that the Air Force had started training an air commando group in April at Eglin Air Force Base in Florida. The 4400th Combat Squadron, under the code name Jungle Jim, consisted of 350 hand-picked volunteers complete with a splashy uniform—Australian bush hat, combat boots, and fatigues. These men were highly trained and combat-oriented, as were the Army's Green Berets; could they be controlled if sent to South Vietnam as teachers and advisers?

In early fall, Kennedy visited the Army's Special Warfare Center at Fort Bragg, North Carolina. His interest dated back to the early days of his administration, when he concluded that the Soviet Union didn't want nuclear or conventional warfare any more than the United States did and was now concentrating on guerrilla war. He was also impressed by a report from Colonel Lansdale on the success of the Viet Cong's guerrilla warfare in South Vietnam.

President Diem's envoy, Defense Minister Nguyen Dinh Thuan, confers in private with President Kennedy at the White House in June 1961. The situation in South Vietnam is becoming precarious.

Beefing up the U.S. Army Special Forces was a personal initiative of President Kennedy. He ordered the forces quadrupled to 4,000 men, gave them back their unique headgear, the Green Beret, ordered new training and new weapons, and in October 1961 inspected units at Fort Bragg to measure their progress.

At Fort Bragg the President gave direct orders: Expand the Special Forces from one thousand to four thousand men, and develop new training manuals and new weapons. Kennedy did two other things: He reinstated the green beret as a unique headgear for the Special Forces and ordered training broadened to include teaching, medical care, and sanitation, in addition to military skills. The Special Forces were going to Vietnam as soldiers and teachers—not to take Vietnam, but to show the Vietnamese how to do it.

During the summer of 1961, the Marines had begun their own OJT (on-the-job training) program. Small groups of officers and noncommissioned officers (NCOs), mostly from the 3rd Division on Okinawa, were flown into Vietnam for two weeks of practice in jungle warfare. In addition, Major General Robert E. Cushman set up a counter-guerrilla training course in northern Okinawa, using instructors from the British Jungle Warfare School in Malaya and the Army's Special Forces School at Fort Bragg.

On the conventional warfare side, the Army's counterinsurgency plan (CIP) was on Kennedy's desk just as he reached the White House. At Eisenhower's order, the Army had spent a year developing it. CIP pledged United States support to an increase of twenty thousand men in the regular South Vietnamese army and a thirty-two thousand-man increase in the Civil Guard, conditional on governmental reforms by Diem. Kennedy quickly approved CIP, but Diem raised one objection after another.

In the meantime, terror in the South Vietnamese countryside continued to rise. By March 1961, U.S. intelligence estimated the Viet Cong strength at ten thousand men, in control of 58 percent of the countryside. Violent incidents were running over six hundred per month. At the end of April, Kennedy, tired of waiting for Diem to move, approved the CIP plan unilaterally. He also authorized one hundred new MAAG personnel, for a new total of 785 Americans serving in Vietnam.

By summer, terrorist activity was rising alarmingly. Diem now wrote Kennedy a long letter. In addition to the Viet Cong's activities, he said, North Vietnamese regulars were infiltrating South Vietnam by the hundreds and must be stopped. Diem asked for more American advisers, more military hardware, and money for 100,000 new troops to raise the Army of the Republic of Vietnam (ARVN) to 270,000.

Kennedy turned to his oldest and most trusted military friend, General Taylor. Maxwell Davenport Taylor, just turned sixty, was the perfect soldier—urbane, intellectual, rugged. He had been Superintendent of the Academy at West Point, teacher of French and Spanish, Commander of the 101st Airborne Division at Normandy, Commander of the American Military Government and Army forces in Berlin in 1950, Commander of the Eighth Army in Korea. Now Kennedy asked him: "How do I answer this letter from Diem?"

The result was the Taylor mission to Saigon, set for mid-October. General Taylor was the man who, after Korea, had said "never again" to an American war on the Asian land mass. To balance the scales, Kennedy sent along Walt Rostow, the administration's resident superhawk and optimist. Taylor and Rostow's assignment was to view the situation in Vietnam and recommend what to do to "avoid a further deterioration in the situation in South Vietnam, and eventually to contain and eliminate the threat to its independence."

After two weeks in Vietnam, Taylor and Rostow stopped on the way home at Baguio in the Philippines to write their report, and reached Washington early in November. The report proposed a fundamental change in American policy in Vietnam. Instead of a strictly advisory role, Taylor proposed a "limited partnership," in which the United States would provide "working" advisors and "working" military units. Specifically, Taylor recommended the quick dispatch of three Army helicopter companies and six to eight thousand ground troops. The helicopters would go into service immediately with the Vietnamese Army, but the troops would be on strictly defensive duty around vital military installations.

Kennedy was upset by Taylor's recommendation to commit U.S. troops to Vietnam; he felt that was just the beginning, or, as he told friends: "It's like taking a drink. The effect wears off and you have to take another." Nor did Kennedy like a suggestion that perhaps the Americans could be disguised as a flood relief party, Vietnam having had terrible monsoon rains that fall. Kennedy vetoed the troop

General Maxwell D. Taylor, on a mission for President Kennedy, meets President Diem in October 1961 in Saigon, and returns to Washington with a fateful report. Based on Taylor's recommendation, Kennedy agrees that U.S. advisers, working in South Vietnam since 1957, may accompany their Vietnamese units into combat. There is no public announcement of this.

proposal, but granted one vital concession: Advisers already in Vietnam could now accompany their Vietnamese units into combat. Kennedy also approved the Army helicopters for Vietnam. A new era in warfare was about to begin.

On November 13, 1961, Defense Secretary McNamara issued a sheaf of orders, all with admonitions such as "with all possible speed," or "proceed urgently." They directed the dispatch of American men and materials to Vietnam for airlift, reconnaissance, photography, a tactical air control system, intelligence, boats and ships for control of inland and coastal waterways, and additional air and ground support systems. On the economic side he ordered better pay, food, and medicine for the military, relief goods for flood areas, and "insertion" of Americans into the South Vietnamese bureaucracy "in types and numbers to be agreed upon by the two governments."

There was no public announcement, but McNamara put it this way in orders to Admiral Harry D. Felt, Commander in Chief, Pacific, the overall military commander for Southeast Asia:

"Political uncertainty of Diem's position and doubt as to his willingness to take steps to make his government more effective must not prevent us from going ahead full blast (without publicity, until political discussions are completed) on all possible actions short of large-scale introduction of U.S. combat forces."

Neither McNamara nor the Joint Chiefs of Staff (JCS) were entirely happy with the Kennedy program; the JCS had been thinking in terms of six American divisions for Vietnam, "to show we mean business," and some of McNamara's thoughts (and actions) were far ahead of Taylor's. Secretary of State Dean Rusk worried about further commitment to "a losing horse," and J. Kenneth Galbraith, a trusted Kennedy adviser, looked on Diem as "a wasting asset."

But on the whole, the Kennedy program was a solid step forward for the American military, which already had set up such code-named operations as Farm Gate (air power) and Ranch Hand (defoliation), and sent in the Army helicopters and the Green Berets. The rest of 1961 was crowded with action.

Jungle Jim, the Air Force commandos, began staging out to Vietnam in October, and by December the outfit was complete at Bien Hoa airfield, just north of Saigon; 151 men and sixteen planes—eight T-28s, four SC-47s, and four RB-26s. All aircraft carried the markings of the Vietnamese Air Force. In addition, the USAF flew out four RF-101s for reconnaissance over Vietnam and Laos. The subterfuge was that Saigon had invited them to take part in an air show.

In November, four other RF-101s had changed base, from Japan to Don Muang air base in Thailand. The Bien Hoa planes flew 67 sorties in their first month; the Thai-based planes, 130. In addition, sixteen C-123s went out in November, along with thirty T-28s on "loan" to the VNAF.

The first Green Beret assigned in Vietnam was a medical sergeant sent up to Buon Enao in Darlac Province (II 11) in November. He learned very quickly, as would many other Special Forces men, that theirs was a curious role. Supposed to be advisers, they were forced to take a much larger role as leaders, counselors, and judges for the Montagnards, an aboriginal people in the highlands. The Green

Berets became the backbone of the CIDG, the Civilian Irregular Defense Group, a valued holding force until the big American buildup came in 1965.

Late in November, President Kennedy approved one more step. He agreed that six C-123s, equipped for aerial spray, could continue on from California to South Vietnam, and there perform "carefully controlled" defoliation experiments. Thus began Operation Ranch Hand, with historic consequences.

About the same time, the Air Force put all its Vietnam operations together as 2nd Advance Echelon (2nd Advon) under the command of Brigadier General Rollen H. Anthis. He arrived in Saigon November 20, 1961, and settled in at the Brink Hotel, in charge of three numbered detachments in Vietnam and a fourth one in Thailand. President Kennedy charged these units with a "training" role, but authorized them to "fire back if fired upon." However, they were firmly instructed to avoid killing or wounding civilians.

U.S. Ambassador Frederick Nolting was surprised, and more so when Anthis told him he (Anthis) was in charge of USAF operating units, not training units. Nolting found it "incomprehensible" that this could happen without his knowledge or Diem's.

The first U.S. helicopter forces arrived in Vietnam on December 11, 1961, with no attempt at secrecy. Anyone who wanted to could watch the USS *Card* (a World War II escort carrier) tie up at the Saigon waterfront with thirty-two Army H-21 helicopters and four hundred men of the 8th and 57th Transportation companies. By January the *Card* was back again with a third Army helicopter company (93rd Transportation Company), but this one was delivered at Da Nang, and the helicopters flew in from far out at sea.

Before 1961 was over, the U.S. Army helicopters were lifting Viet troops into action against the Viet Cong in War Zone D, near Saigon, and McNamara had approved moving a tactical air control system (TAC) to Vietnam to provide "cooperative" use of VNAF and USAF forces in strike, reconnaissance, and transport operations.

The rules of the game now began to get complex for the Americans. As 1961 ended, Washington decreed that Farm Gate aircraft could not engage in combat "except" when a Vietnamese crewman was aboard or when the VNAF was not able to perform certain missions. In coming months, many a bewildered Vietnamese found himself as a "crewman" on a "mission" he knew nothing about. Some could not speak a word of English and had never been off the ground before.

By year's end, American military strength in South Vietnam had risen to thirty-two hundred men, but the increase had not made any difference yet. The Viet Cong's strength had risen to twenty-five thousand men, augmented by perhaps four thousand North Vietnamese infiltrators. Saigon was nearly surrounded by hostile forces and, if Diem was going to be saved, 1962 was the year to do it.

4

Building Up
1962

ARLY 1962 was clearly the time to straighten out American command problems in Saigon. With American troops moving into the country, and thousands more expected, situations like the Air Force's 2nd Advon simply had to be regularized. Washington finally acted on February 8, authorizing the Military Assistance Command, Vietnam (MACV), with a full general in charge. McNamara leaned toward the Army's Lieutenant General Paul D. Harkins. The secretary described Harkins as "an imaginative officer, fully qualified to fill what I consider to be the most difficult job in the U.S. Army." Harkins flew to Florida, where Kennedy was on vacation. The President quickly approved Harkins' appointment, with a fourth star. Kennedy was delighted to discover that Harkins spoke French and wished him luck in his new command.

Harkins flew to Saigon and quickly solved his first problem by making General Anthis chief of all USAF operations in Southeast Asia, under MACV. It was now clear that for that part of the world a full general would be reporting to a full admiral in Hawaii, CINCPAC (Commander in Chief, Pacific), who reported to the Secretary of Defense in the Pentagon, who met nearly every day with President Kennedy in the White House. It was never entirely settled who outranked whom in Saigon, the commanding general or the U.S. ambassador, but it really mattered little (except for an occasional ruffling of feathers) since the ambassador spoke directly to Secretary of State Rusk, who met nearly every day with McNamara and Kennedy. There was never any doubt that Kennedy outranked them all.

Operation Ranch Hand, the defoliation program in Vietnam, finally began January 10, 1962, on a very low key and only after full discussion at the highest levels in Washington and Saigon, including both Kennedy and Diem. The fear was that North Vietnam would try to capitalize on American use of "chemical warfare" against Vietnamese natives. It was decided to let the announcement come from

The American brass arrived in force in 1962. Here, U.S. Ambassador Frederick E. Nolting (right) greets General Paul D. Harkins, the first full U.S. general to command in Vietnam, and Admiral Harry D. Felt, the U.S. Navy's Commander in Chief, Pacific, and, by inter-service agreement, the highest U.S. military authority in Southeast Asia.

Diem, and a cleverly contrived press release appeared the next day in the Vietnamese press (see facsimile). The response from the world press was mostly negative; there was even some opposition within the American military, but that could be controlled.

The first C-123 flight sprayed about two hundred gallons of Agent Purple along Route 15, just east of Saigon. Results were poor. The mixture was not strong enough to kill the heavy jungle foliage, but it did melt the rubber gaskets in the spray machine. Formal missions began January 13 along Route 15, between Ba Ria and Long Thanh, with gradual refinement of technique. It was soon found that spraying must be done between sunset and sunrise, because, when the sun was up, thermal waves caused the spray to rise, rather than fall, and thus disperse too widely to be effective.

OPERATION RANCH HAND

FIRST ANNOUNCEMENT—DEFOLIATION PROGRAM
Vietnamese Newspapers—Jan. 11, 1962

SAIGON (VP)—The Republic of Vietnam today announced plans to conduct an experiment to rid certain key communications routes of thick, tropical vegetation. U.S. assistance has been sought to aid Vietnamese personnel in this undertaking.

The purpose of this operation is to improve the country's economy by permitting free communications along these routes and by making additional land available for cultivation and other uses. In addition, it will facilitate the Vietnamese Army's task of keeping these avenues of communication free of Viet Cong harassments.

Commercial weed-killing chemicals will be used in experiments. These chemicals are used widely in North America, Europe, Africa, and the USSR for such purposes as ridding corn fields of weeds, renovating weed-infested grazing pastures and clearing irrigation ditches.

The chemical will be supplied by the United States at the request of the Vietnamese Government. The Government emphasized that neither of the two chemicals is toxic, and that neither will harm wild life, domestic animals, human beings, or the soil. There will be little, if any, effect on plants outside the sprayed strip.

If the results of this initial operation are satisfactory, extensive operations will be conducted to clear roads and railroads linking key cities of Vietnam. Clearance of tropical growth along these routes will ease greatly the task of maintaining road systems and railroad beds and will permit the construction of new roads.

Spraying was confined mostly to thinly populated areas, and C-47s preceded the operations, telling civilians by voice and leaflets to take cover. There were no complaints from the peasants or the South Vietnamese government, but it was easy to tell where the planes were kept at Tan Son Nhut. Fumes from the defoliants killed all vegetation around the headquarters, including two huge trees.

On February 2, 1962, the Air Force suffered its first action casualties in Vietnam; one of its C-123 spray planes crashed in the jungle, killing three Americans— Captain Fergus C. Groves II, Captain Robert D. Larson, and Staff Sergeant Milo B. Coghill. It was never determined if the cause was enemy action, but from then on Ranch Hand missions had fighter cover. Nine days later an SC-47 crashed on a leaflet-dropping mission near Da Lat (II 14), 150 miles northeast of Saigon. This

Defoliation experiments, using U.S. Air Force C-123s with special rig, began in earnest in 1962. The storm of protests over the so-called Agent Orange came years later, but this official caption contained this line: "Harmless to human and animal life, the chemicals are temporarily effective against the dense vegetation which may be shielding enemy troops from aerial view."

OPERATION RANCH HAND

The Defoliation Spraying Program in South Vietnam
1965–1971

Acres Treated [1]		*Principal Agents Used, in Gallons* [2]	
1962/64	124,493	Orange	11,266,929
1965	221,555	White	5,274,129
1966	765,378	Blue	1,137,470
1967	1,661,885		
1968	1,464,217		
1969	1,442,680		
1970	273,982		
1971	2,303		

Sources: 1. The mean figure of three principal studies: National Academy of Sciences, Department of the Army, and Stockholm International Peace Research Institute.
2. National Academy of Sciences.

time the toll was eight Americans and one Vietnamese. McNamara was angry and embarrassed. Eight Americans to "train" one Vietnamese? The Joint Chiefs of Staff promptly ordered an end to such activities, "except in unusual circumstances."

For the rest of the year Operation Ranch Hand continued its experiments and made some discoveries: It was really hard to kill the jungle and almost impossible to burn it. The spray had to fall under ideal conditions, and even then it often took repeat trips to denude up to three layers of jungle canopy. Meanwhile, complaints and damage claims for lost crops began to come in from Vietnamese farmers.

But there were positives, too. The defoliation program had a strong psychological impact on the Viet Cong, with hundreds surrendering in the first few months. Also, spraying could deny food to the Viet Cong. One helicopter run could destroy an acre of Viet Cong crops in five seconds. McNamara defended this usage of defoliants, pointing out that both sides had been burning each other's crops for years. That November, at harvest time, two Vietnamese helicopter units destroyed 745,000 pounds of food in a few minutes in Phuoc Long Province (III 18), near the Cambodian border. That was enough food to sustain a thousand Viet Cong for a year, Saigon said.

By the end of 1962, Kennedy had dropped most restrictions on defoliation and the Air Force had treated fifty-seven hundred acres in all. Besides aerial spray, the next few years saw wide use of defoliation by American ground troops around bases to destroy enemy hiding places on the perimeters. This was usually done by hand spray. For the first two years, no Agent Orange was used.

Early in 1962, McNamara had ordered a central air control system set up for all of South Vietnam. Within two weeks the U.S. Air Force flew in men and equipment and set up high-frequency radio-teletype circuits between Tan Son Nhut and Da Nang, Bien Hoa, Pleiku, and Nha Trang.

Ironically, the first use of the air control system occurred when two of Diem's own pilots bombed his palace on the morning of February 27. The system quickly disclosed that the pilots had taken off ostensibly to bomb the Viet Cong in the Delta, but had then turned back to bomb the palace. Diem, his brother Nhu, and Mme. Nhu ran for the cellar shelters and were not seriously injured, though Mme. Nhu fell and broke her arm. The pilots, flying old American AD-6s, were angry over personal grievances. Both pilots lived to fight another day, but Diem now feared his own people more than ever.

In March the South Vietnamese government launched its Strategic Hamlet Program, with great fanfare. The idea was not new; a somewhat similar program, the so-called agroville program, had been started three years earlier. Now the government would build standardized villages (forts), enclosed by barbed wire, moats, and punji stakes of sharpened bamboo. Inside were neat thatch huts, school, dispensary, power plant.

The first five villages were quickly set up, like demonstration models, at Ben Cat, just north of Saigon. The farmers hated them. They were too far from market, too far from working fields, and they didn't stop the Viet Cong. In many cases, the guerrillas moved into the hamlets and operated from there. There never seemed to

51

President Diem's Strategic Hamlet program, launched in March 1962, was greeted with enthusiasm in Saigon, but skepticism in the field; nonetheless it went forward, for a time. The Vietnamese surrounded some villages with stockades (top), to protect the huts inside (bottom).

(Above) The United States supplied health services (shown, 1st Special Forces, Co. A, from Okinawa). The Saigon government tries to explain to the women and children, these near Pleiku, why they are being uprooted from their ancient villages. The plan was doomed to fail; the Viet Cong either overwhelmed the crude fortress towns, or joined the villages and subverted them.

be enough money coming from Saigon, or enough room for the population to be served.

Opinion was divided from the start. McNamara thought it a good program, other Americans sent back depressing reports. Diem said he was building "democracy," others thought he was protecting his political interests by dividing the Vietnamese people into controllable groups. The Communists derided the hamlets as "camouflaged concentration camps." American newsmen—there were only a half dozen in Saigon at this time—reported the hamlets were a sham and a failure. But the program went on, and by the fall of 1962 the South Vietnamese government was reporting that some four thousand strategic hamlets were housing 39 percent of the population.

At the same time, several thousand Green Berets and Navy Seabees (construction battalions) began pouring into South Vietnam, spreading out in the central highlands to set up outpost camps for mountain scouting and border surveillance. By the end of 1962 the Green Berets had trained six thousand aboriginal tribesmen who lived there as strike force troops, and another nineteen thousand as hamlet militia and village defenders. The Special Forces were operating in all four corps areas, with a total of twenty-four detachments, and headquarters in Saigon rated a full colonel.

Defense Secretary McNamara arrived in Saigon on April 30 for his first visit to South Vietnam. He spent nearly two weeks in the country, both in Saigon talking with leaders of the Diem regime and out in the countryside. He reported that Viet Cong activity was declining (fewer terror attacks on provincial capitals) and Saigon morale was up. He summed it up neatly in the "whiz kid" language he used: "Every quantitative measurement we have shows we're winning this war."

McNamara was scarcely back in Washington before trouble erupted in Laos. Communist troops were threatening Thailand from the Laotian capital, Vientiane, just across the Mekong River. Heavy fighting broke out in mid-May and Thailand appealed for help. President Kennedy acted swiftly; he was particularly sensitive on Laos. He named the Army's Lieutenant General John L. Richardson commander of Joint Task Force 116 and told him to leave the Russians in no doubt that Thailand would be defended by the United States. Within days the U.S. Seventh Fleet was in the Gulf of Siam, and Marine, Navy, Army, and Air Force reinforcements from all over the world were heading for Thailand. Thailand's huge American-built airfields sprang to life, and within days fifty thousand U.S. Marine and Army troops were on Thailand's northern border, a few miles from Vientiane. Once again the United States and the Soviet Union were metaphorically squared off, this time at a place called Nong Khai on the Mekong River.

Neither Kennedy nor Khrushchev considered Laos worth World War III, and through diplomatic channels they agreed on a mutual pullback. By the end of June, all American forces had withdrawn, but the display of U.S. military power had been impressive.

Another six thousand Americans poured into South Vietnam as 1962 progressed —more helicopter crews, planes, Green Berets, Seabees, advisers, trainers—both

54

Secretary of Defense Robert S. McNamara, personal representative of the Commander in Chief, President Kennedy, arrives April 30, 1962, on the first of his nine trips to Vietnam. (Left) Here, still in his Washington "uniform," McNamara is backed by General Lyman L. Lemnitzer, chairman of the U.S. Joint Chiefs of Staff and General Harkins, commanding general of the U.S. Military Assistance Command in Saigon. The Vietnamese officer is listed as "unidentified." (Below) McNamara quickly changes to more suitable garb and gets out into the field.

From early 1962, American advisers and equipment poured into South Vietnam with the aim of training and arming the Vietnamese to protect their own land. Overseeing this became the primary task of General Paul D. Harkins (center), top U.S. Army commander, shown here with General George H. Decker (right), U.S. Army Chief of Staff.

Civil guards at Hao Cain are instructed in the use of "grease guns."

Even women were pressed into service in this euphoric period of "civil defense" against the Viet Cong. In fact, some of them were Viet Cong, or more sympathetic to the Communists than to the Saigon regime.

M. Sgt. John M. Stover critiques a Vietnamese patrol on return from a mission.

General Maxwell Taylor greets native officers at Tuy Hao, Phu Yen Province, on one of his visits to the field.

More of the haul: The enemy's handmade weapons, crude but deadly, are displayed by M. Sgt. Sterling Cole of U.S. MAAG (Military Assistance Advisory Group). Most of these official U.S. pictures during 1962 carried a ritual disclaimer such as: "These U.S. personnel are not in a combat status and are instructed not to fire unless fired upon."

Some 300 Vietnamese rangers and civil guards, delivered in ten U.S. H-21 helicopters, make an offensive sweep across the Plain of Reeds, west of Saigon, in August.

Part of the haul, Viet Cong prisoners are lined up and await interrogation.

A Vietnamese Ranger knocks down a propaganda sign "left by retreating Viet Cong rebels." This meant the Viet Cong had lived to fight another day.

military and civilian. The first U.S. Marine helicopter detachment reached Vietnam in April, setting a pattern for many future troop movements. HMM-362 (Helicopter, Marine, Medium) moved in to Soc Trang, in the Delta, with twenty-four medium helicopters, in Operation Shufly, taking over an abandoned World War II Japanese airfield eighty-five miles southwest of Saigon. Soc Trang had the only hard runway in the Delta.

A four-hundred-man ARVN (Army of the Republic of Vietnam) battalion set up a defensive ring around the airstrip at dawn, and the first plane (a Douglas R-4D Skytrain) flew in from Okinawa with advance elements. It was quite a day. General Harkins and his Vietnamese counterpart, Brigadier General Le Van Nghiem, flew down from Saigon; Major General John P. Condon, commanding general of the 1st Marine Aircraft Wing, came over from Okinawa, ready to greet the headquarters' commander, Colonel John F. Carey, who had won his Navy Cross at the Battle of Midway in World War II. Colonel Carey stepped from his plane at 0800; there was a brief ceremony of handshakes and salutes; and Carey's party of eighteen officers and 193 enlisted men set to work.

In short order a base sprang up—seventy-five hardback tents, a TAFDS (fuel dispensing unit), a MATCU (Marine airfield traffic control unit) equipped with TACAN (tactical air navigation) and GCA (ground control approach) systems, a Navy doctor, dentist, and chaplain, trucks, and a water purification unit. In five days everything was ready, including radio and teletype connections to both Saigon and Okinawa.

At dawn on April 15, Lieutenant Colonel Archie J. Clapp (veteran of Iwo Jima and Okinawa; Navy Cross at Midway) set the first helicopter down at Soc Trang, flying in from the USS *Princeton,* at sea. By afternoon, the full squadron was ashore, with all its gear, the twenty-four helicopters, three Cessna OE-1 observation planes, and an R-4D transport. The next day "Archie's Angels" began looking over the territory, and a vast one it was. HMM-362's assignment ran from Saigon to Ca Mau, the southernmost tip of Vietnam, two hundred miles north/south, and the entire delta east/west, one hundred and fifty miles at the widest point. In that area, crisscrossed by thousands of canals and streams but few roads, Diem's government held just three large towns: Soc Trang, Can Tho, and My Tho. The Marines had come to Vietnam, but Soc Trang was "advisory," not war.

The real war in the north was three years away, and the Riverine War, here in the south, was four years off. Nevertheless, "Archie's Angels" began "advisory" missions Easter Sunday morning, April 22, 1962, flying four hundred Vietnamese soldiers into action in Operation Lockjaw. The U.S. Army's 57th Helicopter Company, based at Tan Son Nhut, joined in Operation Lockjaw, which went off well. Lockjaw was the first of thousands of such missions, most of them recorded only in service records. As a footnote, the Army helicopters carried machine guns, the Marines only side arms and two hand-held .45-caliber submachine guns (M3A1s). Helicopter warfare was but an infant.

In Washington an extremely important military development was under way. Defense Secretary McNamara had been looking at the Army's air arm, and on

58

April 19, 1962, he issued a now famous memorandum. He found that the Army's use of aircraft was dangerously conservative and he wanted maximum action immediately. He ordered a mix of integrated aircraft types looking toward maximum mobility for ground forces. It was a coup for the Army over the Air Force because it confirmed that, within a combat zone, the Army must control not only helicopters, but transport, observation, reconnaissance, and fighter aircraft.

The Army had long been experimenting with support aircraft of many types; now it could order the planes it wanted and begin integrating them into the new Army— air-mobile and airborne. By August the profile of the Army assault division was ready. It would have 459 aircraft, instead of 100; a total of 1,100 ground vehicles instead of 3,452. It would also have 105-mm howitzers and Little John rockets, transportable in helicopters; twenty-four armed Mohawks, and thirty-six Huey helicopters. One third of its assault elements could move at one time. Army aviation as a whole would need 8,900 aviators by 1963, and 20,600 by 1968. These were exciting times for the Army, and Vietnam was the place to try it all out.

In July McNamara authorized two more Army helicopter companies for Vietnam, and soon approved more planes for the South Vietnamese Air Force and for the U.S. Air Force's operation Farm Gate in training and supporting the growing VNAF. The new Huey gunships were arriving by fall, along with Mohawks and Caribous. The Mohawk (OV-1) was brought in to provide air surveillance for the ARVN and was a hit from the start. It was a twin-engine plane with a wingspread of only forty-two feet, and good speed (255 knots maximum), well suited for its mission of visual and photographic reconnaissance.

The U.S. Army's 23rd Special Warfare Aviation Detachment (surveillance), consisting of three flight teams, headquarters, and photo processing section, arrived at Nha Trang October 16, 1962, to support the ARVN 9th Division and the Railway Security Agency. Each team had two armed Mohawks, four pilots, and seven enlisted support specialists. The American rules then specified that a Vietnamese observer must be along on all missions, no weapons could be over .50 caliber, and they could be used only in defense.

Without question, the Mohawks reduced Viet Cong activity immediately and produced a wealth of intelligence, both visual and photo. Camouflaged buildings showed up, people were sighted where they shouldn't have been, and some could be identified from the air. The Mohawks were very quiet and soon were directing artillery fire, increasing the volume of such fire tremendously. Suddenly, every ground unit wanted Mohawks and clamored for greater offensive use.

The Caribou was a big plane for the Army (twin engine, wingspread of ninety-five feet, crew of three, and room for thirty-two passengers), but a useful one because it could handle supplies and troops into and out of rough airstrips. (One landing, at Tra My in I Corps, was on a strip 830 feet long, at the bottom of a valley surrounded by high hills. That one took the pilot three tries, and he finally came to rest eight feet from an embankment at the end of the runway.)

The Caribou was about half the size of the Air Force's smallest standard fixed-wing plane, the C-123, but the C-123 was denied many airstrips in Vietnam because

American Equipment

The USS Card, *a weary World War II escort carrier, did yeoman service transporting choppers to the war zone after a humiliating start. The Viet Cong sank it in the Saigon harbor with a limpet mine, in plain view of civilian gawkers, but the* Card *quickly rose to sail again and again.*

In early training, South Vietnamese regulars learn to fight out of choppers in both rice paddy (above left) and mountain jungle (above right).

South Vietnamese regulars move on to mass maneuvers (below left), and wing off to trap "Charlie" before he can escape (below right).

By February 1962, some 18,000 Vietnamese, such as these, had been trained in split-second loading (average time, 17 seconds).

American advisers trained Vietnamese pilots, such as this one, who is shown landing a T-28 trainer-fighter at Nha Trang.

(Center) The O-1E Bird Dog (shown minus jungle camouflage) played a big role in spotting the enemy, directing fire, assessing bomb damage, and chasing the Viet Cong. (Bottom) The new OV-10A Bronco was heavily armed for reconnaissance, pursuit of fleeing troops, transportation, and other odd jobs.

of its size. The Caribou, by contrast, was using 77 percent of all airstrips in South Vietnam by 1963, and was extremely useful in support of the Green Berets and all isolated strongpoints in the country. In the first six months of 1963, the Caribou flew over nine thousand sorties for the Army, delivered nearly four thousand tons of supplies, and carried almost fifty thousand passengers.

The Army also sent in its U-1A Otters and O-lF Bird Dogs; the former could carry up to ten passengers, and the latter, the smallest plane in the Army's inventory, only a pilot and observer. By midsummer the Otters and Bird Dogs were scattered from Hue to the Delta, and everybody called for more.

In September, the Marine helicopter squadron at Soc Trang, in the Delta, changed places with the Army helicopter company at Da Nang airfield, in the north. The change was made partly because the Marine helicopters worked better than the Army's at the higher altitudes in I Corps, but the change established the Marine presence in I Corps, where the Marines would fight out the rest of the war.

American animals go to war, too. M. Sgt. Johnie Pate of San Antonio, Texas, introduces the bloodhound to Warrant Officer Truong Van Be at a dog training center near Saigon.

The helicopter was already changing the shape of that war. Within a matter of months, Viet Cong morale plummeted. Suddenly the South Vietnamese had the upper hand; they could drop troops all around the Viet Cong concentrations and close in for the kill. The U.S. Army and Marines were delighted with the new weapon and called for more helicopters, and better ones.

Fortunately, the UH-1B, the first of the improved Hueys, was already on the way. This bird, the Army's standard utility helicopter, began reaching Vietnam in mid-1962 as the UH-1A, but in September the UH-1B overtook it and became the standard. Huey B had more firepower—four factory-installed M-60 machine guns and eight clusters of 2.75-inch rockets—than the Huey A and went into full service immediately, riding shotgun for the troop carriers, the H-21s. There was one big hobble—the Hueys were forbidden by Washington to fire until fired on. It didn't take the Viet Cong long to figure that one out—they simply withheld fire until the helicopters were hovering to land, then opened fire to destroy them. This was the beginning of a long line of rules that restricted American air power throughout the war. The rules were constantly changing, but they were always there.

Nonetheless, the helicopter badly frightened guerrillas and the Viet Cong quickly issued a tactics book, trying to teach its forces, both guerrilla and regular, how to combat the whirlybirds. The Communists never did develop a fully effective counterweapon, but hot days of battle lay ahead for the helicopter.

Vietnam was not the headline news in 1962; the Cuban missile crisis was. The Soviet Union, in order to probe the outer limits of American intentions, had secretly constructed forty launch pads for nuclear missiles in Cuba and was in the process of loading them, two missiles per pad. Even as the crisis blew up in October, Soviet ships were bringing more missiles. Obviously, the United States would not permit such a threat only ninety miles from American soil.

President Kennedy quickly built up a force of more than a hundred thousand troops in Florida, including both the 82nd and 101st Airborne divisions, a Navy-Marine amphibious force of forty thousand men, and a ring of ships around Cuba including eight aircraft carriers and sixty-eight squadrons of fighter planes. It was the largest American assault force assembled since World War II.

On October 22, Kennedy gave Khrushchev a forty-eight-hour ultimatum: remove all Russian missiles from Cuba or take the consequences. The Soviet Union capitulated; the most portentous crisis of the nuclear age was over.

In Vietnam, as 1962 ended, Robert Kennedy stood in Saigon and proclaimed, "We are going to win"; General Taylor stated that "a great national movement to destroy the Viet Cong" was under way; the New York *Times* said Vietnam "is a struggle this country cannot shirk"; and President Kennedy drafted a 1963 State of the Union message that would say, "The spearpoint of aggression has been blunted in South Vietnam."

5

The 1963 Debacle

THE YEAR 1963 opened with a victory, which the American media ignored, and a defeat, which the media vastly overplayed.

On the morning of January 2, ARVN forces with American air and helicopter support attacked a series of nine Viet Cong posts in Tay Ninh Province (III 21), west of Saigon. All planes available—twenty-six VNAF AD-6s, sixteen U.S. B-26s, and twenty-four T-28s—softened up the combat zone, and 1,250 South Vietnamese paratroopers dropped in to clean it up. Weapons and documents were captured, and at least four hundred Viet Cong, possibly eight hundred, were killed.

At the same time, at a tiny place called Ap Bac, thirty-five miles southwest of Saigon, a small operation turned into a debacle. The target was a radio station serving the Viet Cong Central Post for South Vietnam. About two hundred guerrillas were believed to be guarding the radio. The plan was to smash this outpost with a force of about two thousand South Vietnamese—helicopter troops from the north, mechanized infantry from the south.

Everything that could possibly go wrong did. No air cover was available; it was tied up at Tay Ninh. The enemy was far stronger than expected; at least battalion-size, instead of company-size. The helicopter troops sat down out of position. Liaison was bad; orders conflicted; there was some cowardice and a great deal of confusion.

The Viet Cong quickly pinned down the helicopter troops, put the armored company out of action, and escaped the trap leaving only four dead. The next day, South Vietnamese forces searching for the enemy fired on each other, refused to attack when ordered to, and moved in wrong directions. Three Americans, all helicopter crewmen, were killed, and six wounded; sixty-five South Vietnamese were killed, and one hundred wounded; three helicopters were lost and two were damaged.

In early 1963, training and village defense continued, with native forces building moats and setting punji stakes (sharpened bamboo) around the hamlets.

A minor military event, Ap Bac became a spectacular media event, providing American correspondents in Saigon an opening to blast both the Diem regime and the growing American involvement in the war. The dispatches—particularly those of David Halberstam of the New York *Times*—infuriated the military and displeased the administration, including President Kennedy.

Thus, Ap Bac became the opening gun in the "media war," leading to administration thoughts of battlefield censorship and to Admiral Felt's acerbic comment to one American newsman: "Get on the team!" Censorship was never imposed because it was impractical, and Vietnam became unique as a war that anyone could attend simply by buying an airline ticket to Saigon.

The real importance of Ap Bac was that it exposed serious military command problems, both within the American command and between the Americans and the Diem regime. The former problems—such as who should control air cover, the Army or the Air Force, and how?—were gradually solved by conference and compromise. The basic problem—that the United States was running a war for another country, which had sovereign control—never could be solved.

The Joint Chiefs of Staff, meeting January 7, 1963, ordered General Earle G. Wheeler, the Army chief of staff, to lead a party of senior officers to Saigon and "form a military judgment as to the prospects for a successful conclusion of the

Vietnamese training in the field: Troops are shown at chow (top); staging out of Can Tho in the Delta (center); and reviewing operations at the sand table (bottom).

conflict within a reasonable period of time." The mission spent the last two weeks of January in Vietnam and concluded that, on the whole, things were going well there and the United States should continue its present course. General Wheeler said that the situation had been "reoriented, in the space of a year and a half, from a circumstance of near desperation to a condition where victory is now a hopeful prospect."

At the same time the Viet Cong was seeing Ap Bac as its first good news in a year. The guerrilla leaders looked on it as the basis for a new war strategy—knock out an enemy strongpoint, then annihilate the enemy reinforcements as they arrive.

But the real impact of the Wheeler mission came from discussions with General Harkins in Saigon. Part of the explanation for Ap Bac, Harkins said, was the rule that helicopters could not fire until fired upon, and the Mohawks were unarmed. Soon after Wheeler returned to Washington the Joint Chiefs of Staff changed that: The Mohawks could now carry 2.7-inch rockets, and helicopters could "engage clearly identified Viet Cong elements which are considered to be a threat to the safety of the helicopters and their passengers."

That announcement caused a media event around the world. Hanoi demanded that the International Control Commission expel American air forces from Vietnam. Secretary of State Rusk, Secretary of Defense McNamara, and President Kennedy were besieged by newsmen, and fire came even from the Democrats, the president's own party. Senate Majority Leader Mike Mansfield said that after $4 billion of American aid "the same difficulties remain, if, indeed, they have not been compounded." He said Vietnam was more removed than ever from "popularly responsible and responsive government."

Nonetheless, both Army and Air Force resources expanded sharply in 1963. The Air Force's Southeast Asia Airlift System by mid-year was operating forty-eight C-123s, from both Tan Son Nhut and Da Nang; thirty-two C-47s, and thirty-two Army Caribous, making regular deliveries to four major depots, twenty-nine other distribution points, ninety-five different airfields, and sixty-five drop zones. It was also training Vietnamese helicopter pilots, graduating the first class of fifteen at Tan

General Earle G. Wheeler, the Army's new Chief of Staff, returns from touring Vietnam and tells a Washington news conference in early February the situation has improved from "near desperation," and "victory is now a hopeful prospect," though aid to the rebels from the Soviet Union and Communist China is a potent threat.

67

American losses begin to mount as U.S. commitment grows. At Tan Son Nhut, U.S. Army chaplain Lieutenant Colonel Thomas E. Waldie conducts a memorial service for Captain James E. Wenzel and Lieutenant Timothy M. Lang, 118th Aviation Co., Bien Hoa, killed while supporting ARVN troops.

Son Nhut in June. Another training center opened at Nha Trang in September, and airport support squadrons were activated at Qui Nhon and Can Tho. The 19th Tactical Air Support Squadron at Bien Hoa began training Vietnamese pilots in forward air control, reconnaissance, combat support, and observation. The Nha Trang center turned out Vietnamese pilots with eighty hours' flying time.

By mid-year, the Air Force alone had nearly five thousand people in Vietnam. The Americans were supposed to be merely advisers, but the press was reporting more and more Americans in combat missions. When the Viet Cong had shot down a B-26 on February 3, killing Captain John P. Bartley and Captain John F. Shaughnessy, Jr., it was hardly a "training mission," and three days later Major James E. O'Neill was killed in a crash. But Ambassador Nolting in Saigon and Secretary of State Rusk thought it better to maintain some fictions, Rusk asserting publicly that the Americans were "strictly limited to advisory, logistic, and training functions."

Strains were also showing in the Saigon regime. Diem himself was being seen less often, and his brother Nhu and Mme. Nhu seemed to be assuming more voice and power. After Ap Bac, Mme. Nhu had lashed out at American newsmen, implying they cared nothing for Vietnamese lives sacrificed there, only American lives. Harking back to the palace bombing of February 27, 1962, she said American reports of that episode showed "ill-concealed regret that the bombing had failed in its objective," despite the fact that she and her children were endangered. Even the Wheeler

On July 4, Brigadier General Joseph W. Stilwell, Jr., (left) dedicates Camp Holloway, near Pleiku, to the memory of Chief Warrant Officer Charles E. Holloway, an Army helicopter pilot killed on his first flight in Vietnam; a "missing man" ceremony (below) is held by men of the 52nd Aviation Battalion.

The Diem dynasty gathers, in early summer, for what turns out to be its last family portrait. Standing are President Diem, second from left; his brother Ngo Dinh Nhu, far left; and Madame Nhu, near center in white turban. Others standing are brothers or in-laws of Diem, a lifelong bachelor. Seated are Diem's mother and four Nhu children.

report commented on "mutual dislike and distrust" between the Vietnamese government and the American press.

By April, Nhu was hinting that American forces in Vietnam should be cut, by perhaps two thousand or more. Diem found the Special Forces "particularly irritating" because he saw them as undermining his authority in the countryside. He also feared that American efforts to expand their intelligence sources were really aimed at him, instead of the Viet Cong.

Diem never requested a cut in American forces, but other events were working that way. Sir Robert Thompson, the British counterinsurgency expert who earlier had defeated insurgent forces in Malaya, perceived that the South Vietnamese were "beginning to win the shooting war against the Viet Cong," mainly due to the helicopter advantage.

Admiral Felt advised the Joint Chiefs of Staff: "If things go right by the end of 1963 we should take 1,000 military out of RVN at one time." This would show, said Felt, that (1) the Republic of Vietnam was winning; (2) the steam was out of the anti-Diemites; and (3) U.S. intentions were honest.

But serious trouble for the Diem regime broke out in May. The Buddhists had suffered for years under Diem's rule and decided the time had come to make a show of their resentment. They chose May 8, Buddha's 2,527th birthday, and the sacred imperial city of Hue.

In a carefully planned demonstration, thousands marched through the streets waving religious flags and carrying banners, some of them in English so that the American media could spread their message. Religious flags had been prohibited back to the time of French rule, but Diem often bent the rule for the Catholics. In a nation 85 percent Buddhist, he had allowed the papal flag a few days earlier in parades celebrating the twenty-fifth anniversary of the ordination of his brother, Ngo Dinh Thuc, a priest in Hue. There were many other grievances of long standing, including the fact that Diem decreed Catholic chaplains for the armed services, made up largely of Buddhists, but prohibited Buddhist chaplains.

As the throng of Buddhists massed in the center of Hue, armored cars appeared at the street corners and opened fire. In the stampede and panic that followed, hundreds were trampled and at least ten people died, including several women and children.

The Vietnamese nation was outraged, and disorders broke out in other cities. Even Diem was shaken, though he denied any complicity. He declared that the disorders were part of a communist plot, carefully fomented to weaken his government. Mme. Nhu said the Americans were at fault and had manipulated the Buddhists. From Saigon, General Harkins ordered all Americans to preserve strict neutrality, in particular not to transport any of Diem's troops on anti-Buddhist missions.

Reaction against Diem was strong in the United States, even among those who normally supported him. President Kennedy was particularly sensitive on the issue of religious tolerance, having recently become the first Catholic president in American history. For the first time, Kennedy seriously contemplated the idea that the Diem regime must go.

As the summer heat rose, so did the nation's temper, culminating on June 11 in a spectacular event in the streets of Saigon. Shortly after 9 A.M., a gray sedan moved slowly along a main street, followed by some two hundred and fifty Buddhist priests and nuns, chanting in unison. At a busy intersection, the car stopped and an aging priest alighted. This was Quang Duc, a venerable of the Buddhist church. He walked slowly to the center of the street and assumed the lotus position. The crowd fell silent. Another monk approached him carrying a plastic container filled with gasoline. He poured it over Quang Duc, soaking his head and face and his saffron robes. Quang Duc sat motionless for a few seconds, then slowly extracted a match

With Diem's power waning, the troubles of summer made scenes like these common in South Vietnam. The city of Hue is under martial law in August (top), and yet another Buddhist monk burns himself to death in Saigon in September (above), the sixth such immolation in protest against Diem's pro-Catholic rule.

from inside his robe and struck it. He was instantly engulfed in flame as the crowd moaned and many fell in the street in prayer. Quang Duc, seventy-three, was now a saint among Buddhists, chosen for this honor because he was the oldest among the volunteers. He remained upright in the flames for long minutes, finally falling backward as his flesh blackened. It was the first of the self-immolations, and it stunned the world.

Mme. Nhu figuratively consigned the Diem regime to the flames when the press quoted her as saying, "Let them burn, and we shall clap our hands." This destroyed the last support the Diems had in Washington. Late in June President Kennedy appointed Henry Cabot Lodge as ambassador to Saigon, replacing Frederick Nolting, long a staunch supporter of Diem. No one in Washington could see who might succeed Diem, but Vietnamese military leaders in Saigon were already plotting. They, too, had grievances, and could read plainly that if Diem did not step down, American aid would stop.

The public disorders would not die down, and by early August six more Buddhists had committed suicide, four of them by immolation. Mme. Nhu, unrepentant, declared "all the Buddhists have done for this country is to barbecue a monk." American wags in Saigon changed their slogan, dropping "Sink or swim with Ngo Dinh Diem" in favor of "You cannot win with Ngo Dinh Diem."

Actually, it was Nhu who was now in charge. As Diem retreated more and more into his private world, Nhu came to the forefront as the "evil genius" of the regime. Rumors floated everywhere—that Nhu was a slave to opium, that he was secretly plotting with Ho Chi Minh to oust the Americans.

Then came "the night of the pagodas," when Nhu ordered his own police to sack Buddhist shrines on the night of August 20–21. Led by Colonel Le Quant Tung, police and some military units struck shortly after midnight against Xa Loi, the most sacred pagoda in Saigon. Other forces raided pagodas in all major cities of South Vietnam, breaking down doors, smashing statues and shrines, arresting over a thousand monks, and injuring scores. The raiders, in full battle gear, shouted in hate as they sacked the pagodas, the frantic tower gongs awakening the cities.

Mme. Nhu denounced the Buddhists as "hooligans in robes," but she and her husband had gone too far. In Washington, her own father, Tran Van Chuong, resigned as ambassador to the United States and returned to Saigon. Diem's foreign minister resigned and shaved his head like a Buddhist monk, and Tri Quang, leader of the Buddhists, took refuge in the American embassy. Nhu blamed the "night of the pagodas" on the Vietnamese Army, but few believed that.

At this very time, Lodge and Nolting were meeting in Honolulu so the retiring ambassador could brief Lodge on the situation in Vietnam. (Nolting quipped bitterly that he had been "disLodged.") When word reached them of the pagoda raids, Nolting is said to have remarked of Diem, "but he promised me, he promised me." When Lodge later arrived in Saigon, Nolting having returned to Washington, his first act was to visit the Xa Loi pagoda. This upset Diem, as it was no doubt intended to do. The first rumors to reach Lodge were of impending coups—either the military against Diem, or vice versa. On August 24 a cable from Washington left no doubt about the Kennedy administration's policy: "We wish to give Diem reasonable opportunity to remove Nhus, but if he remains obdurate then we are prepared to accept the obvious implications that we can no longer support Diem."

Within the next few days, events moved swiftly. A military clique headed by Generals Tran Van Don, titular head of the South Vietnamese armed forces, and Duong Van Minh established communications with the United States embassy, with Colonel Lucien Conein of the CIA as go-between. The generals said they were prepared to move against the Diem regime and wanted assurances of approval by the Americans. Ambassador Lodge gave assurances and on August 29 cabled Washington: "We are launched on a course from which there is no respectable turning back; the overthrow of the Diem government."

On the same day, Admiral Felt alerted two battalions of Marines on Okinawa and moved American naval and air forces closer to Vietnam. Cambodia had broken relations with South Vietnam two days earlier, because of the outrages against the Buddhists. Felt wanted to be ready, if necessary, to protect American interests in the area and evacuate the nearly four thousand American civilians—including eleven hundred civilian employees and over fifteen hundred dependents, mostly women and children.

After waiting five days, Ambassador Lodge went to the palace on Monday, August 26, to present his credentials to Diem. Lodge also delivered a message from Washington—it was the American view that the Nhus must leave the Vietnamese government within "a reasonable time." As the conversations progressed, Diem's manner became colder and, Lodge reported later, he clearly conveyed a feeling that the United States had no right to interfere in his government. In effect, the Nhus were his business and he would not oust them. This doomed the Diem regime; the United States would no longer support it, and it could not stand alone.

The end was delayed as the generals held off their revolt, nervous over interior conspiracies and subplots, and ever seeking stronger assurances of American support. They seemed to receive such assurances in President Kennedy's nationwide television interview with Walter Cronkite on September 2. The President said the Diem regime had "gotten out of touch with the people," and he clearly signaled an end to the Nhus when he called for changes in "policy and personnel." This was the first time Kennedy had publicly spoken against the Diem regime, but it did not mean the end of American support for South Vietnam. "I don't agree with those who say we should withdraw," the President said. "That would be a great mistake. We must be patient. We must persist."

The President had just sent yet another mission to Vietnam, this one led by Major General Victor H. Krulak, the Marine Corps's leading expert on guerrilla warfare, and Joseph Mendenhall, a State Department expert on Vietnam. They flew twenty-five thousand miles, spent four days in Vietnam, spoke hardly a word to each other, and reported to the President on September 10. General Krulak said in effect that all was going well in Vietnam; Mendenhall depicted Vietnam in the gloomiest of terms. President Kennedy said: "Are you sure you two gentlemen were in the same country?"

Their report had little value, except to illustrate one of the great problems of Vietnam: the difficulty of the American commander in chief in getting at the truth, in getting the facts necessary to make informed decisions. In no other foreign war in American history were so many decisions, even minor decisions, made by the President. Yet the information reaching the President was always strained, winnowed, hammered, and shaped by powerful forces—the military, diplomats, civilians, special interest groups—mostly honest, mostly well-intentioned, but all skewed in some degree from true objectivity. Ultimately it came down to one man.

Kennedy decided to send yet another mission, this time the two men he trusted most: McNamara and Taylor. They arrived in Saigon in late September and soon learned it was a snake pit of plots and counterplots. Lodge had taken a strong hand in supporting the overthrow of the Diem-Nhu regime, deliberately bypassing General Harkins, who was furious. Lodge and Conein now definitely held the upper

After a second trip to South Vietnam in late September, Secretary McNamara and General Taylor report to President Kennedy their hope that a thousand Americans can be withdrawn from Vietnam by the end of 1963, and nearly all Americans will be out by the end of 1965.

hand in the conspiracy to overthrow the regime, but moods and actions seemed to be changing every day, both in Saigon and in Washington.

McNamara and Taylor returned to Washington with a report replete with contradictions, and some questionable military predictions. They confessed to seeing great military progress and recommended recalling a thousand American advisers by year's end. They foresaw the withdrawal of nearly all Americans by the end of 1965. This was good news to President Kennedy, already thinking of his 1964 campaign for reelection, and this news may in fact have been included in their report at the President's own suggestion.

Events in Saigon were moving inexorably, and by mid-October the scenario was essentially complete. Colonel Conein was in close touch with General Minh, who had emerged as leader of the rebel Vietnamese group, and it was clearly understood that the Americans would have no direct part in the coup but would do nothing to thwart it. That is the way it went off.

On Friday, November 1, Ambassador Lodge, General Harkins, and Admiral Felt went to the palace to call on Diem. The meeting lasted from 10 A.M. until well after noon. Diem rambled on in his conversation, as he always did. In the meantime, the generals were moving, their coup set for 1:30 P.M. Lodge returned to his quarters for lunch and Harkins accompanied Felt to the airport to see him off.

At the appointed time, the rebels quickly seized the Saigon police headquarters, attacked the garrison of the palace guard a few blocks from Gia Long Palace, and threw a full division of troops around the palace itself. Diem remained calm, believing his forces were already in action to thwart the coup. Twice during Friday afternoon the rebels called on Diem to surrender; he refused, unaware that his forces, rushing toward Saigon, had been cut off and routed.

At 3 P.M. Diem called General Don, a leader of the plot, offering to talk. "It may be too late for that," said Don, knowing full well that it was.

Shortly after 4 P.M., Diem telephoned Ambassador Lodge, asking what the United States planned to do. Lodge parried, saying it was early morning in Washington, adding; "Now I am worried about your physical safety. I have a report that those in charge of the current activity offer you and your brothers safe conduct out of the country if you resign. Had you heard this?" Diem said he had not, and Lodge said, "If I can do anything for your physical safety, please call me." Diem's final words were, "I am trying to restore order."

That was impossible. The rebels had won control of Saigon and at 4 A.M. Saturday they attacked the palace. The city was aflame, and tracers filled the night sky. The few remaining palace guards, "Diem's Angels," held out as long as they could, but at 6:37 A.M. they ran up the white flag.

The birds had flown; Diem and Nhu had escaped from their cellar bomb shelter by a secret passage and made their way to a safe house in Cholon, the Chinese section of Saigon. Diem, exhausted and frightened, telephoned General Minh at 6 A.M., attempting to negotiate. Minh refused, and Diem called him twice again, finally agreeing to leave the country. They agreed to meet at St. Francis Xavier church in Cholon.

The fall of Diem, and the end to American hopes for quick victory in Vietnam, nonetheless bring joy in Saigon. The despot's palace is wrecked (top); the victors celebrate with tank crewmen (center); and the city's streets show some of the carnage of the fighting (bottom).

For President Diem (foreground) and his brother Nhu there was bloody death by unknown hands. Their bodies, clothed in priest's garb, were found in this armored personnel carrier on the morning of November 2, 1963. The promised safe conduct to Tan Son Nhut airport had been brutally terminated.

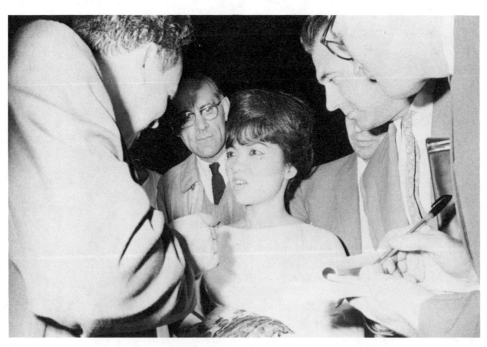

Ever the survivor, Madame Nhu flees to Europe and lives out a tragic life in Rome, bitter to the end at her countrymen and the Americans she hated.

Shortly after 9 A.M., an M-113 armored car and a jeep arrived at the church. Diem and Nhu entered the armored car and it set off for rebel headquarters in Saigon. When the M-113's door was opened, inside were the bloody bodies of Diem and Nhu. Their hands were wired together behind their backs, and they had been sprayed with bullets and stabbed repeatedly.

When the news reached Washington, President Kennedy was in a meeting with the National Security Council. A messenger entered, presented the President with a slip of paper. Kennedy read it, the blood drained from his face, and he left the room without a word.

No one had expected such violence, least of all Kennedy. There was great shock in American circles, both in Washington and in Saigon. But among the Vietnamese there was jubilation; a tyrant had been overthrown. Crowds celebrated in the streets of Saigon and other cities, and in the countryside the peasants tore down the hated Strategic Hamlets. Lodge cabled Kennedy: "The prospects now are for a shorter war."

The Viet Cong moved in swiftly, mounting over seventy attacks on outposts and hamlets in the first week. The South Vietnamese civil guards and self-defense corps seemed utterly demoralized, and the Viet Cong killed nearly three thousand local

American leaders gather in Honolulu in November and prepare another optimistic report. From left: David E. Bell, director of the Agency for International Development; Secretary of State Dean Rusk; Secretary of Defense McNamara; Henry Cabot Lodge, Ambassador to South Vietnam; General Taylor, Admiral Felt, and General Harkins. This photo was taken two days before the assassination of President Kennedy in Dallas.

officials in November. Only the U.S. Air Force gave any serious support to the populace, flying nearly six hundred sorties against the Viet Cong.

As Washington gradually recovered, President Kennedy held the first strategy meeting of his reelection campaign on November 12. Lyndon Baines Johnson was not invited, even though the meeting decided Kennedy would go to Dallas ten days later. There was a serious rift in the Democratic party in Texas, and Kennedy asked Johnson to meet him there and help heal the wounds. It was not decided then, nor was it ever, whether Johnson would again be Kennedy's running mate in 1964.

As to Vietnam, Kennedy announced on November 14 that he was sending McNamara and Secretary of State Rusk to Honolulu on November 20 to discuss American involvement, in view of the new situation in Saigon. Ambassador Lodge, Generals Taylor and Harkins, and Admiral Felt would also be at the meeting. "Now this is our objective," the President said. "To bring Americans home, permit the South Vietnamese to maintain themselves as a free and independent country, and permit democratic forces within the country to operate."

On November 22, 1963, President Kennedy was assassinated in Dallas in one of the most dramatic moments of the twentieth century. Through the eyes of television, the whole world could watch as the life of this charismatic young man was snuffed out.

Within hours Vice-President Johnson took the oath of office as the thirty-sixth president of the United States and flew toward Washington in Air Force One. Somewhere in the bundles of official papers thrust at him was the report from the Honolulu meeting. Defense Secretary McNamara and Secretary of State Rusk confirmed a main recommendation of the McNamara/Wheeler mission—the withdrawal of American forces from Vietnam should begin. The first three hundred Americans departed from that country on December 3, and another seven hundred left ten days later.

Part II

VICTORY AND DEFEAT

6

"Johnson's War" 1964

T<small>HE SAIGON</small> assassinations of President Diem and his brother worked a profound change within Vietnam, as did the Dallas assassination of President Kennedy in American affairs. These changes, in two nations ten thousand miles apart, began to become apparent in 1964, setting the stage for tragic events to follow.

In Vietnam, Diem's government was replaced by a military government. For the next four years there was constant turmoil in Saigon as ever-shifting military cliques struggled for power. In Washington, Johnson came to the White House with two main objectives: the launching of his domestic programs under the banner of The Great Society, and election to the presidency in his own right. In his first State of the Union message on January 8 he declared "unconditional war on poverty." He said nothing about the other war, Vietnam, and in an election year he intended to keep as quiet about that as he could. That didn't mean that nothing was going on in Vietnam; in fact, it was a busy and significant year.

The ARVN kicked off January 18 with the largest helicopter operation to date; 115 choppers dropped a thousand Vietnamese troops into Zone D, which had been VC country for years. The operation went well except for one detail: it didn't bag a single guerrilla insurgent.

A few days later, William Childs Westmoreland stepped down from the regular Pan Am flight at Tan Son Nhut, briefcase in hand, his business suit rumpled from the long flight. He looked for all the world like an American executive, come to take charge of one of his firm's important properties. In a way, that was correct.

Lt. Gen. Westmoreland was arriving as prospective commanding officer of U.S. military forces in Vietnam. He went directly to lunch at General Harkins' villa, which would shortly become Westmoreland's home for the next four years. Ironically, the villa was located on Tran Quy Cap Street, named in honor of a Vietnamese scholar and patriot whom the French had beheaded.

Nearby was the Cercle Sportif, a social club with swimming pool and tennis courts, a reminder of palmier days under French colonial rule. Saigon, with its tree-lined boulevards, did look somewhat like "the Paris of the Orient," and here, within a few weeks, the general would be joined by his wife, Katherine Van Dusen Westmoreland (Kitsy) and two of their children, Rip, ten, and Margaret, nine. Their third child, Stevie, a daughter back home in boarding school, would join them in June. Ambassador Lodge and his wife Emily, who lived nearby, helped the Westmorelands settle in. It all seemed, somehow, much like any other peacetime overseas assignment.

That world blew away within two weeks. On February 3, terrorists attacked a military compound in a hill city called Kontum, 250 miles northeast of Saigon. It was a vicious little attack and the first direct assault on an American installation, for Kontum was home to a group of U.S. Army advisers working with the South Vietnamese Army. One American soldier was wounded. Was this a VC message to the new American commander?

Within days General Westmoreland was out in the field, in obedience to one of his own basic command tenets: a commander should see his men frequently, and they should see him. In addition, he wanted a look at the battleground he would command within months, upon Harkins' retirement.

Just over six feet tall, handsome, erect, slightly graying, Westmoreland looked every bit the Army's top field soldier. He had made the landings at Casablanca and Normandy, commanded airborne troops in Korea, been the youngest major general in the Army, commanded the 101st Airborne Division for two years, been superintendent of West Point. Here was a man who clearly knew where he was going, and he was still two months short of his fiftieth birthday.

When he looked closely at his new command, Westmoreland saw a long, slim land with a seacoast of nearly nine hundred miles, from the demilitarized zone (DMZ) in the north, southward around the Mekong Delta, and back up to the Cambodian border at Ha Thien. That was his rear. His front was the fifty-mile DMZ at the north, his only direct contact with North Vietnam, and another six hundred miles of mountain and jungle border with Laos and Cambodia. It came to his mind that the Western Front in World War II was about the same length as his land front in Vietnam, and it had taken 4.5 million troops to man the European front.

Even Korea, with only a 123-mile front across the waist of the country, had required nearly a million UN forces. Almost at once Westmoreland thought his best defense might just be a straight east-west line along Route 9 near the DMZ, from the South China Sea to the Thai border at Savannakhet. That would be about one hundred and fifty miles, and would deny the enemy the trails already being used to infiltrate South Vietnam. Such a line might be manned by a United Nations force, as in Korea. The general passed some of these thoughts up the chain of command, and heard no more of them.

Lieutenant General William Childs Westmoreland (center), who took over the American field command in 1964, at first hoped Vietnam could become a United Nations initiative, as the Korean War had been. A few nations did send military help. As shown at left, Westmoreland and Vinh Tho, South Vietnam's foreign affairs leader, welcome the first ROK serviceman; and shown below, a South Korean MASH unit disembarks from a Royal Australian Air Force plane at Vung Tau. The United Nations concept never blossomed, but fighting units from Australia, South Korea, and a few other nations did give the United States valiant fighting support.

Westmoreland also remembered his last meeting with General MacArthur at the old soldier's apartment in the Waldorf Astoria hotel in New York. MacArthur had told him a great many things about the Orient, such as the importance of "face." (Westmoreland was careful about that; in keeping with Oriental tradition, he always walked on the left side of General Cao Van Dien, chairman of the Joint General Staff of South Vietnam, thus showing deference. Also, he never summoned high-ranking Orientals to see him; he called on them instead.)

MacArthur advised him to have plenty of artillery, for the Oriental "greatly fears artillery." The Vietnamese officers, he said, should be treated "as you did your cadets; be understanding, basic in your advice, patient, work with them to develop their sense of responsibility and their ability to make decisions."

Westmoreland picked up a good deal more useful information on his country tours, as on his visit to a Special Forces camp in Darlac Province where he found the American captain using rented elephants to carry supplies for his patrols. That was initiative and adaptation. Another time Westmoreland's interpreter told him a farmer was really happy that Americans had given him a sow and a boar because now he was increasing pork production. What the farmer actually said was that he had sold the animals and pocketed the money. The interpreter was afraid of the general, but fortunately one of Westmoreland's aides understood Vietnamese.

There were more serious problems; for example, the Vietnamese manpower situation. When McNamara was back in Saigon in March (his second trip in three months), the military clique then in power agreed to increase the ARVN by ninety thousand troops, which the United States would pay for. This sounded good, but exposed some other problems. The Vietnamese Army was getting about three thousand volunteers a month, but desertions were running five thousand or more per month. The Vietnamese did not like military duty without their families, and if the families could not accompany them they dropped out. Desertion was particularly high at the time of the rice harvest. The Vietnamese draft started for males at age twenty, while in the United States it was eighteen. This later became a highly emotional issue in the United States when young Americans were dying and Vietnamese the same age were escaping service. Saigon refused to lower its draft age. But for 1964 the Vietnamese Army rose to the goal of 230,000 regulars and another 270,000 part-timers in the Regional and Popular Forces. In the same period, the VC was also growing, to a total estimated at 170,000. This in spite of twenty thousand guerrillas killed or captured, and another seventeen thousand surrendering in amnesty programs. In addition, some twelve thousand North Vietnamese regulars infiltrated south during the year.

In March 1964 the first American regular was taken as a prisoner of war, opening an especially grisly chapter in the Vietnam experience. Army Captain Floyd J. Thompson, thirty, took off on March 26 in the observer seat of an O-1 Bird Dog, with Air Force Captain Richard Whitesides at the controls. Thompson commanded the Special Forces camp at Khe Sanh, and guerrilla activity had been rising; he needed a look-see outside his perimeter. A short time after takeoff there was heavy ground fire and the plane crashed in flames. Thompson ran from the wreckage, into the arms of the VC. No trace of Whitesides was ever found.

South Vietnamese military strength grew in 1964, despite a succession of unstable governments in Saigon, but so did the rebel Viet Cong army. In March, Secretary McNamara once again rallied the natives—here shown at Bac Lieu, in the Delta— on his second visit for President Johnson in two months.

Thompson spent months in the jungle with his captors, and at first relations were fairly good; they just wanted to "reeducate" him. By August the enemy was using brutality and torture, and Thompson was headed for a North Vietnamese prison and nearly nine years of captivity. Waiting for him at Fort Bragg were his wife and three daughters. Prison was an eternity for Jim Thompson and his loved ones, and a unique and troubling experience for America. Before it was over, the American POWs, nearly a thousand of them, became a major bargaining chip for the North Vietnamese in the Nixon-Kissinger "peace with honor" campaign.

The reality of spring 1964 was that the enemy was getting stronger and his weapons better. Russian and Chinese rifles and machine guns were showing up, in particular the AK-47, a superb automatic assault weapon. It was easily recognized in battle by its high rate of fire and a sound like vomiting, reminiscent of the German burp guns of World War II. The enemy also was getting rocket launchers, mortars, and recoilless rifles. Most of this armament was reaching the VC by sea, smuggled south around the DMZ by hundreds of junks and sampans. The weapons were easily landed on the long, guerrilla-controlled coast from Da Nang to Vung Tau, a seaside resort near Saigon that the French had called Cap St. Jacques. At the same time, the ARVN was still using American M-1 semiautomatic rifles and M-2 light carbines left over from World War II.

Not all VC escape. South Vietnamese soldiers guard Communist prisoners awaiting airlift from the battle area (left), and an outpost commander (below) looks over a haul of captured enemy weapons, including Russian, Chinese, and homemade ones.

South Vietnam's American-supplied planes—also World War II vintage—were literally falling apart. All B-26s in Vietnam were ordered out of combat in February, after the wings fell off one of the old bombers. The T-28s (World War II trainers) also had to be phased out, to be replaced by the newer A-1H attack planes. (Not quite quickly enough: Captain Edwin G. Shank, Jr., was killed March 24 when a wing sheared off his T-28 in flight, and Captain Robert Brumett went down two weeks later when his T-28 failed to come out of a dive.)

On April 12, the Viet Cong destroyed the town of Kien Long, near Vi Thanh, the capital of Choung Thien Province (IV 40), far south in the Mekong Delta. On May 2 guerrilla swimmers placed a mine on the hull of the USS *Card,* a converted World War II "jeep" carrier, and sank it in plain sight of anyone who cared to visit the Saigon waterfront. A crowd gathered, including Ambassador Lodge, and a few minutes after he left, a Viet Cong bomb wounded eight American servicemen and a civilian spectator. Fortunately the *Card*'s cargo of new American planes and helicopters had already been unloaded. The vessel was refloated and limped off home with a cargo of scrap choppers and planes.

McNamara was back in Saigon again on May 11 (his third trip for President Johnson since December), and this time General Westmoreland gave him an earful. If the United States wished to stay in Vietnam, the general said, America would need infinite patience and must face the fact that Vietnam could become "a bottomless pit" for American lives and resources. In Westmoreland's personal belief, this was no place for Americans to fight—too much disease, heat, reptiles, and vermin, not to mention that the natives were none too friendly. McNamara did not really want to hear this, nor did President Johnson. The President was shepherding the Civil Rights Act of 1964 through Congress. (He would sign it on prime time TV on July 2, but too late to prevent the "long hot summer" of black riots in Harlem, Rochester, Jersey City, Philadelphia, and elsewhere.)

Furthermore, it was an election year and Johnson was saying as little about Vietnam as he could. For example, there was no public announcement of Operation Yankee Team, which started in May. Yet the orders authorized U.S. Air Force and Navy planes to fly "reconnaissance" missions over the Laos panhandle. Some of the escorts could carry "ordnance" (bombs) and were permitted to "expend" (drop) them if the targets were positively enemy and considerably outside South Vietnam. Word of this began to leak out in late May, and there were some close calls. (One American pilot was downed and captured, then escaped; another was downed and rescued by helicopter, but no Americans were killed.)

McNamara's message to Westmoreland was stern: Americans must stop flying combat, even with Vietnamese aboard, and go back to training only. The rules had been slightly relaxed in March. Strike aircraft were authorized to operate to the South Vietnamese border if it was a road or river; up to two thousand meters of the border if directed by a forward air controller (Vietnamese), or up to five thousand meters if not. But now a new phase was beginning. President Johnson was suggesting that two or three hundred American troops be brought home and replaced by civilians to change the emphasis toward "the art of peace." At about the same time, Ho Chi Minh was sending new legions of construction workers into Laos and down the panhandle to expand the supply trails. Ho's radio transmissions also announced that if the United States had any ideas of pressing north, he had "powerful friends ready to help" North Vietnam.

As a matter of fact, the United States was pressing a bit, on two fronts. One campaign, under the cover name SOG (Studies and Observation Group), began as early as January 1964. At first it was financed and run by the CIA as a "joint unconventional warfare task force" or, bluntly, secret agents. By February, five- or six-man teams of South Vietnamese volunteers were being parachuted into Laos (Operation Leaping Lena) to reconnoiter the Ho Chi Minh trail. Most of these agents never came back, presumably they were killed, captured, or had defected. Eventually SOG would be turned over to the U.S. Army and would grow to some two thousand Americans and eight thousand indigenous troops, with its own air force (90th Special Operations Wing), Navy SEAL (sea, air, land commando groups) teams, PT boats, UDTs (underwater demolition teams), and its own headquarters and training facilities. This American effort was always volunteer, and always had a waiting list.

The most interesting offensive took place on the east coast—amphibious assaults by South Vietnamese forces. By midsummer, the South Vietnamese were ranging up the coast nearly to Haiphong, a course of action that would lead directly to the Tonkin Gulf incident.

It was a busy summer at the command level. In June General Harkins retired, as planned, and Westmoreland took charge, picking up his fourth star. General Maxwell Taylor became ambassador at Saigon, so Lodge could go home for the presidential election campaign. In Pearl Harbor, Admiral Ulysses S. Grant Sharp, Jr., fifty-eight, U.S. Naval Academy class of 1927, relieved Harry Felt as CINCPAC (Commander in Chief, Pacific), and General Hunter Harris, Jr., became Commander in Chief, Pacific Air Forces.

President Johnson muddied the command waters a bit with his personal letter to General Taylor outlining "my desire that you have and exercise full responsibility for the effort of the United States Government in South Vietnam," making plain this included "the whole military effort." Taylor, ever the diplomat, stopped in Honolulu on the way out to assure Admiral Sharp that he (Sharp) had "no reason for concern" and had full rein in "the day-to-day business of the military effort." Taylor told Westmoreland the same thing in Saigon, but clearly Taylor was to be in charge. Taylor was one of the very few military who had Johnson's full trust, and the President had twisted his arm to take the Saigon job for one year.

It was also a bloody summer, with the Viet Cong on rampage from the Delta to the DMZ. In the worst attack, the guerrillas struck the Green Beret camp at Nam Dong, in the mountains of Thua Thien Province (I 2) near the Cambodian border, about fifty miles west of Da Nang. The battle opened at 2:30 A.M. on July 6 with heavy mortar fire, and from then until dawn, Captain Roger Hugh C. Donlon led the defenders in a fierce battle for survival. Two American and one Australian advisers were killed, along with fifty-five South Vietnamese irregulars. Donlon, suf-

In the boondocks, guerrilla warfare was constant and deadly. Here loyal South Vietnamese celebrate the fiftieth defense of their outpost (above), and the province chief immediately rewards its heroic defenders (below).

Americans deliver the Vietnamese troops to battle in C-123s (left) and Marine helicopters (below).

fering multiple wounds, was still alive and in command when reinforcements arrived soon after daylight. Within hours there was another visitor, General Westmoreland himself. Captain Donlon was cited for his bravery and won the Army's first Medal of Honor in Vietnam.

But Nam Dong also revealed severe problems within the South Vietnamese armed forces. When the first South Vietnamese fighter planes arrived over the outpost at dawn, they could not fire because their forward controller could not make radio contact with the ground to verify the target. Westmoreland was "deeply concerned" at such occurrences, which were costing American lives. He ordered Army helicopters on night alert, and asked Washington for more Special Forces, one Army helicopter company for each Vietnamese division, and more armed helicopter companies.

At the core was the whole question of Americans in "combat." On March 8, Colonel Thomas M. Hegert, deputy chief of the MAAG Air Force Section, was killed when his A-1H was shot down. It turned out he was flying a Vietnamese plane as wingman for a Vietnamese pilot, and they had made a dozen passes over the target before Hegert's plane went down. Investigation turned up the fact that some ninety other American pilots were flying Vietnamese planes, under a few bent rules: the American "advisers" could not lead a flight; fire first, or continue in battle if the Vietnamese leader aborted.

On March 24, Captain Edwin G. Shank, Jr., was killed in a crash during a bomb run near Soc Trang, in the Delta. Letters he had written home complained that American equipment (a T-28, in his case) was in poor shape, and that Americans were regularly flying combat, taking Vietnamese students along as "sandbags." These letters reached the press and congressmen in April. The official explanation was that the Americans were flying combat so as not to take Vietnamese away from their training. General Moore suggested that the sham of Vietnamese "sandbags" be ended.

Washington's answer was that Americans must stop flying "combat," except for "bona fide operational training missions against hostile targets to prepare the participating VNAF personnel for eventual replacement of U.S. pilots." As for helicopters, where American Army and Marine personnel were regularly mixing it up with the enemy, that could continue but weapons could be fired only in self-defense. "Armed helicopters will not be used as a substitute for close air support strikes," the rules said, adding, "Helicopters are for use as transport."

When the Air Force asked for clarification, the answer from MACV was that pilots should be "more circumspect" and be sure that any Vietnamese aboard were actually in training and not just "sandbags." The Air Force paid attention, and the number of Americans in combat declined; twenty-nine Americans had been killed in action up to this time. By May, three Vietnamese fighter squadrons were in action, two pilots per plane, and McNamara wanted to add three more squadrons by February 1965.

This sounded good, but there were many problems. The Vietnamese could not fly at night; many did not speak enough English to communicate with other planes or

Americans also fought weather and jungle conditions. An American helicopter (above) checks out the terrain in central South Vietnam in the fall, after the area's worst typhoon in a hundred years. An Air Force C-123 spray plane fights the never-ending battle against the jungle (below).

the ground; and the radio nets were slow and unreliable. In addition, only Vietnamese could call fire, and they often refused to do so, or to let Americans do so, even though targets were clearly identified. As Nam Dong had shown, the results could be deadly.

In July, defoliation was continuing and Operation Ranch Hand became an official part of the Army. After three years of temporary status it was now Detachment 1, 315th Troop Carrier Group, with tested equipment and tactics. A great improvement, introduced in August, was a spray system that could deliver three gallons of defoliant per acre in one pass. The old system had required two passes over the target, which gave the enemy time to prepare for the second pass, increasing the danger to the C-123s and their crews. The new system, with spray booms under each wing and the tail, also sharply increased the acreage that could be treated.

Ranch Hand was ready, but the Vietnamese pilots were not. They refused to fly against the Viet Cong's two best crop areas—War Zone D near Saigon and Phuoc Long Province (III 18), on the Cambodian border to the north: too much ground flak for them. General Taylor fixed that, using the broad authority President Johnson had granted him. The C-123s piloted by Americans, with South Vietnamese "aircraft commanders" aboard, executed "Big Patch" in Zone D in October and "Hot Spot" in Phuoc Long in November. MACV rated the operation highly successful, claiming 7,620 acres of Viet Cong crops destroyed. Crop destruction seemed much more effective than defoliation, but the future of both programs was assured.

Still, the Viet Cong was striking everywhere—assaulting the Special Forces camps at Plei Mrong, near Pleiku (II 8); Polei Krong in Kontum Province (II 6); and Hiep Hoa in Long An Province (III 27), only a few miles from Saigon. In the Delta, the Viet Cong took virtual command of Chuong Tien Province (IV 40), and severely mauled South Vietnamese forces at Ben Cat, twenty-five miles north of Saigon in Binh Duong Province (III 23).

Westmoreland began talking with his staff about the dangers to his two main airfields, Tan Son Nhut and Da Nang, and the need for more troops, more ports, more helicopters, more supplies. No word was yet passed to Washington; Johnson had his eye only on his Great Society and the upcoming Presidential election. Tonkin changed that.

By early summer, South Vietnamese commando units were making coastal raids by boat north of the DMZ, probing the North Vietnamese shore defenses with U.S. Navy support never far offshore. On Friday night, July 31, the commandos raided the small islands of Hon Me and Hon Ngu, north of the city of Vinh, seeking to destroy North Vietnamese radar and radio stations. The next night they attacked an enemy PT base at Loc Chao, near Thanh Hoa, a major enemy city only seventy-five miles south of Hanoi.

At the same time, thirty miles at sea, the American destroyer USS *Maddox* was working her way north into the Gulf of Tonkin. She was in international waters and was executing what the Navy called a De Soto patrol.

Admiral Sharp explained later that De Soto was a standard procedure, used by

In a typical incident, the Viet Cong blasts a government truck convoy, attacks the defenders, and runs off with the supplies before help can arrive.

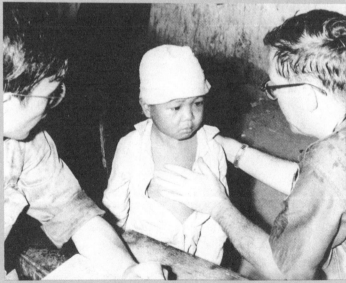

Vietnamese children live with terror and disease. This Montagnard woman (left) tries to protect her children in a Viet Cong village. Her husband has fled to the hills with his VC unit. An American doctor, Army Captain Carl A. Schweers, Jr., treats a suspicious patient (right).

the Navy in many parts of the world, in which a vessel using special electronic gear would approach a hostile coast seeking intelligence of the enemy's physical and electronic equipment. In this case, the *Maddox* was the snoop vessel, and Sharp had permission from the Joint Chiefs of Staff for the Tonkin patrol.

De Soto patrols succeeded best if the enemy felt goaded into attacking the snoops; he then opened up with all his armament and electronics and exposed his power to the snooper. This gambit worked perfectly on the hot Sunday afternoon of August 2. Three of North Vietnam's new, high-speed Swatow patrol boats, of Russian design, roared out of Loc Chao, heading for the USS *Maddox,* some twenty-eight miles at sea, clearly in international waters. The USS *Maddox,* which had just turned south, opened warning fire as the three torpedo boats approached, and called in air cover from the carrier USS *Ticonderoga,* operating north of the DMZ.

As the patrol boats bore down on the USS *Maddox,* the destroyer shifted to destructive fire and four F-8E Crusaders from the carrier also attacked. In the melee, one North Vietnamese boat passed astern of the *Maddox,* firing machine

The blowup comes in the Gulf of Tonkin, as North Vietnamese gunboats attack the American destroyer Maddox *in international waters on Sunday afternoon, August 2. This photo, showing a Russian 37-mm antiaircraft gun manned by North Vietnamese sailors, was copied from the Soviet magazine* Starshina Serjant.

guns, and another launched a torpedo that came within two hundred yards of the destroyer. The Crusaders laid on Zuni rockets (unguided) and 20-mm cannon fire, and all three boats were sunk or badly damaged. The *Maddox* sustained one bullet hole in the transom; none of the crew of two hundred seventy-five was hurt, and no planes were lost. It was a good afternoon's work for the *Maddox*. As Admiral Sharp said later, a little mixup like that offers "a fine time to pick up information on what the enemy has and how it operates." But this was only a beginning.

Within hours the State Department dispatched a warning to Hanoi: Grave consequences "would inevitably result from any further unprovoked offensive military actions against U.S. forces." The Navy ordered another carrier, the USS *Constellation,* to make its way from Hong Kong, four hundred miles away, to back up the *Ticonderoga.* A third carrier, the USS *Kearsarge,* was ordered to the scene at best speed, accompanied by an ASW (antisubmarine warfare) team of specially equipped destroyers.

The Air Force began moves on its worldwide checkerboard, advancing planes from Okinawa, the Philippines, and other bases toward Vietnam. F-102 jet interceptors zoomed in to Da Nang and Tan Son Nhut; more fighters landed on all the U.S. airfields in Thailand; and thirty-six B-57 bombers arrived at Tan Son Nhut. Another destroyer, the *C. Turner Joy,* was sent to join the *Maddox.* All Army and Marine troops in the Pacific were placed on alert.

The *Maddox* and the *Joy,* now a TG (task group) under command of Captain J. J. Herrick, continued the De Soto patrol in the Gulf of Tonkin, midway between North Vietnam and the Chinese island of Hainan, where the Communists had both air and naval bases. On Tuesday afternoon, August 4, the destroyers were patrolling in overcast weather about sixty miles off Thanh Hoa and seventy-five miles south of Haiphong. Late in the afternoon, the *Joy*'s radar picked up blips that were assessed as torpedo boats paralleling the destroyers. An hour later, the *Maddox* reported radar fixes on two boats and three planes, but the *Ticonderoga* could find no plane targets in the low ceiling.

At 9:30 that night both destroyers picked up radar blips closing in on them at over forty knots, and torpedo wakes were picked up at 9:52. The destroyers opened fire at six thousand yards, and for the next two hours there was a good deal of confused maneuvering and reporting—radar blips, searchlights, torpedo noises on sonar. By midnight all enemy blips had disappeared. The destroyers reported they had "observed numerous hits on the enemy boats," and some of the *Joy* crew reported they saw a "thick column of black smoke."

No one was really sure what happened. The North Vietnamese said their boats weren't even out that night, but Admiral Sharp, pressing for permission to make a punitive air strike, concluded that "there was enough information available to indicate that an attack had, in fact, occurred." He telephoned McNamara in Washington that "the weight of evidence (including some radio intercept intelligence) supported our conclusion."

Permission for retaliation was granted, and Wednesday afternoon sixty-four planes took off from the *Ticonderoga* and *Constellation,* including F-4 Phantoms,

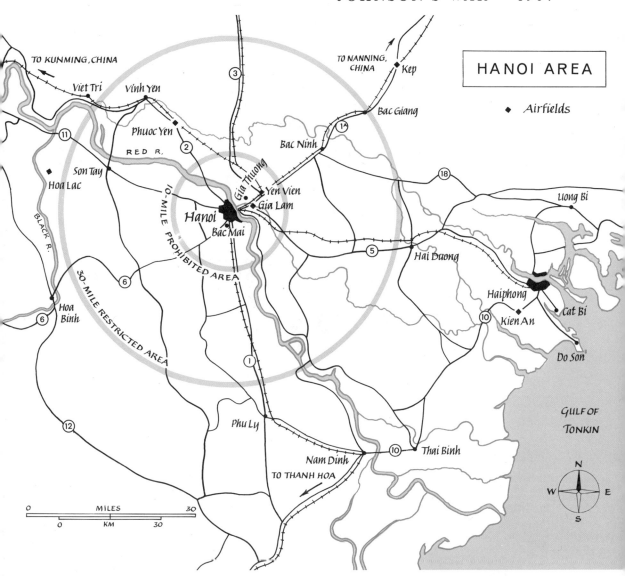

F-8 Crusaders, and A-4 Skyhawks, all jets, and some A-1 Skyraider prop planes. In the next five hours they bombed PT nests at Quang Khe, Phuc Loi, Loc Chao, Hon Gai, and the enemy's main oil storage depot, located at Vinh. The pilots claimed twenty-five PTs destroyed, over half the North Vietnamese force, seven AA batteries silenced, and twelve of the fourteen oil tanks at Vinh in flames, with smoke rising to fourteen thousand feet.

At the same time, near midnight Tuesday in Washington, President Johnson was intoning on radio and television:

"My fellow Americans, as President and Commander in Chief, it is my duty to the American people to report that renewed hostile actions against United States

99

The war goes electronic, as U.S. Army technicians install a satellite dish at Tan Son Nhut airfield, outside Saigon, in October.

ships on the high seas in the Gulf of Tonkin have today required me to order the military forces to take action in reply . . . That reply is being given as I speak to you tonight. Air action is now in execution against gunboats and certain supporting facilities in North Vietnam which have been used in these hostile operations . . . Our response for the present will be limited and fitting . . . We still seek no wider war . . ."

Two planes were lost that day. Lieutenant (JG) Richard Sather, twenty-six years old, of Pomona, California, was killed when his Skyraider plunged into the gulf off Loc Chao. Lieutenant (JG) Everett Alvarez, twenty-six, of San Jose, California, flew his A-4C jet from the *Constellation* against Hon Gai, fifty miles northeast of Haiphong, and only fifty miles from the Chinese border. In his second pass across Hon Gai harbor, flak set his plane afire and Alvarez bailed out. He landed in the water near some small fishing boats which quickly closed in on him. The fishers, both men and women, were in a rage at the American attack, and Alvarez feared they were going to drown him right there. They saved him, the first Navy POW, for nearly eight years of hell in North Vietnamese prisons.

On the same day as the raids, President Johnson sent to Congress a resolution prepared some weeks earlier against just such a happening as the Tonkin incident. With more than a dash of irony, the resolution was introduced in the Senate by

Senator J. William Fulbright, soon to become one of the more acidic critics of Johnson and the war. Two days later, with minimum debate, the so-called Southeast Asia Resolution passed; the vote in the Senate was 88–2, and in the House, 416–0. The dissenting votes were cast by two Democrat mavericks, Wayne Morse and Ernest Gruening.

The resolution had three operative parts; it resolved that

1. "the Congress approve and support the determination of the President, as Commander in Chief, to take all necessary measures to repel any armed attack against the forces of the United States and to prevent further aggression";
2. the United States "is, therefore, prepared, as the President determines, to take all necessary steps, including the use of armed force, to assist any member or protocol state of the Southeast Asia Collective Defense Treaty requesting assistance in defense of its freedom";
3. the resolution "shall expire when the President shall determine that the peace and security of the area is reasonably assured . . . except that it may be terminated earlier by concurrent resolution of the Congress."

It was not a declaration of war, and none was ever voted on. Congress could have rescinded the resolution at any time, but did not do so until the last day of 1970. In many ways, a declaration of war would have had better consequences for the United States. A declaration is clearly understood by all nations; it gives notice, confers powers, and prohibits certain actions. The POWs suffered for lack of a declaration. Their guards sneered and beat them when they invoked the protection of the Geneva Convention. There is no declaration of war, said the tormentors, therefore no Geneva Convention.

Between December 1961 and August 7, 1964, the day the Tonkin resolution passed, 181 Americans had been killed in Vietnam. Another 84 had died there outside of combat, and about a thousand had been wounded in battle. On August 7, 16,323 U.S. military servicemen were in South Vietnam, and more were arriving daily.

Also on this date, U.S. reconnaissance planes returned to Da Nang with disturbing photos. Thirty-nine jet fighters were parked on the aprons at Phuc Yen, a principal air base just outside Hanoi. They were Russian-designed MIG-15s and -17s, apparently just flown in from China and the first seen in North Vietnam. The Chinese had more, of course, at their bases on Hainan Island and along China's Gulf of Tonkin coastline north and east of Hanoi.

General Hunter Harris, Jr., Commander in Chief, Pacific Air Forces, recommended his planes be allowed to wipe out the MIGs in North Vietnam as a "sharp lesson" to the Communists. His fighters from Thailand and Da Nang could do this easily with cluster bombs and rockets, he said, and clean up with individual killer sorties. Admiral Sharp passed his request to Washington and it was never heard of again.

The U.S. Navy made one more foray into the Gulf of Tonkin, this time using the destroyers *Morton* and *Edwards.* They fired on radar contacts the night of Septem-

SOUTHEAST ASIA RESOLUTION

Public Law 88-408
Adopted August 7, 1964. Signed by President Johnson August 10, 1964.
Senate vote, 88-2; House vote, 416-0.

Whereas naval units of the Communist regime in Vietnam, in violation of the principles of the Charter of the United Nations and of international law, have deliberately and repeatedly attacked United States naval vessels lawfully present in international waters, and have thereby created a serious threat to international peace; and

Whereas these attacks are part of a deliberate and systematic campaign of aggression that the Communist regime in North Vietnam has been waging against its neighbors and the nations joined with them in the collective defense of their freedom; and

Whereas the United States is assisting the peoples of Southeast Asia to protect their freedom and has no territorial, military or political ambitions in that area, but desires only that these peoples should be left in peace to work out their own destinies in their own way: Now, therefore, be it

Resolved by the Senate and House of Representatives of the United States of America in Congress assembled, That the Congress approves and supports the determination of the President, as Commander in Chief, to take all necessary measures to repel any armed attack against the forces of the United States and to prevent further aggression.

Sec. 2. The United States regards as vital to its national interest and to world peace the maintenance of international peace and security in Southeast Asia. Consonant with the Constitution of the United States and the Charter of the United Nations and in accordance with its obligations under the Southeast Asia Collective Defense Treaty, the United States is, therefore, prepared, as the President determines, to take all necessary steps, including the use of armed force, to assist any member or protocol state of the Southeast Asia Collective Defense Treaty requesting assistance in defense of its freedom.

Sec. 3. This resolution shall expire when the President shall determine that the peace and security of the area is reasonably assured by international conditions created by action of the United Nations or otherwise, except that it may be terminated earlier by concurrent resolution of the Congress.

ber 17, and for the next few days Air Force and Navy planes were hoping for attack orders. After a welter of conflicting orders, they were ordered to cool off; the Navy said it couldn't be sure the enemy had taken any action. From then on, the Navy stayed out of Tonkin and surveillance fell to a weekly flight over the gulf by an Air Force RB-47 electronic intelligence plane.

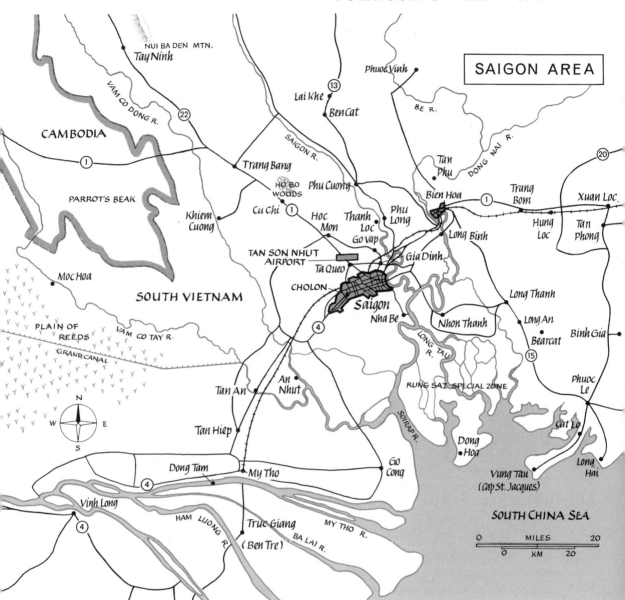

SAIGON AREA

At home, as the presidential election campaign heated up, Johnson was not concerned about winning, but about winning *big*. He wanted a "mandate" for his Great Society. During the last forty-two days of the campaign he traveled sixty thousand miles and made over two hundred speeches. He was satisfied to let the Republican candidate, Senator Barry Goldwater, a reserve general in the Air Force, play the role of hawk. As for himself, Johnson summed up Vietnam in a few words.

"We are not about to start another war and we're not about to run away from where we are," he said. The United States would help the South Vietnamese but there would be no "committing a good many American boys to fighting a war that I think ought to be fought by the boys of Asia to help protect their own land."

On election day, November 3, Johnson obliterated Goldwater in both popular vote (forty-three million to twenty-seven million) and electoral votes (four hundred eighty-six to fifty-two). He had his mandate at home, but halfway around the world, in Vietnam, events were conspiring to destroy Johnson and his presidency, and to humiliate America before the world.

It began late on Saturday night, October 31, 1964, just three days before Johnson began his "victory celebration." A small party of Viet Cong carefully worked its way toward the Bien Hoa air base, twenty miles northeast of Saigon. Approaching from the north, the party stopped about four hundred yards out from the main runways and began setting up six 81-mm mortars. At 12:25 A.M. the order to fire was given. Within ten minutes the mortars got off seventy to eighty rounds. The squad dismantled the mortars and disappeared, unchallenged by anyone.

Bien Hoa, a major American air base, burst into flames. The B-57 jet bombers, so recently flown in from the Philippines to help quell the Viet Cong insurgency, were the main target, but the mortars also ignited fuel and ammunition, vehicles, houses, and the mess hall. South Vietnamese pilots and crewmen, American advisors—everyone on the base—rushed from bed and fought till after dawn to save what could be saved.

Four Americans were killed and seventy-two more wounded in the raid; and two South Vietnamese died and about a hundred were wounded. Of the precious twenty bombers, five were destroyed, eight badly damaged and seven more damaged. Not a single bomber escaped some damage. In addition, one H-43 helicopter was destroyed and three more damaged, three A-1Hs were destroyed and three more damaged, along with two C-47s. Search parties combing the surrounding area found no trace of the attackers.

The American military command was shaken. Besides the material damage, in the millions of dollars, the Bien Hoa raid had exposed a basic problem: Who was responsible for protecting American air bases? The Bien Hoa raid was a precedent in USAF history. Since the days of World War II, air bases had always been in rear areas, immune from insurgent attack. In Vietnam, there were no rear areas, yet a half-dozen giant American air bases were already emerging, from the DMZ to the Delta, and more were on the drawing boards. Who would protect them?

The Air Force had raised the question as early as 1961, but there was no answer then or, tragically, throughout the war. The Air Force contended its job was to fly planes and take the war to the enemy. The Army said its job was ground combat at the front, fighting the enemy, not guarding real estate; that was South Vietnam's job. The enemy, elated with the Bien Hoa results, began training special squads of mortarmen and sappers.

In the next eight years of war these expert squads killed over three hundred Americans and South Vietnamese, wounded over twenty-two hundred more, destroyed one hundred planes, and damaged another twelve hundred. The U.S. military never settled the question of who was to guard American air bases in enemy

Americans become the target of VC raids as 1964 comes to a close. The murderous night mortar raid on Bien Hoa airfield on November 1 destroyed at least 13 B-57s, recently flown in from the Philippines, and killed or wounded 76 American servicemen.

territory, though it might be noted that in I Corps, where the Marines ruled, the Marines guarded the bases. It might also be noted that General Curtis LeMay, the Air Force chief, fulminated from Washington to Hong Kong, but never visited Vietnam, though General Westmoreland said he had invited him.

Bien Hoa was not an isolated event. In the fall of 1964, the Viet Cong activated its first formal division, the 9th, and now had Saigon virtually surrounded, from Vung Tau on the coast all the way west into Cambodia. It was receiving supplies by water at dozens of points along the coast from Da Nang to the Mekong, and on the west down the rapidly developing Ho Chi Minh trail.

A little earlier, in late summer, the first North Vietnamese regulars had begun to go south, some as organized units, others as cadres to train the Viet Cong. The first North Vietnamese regiment arrived in Kontum Province (II 6) and by mid-November the ARVN had lost control there and in Binh Dinh Province (II 7), which bordered the sea coast and controlled all roads and the only railroad between

General Westmoreland (second from right, left photo) and General Taylor (in shirt-sleeves, right photo) rush out from Saigon to inspect the damage, both material and psychological, at Bien Hoa.

Saigon and Da Nang. Westmoreland felt at fault here; he had badgered the ARVN to send out small units to "pacify" the villages. The Viet Cong knocked off these units one by one. There were bitter memories for the military, of the American media trumpeting advice on how to run the war—break up into small units and "pacify."

Early in December, General Westmoreland returned to the United States for his father's funeral. Afterwards he was ordered to stop in Washington to talk with the Joint Chiefs of Staff. He did so, but neither President Johnson nor Secretary of Defense McNamara asked to see him. The general did talk with the Deputy Secretary of Defense, Cyrus Vance, and told him he badly needed more American troops to guard American installations.

On Christmas Eve, two Vietnamese parked an old car in front of the Brink Hotel, a billet for American officers in downtown Saigon. They told a guard they were waiting for an American officer, but soon sauntered off out of sight.

Just before 6 P.M. the car blew up, severely damaging the six-story hotel and setting it afire. A U.S. Navy officer and an American civilian were killed, and sixty-six other Americans were wounded. Once again, the Americans were surprised, humiliated, and enraged.

In the final humiliation of the Americans in 1964, VC terrorists blew up the Brink Hotel in downtown Saigon on Christmas Eve. The hotel had been taken over as a barracks for Americans. Two Americans were killed and 66 others wounded in the blast and fire.

The Viet Cong 9th Division closed out the year by destroying two South Vietnamese regiments in a battle at Binh Gia, thirty-five miles southeast of Saigon. The guerrillas, using the newest Russian and Chinese weapons, badly mauled some ARVN armored units sent to rescue their comrades. The Viet Cong now felt it owned Saigon and its environs. This battle was accepted by the Viet Cong as the official point when insurgency changed into conventional warfare. Westmoreland agreed, saying Binh Gia "meant the beginning of an intensive military challenge which the Vietnamese government could not meet with its own resources."

7

The Call to Combat 1965

THE CUSTOMARY cease-fire for the 1965 Tet (New Year's holiday) expired at midnight Saturday, February 6. Two hours later, about one hundred Viet Cong struck the American military compound near Pleiku and its airstrip four miles away at Camp Holloway. The action lasted only fifteen minutes, but eight Americans were killed, one hundred twenty-six Americans were injured, and the bases were badly damaged. The carefully trained Viet Cong squads ran among the parked helicopters and planes, setting explosive charges. Within minutes, more than a score of aircraft were destroyed.

The raid made no great impact on the military in Vietnam, but had a critical effect in Washington, Hanoi, and Moscow. McGeorge Bundy, a national security advisor to President Johnson, happened to be in Saigon. Alexey Kosygin, the Soviet premier, was in Hanoi; there is some evidence that he was preparing to urge Ho Chi Minh to move toward the negotiating table. Bundy flew up to Pleiku with General Westmoreland, early on February 7, and was appalled at the havoc a few Viet Cong could make and the rudimentary defenses of an American "base."

When Bundy's report on the raid reached Washington, along with one by General Taylor, filed independently, the conclusions were identical—it was time for sustained reprisals. President Johnson convened the National Security Council at 7:45 P.M. Saturday (Washington time). "I've had enough of this," he said. "They [the VC] are killing our men while they sleep in the night. The worst thing we could possibly do would be to let this go by. It would open the door to a major misunderstanding." He approved carrier air strikes into North Vietnam.

Shortly after noon Sunday, in poor weather, the carriers *Coral Sea* and *Hancock* launched forty-nine planes, A-4 Skyhawks and F-8 Crusaders, against barracks, rail lines, and other military targets at Dong Hoi, fifty miles up the coast from the DMZ. The next day, with clearing weather, some thirty South Vietnamese A-1s (with USAF F-100s flying cover) hit North Vietnamese barracks at Chap Le, only ten miles above the DMZ. Piloting one of the A-1s was Air Marshal Nguyen Cao Ky, thirty-four, soon to emerge as prime minister of the Republic of Vietnam.

The raids had some small material effects, but a monumental effect in Hanoi. Premier Kosygin gave up all thought of bringing Ho to the bargaining table. As it came out in formal language over Radio Hanoi, Kosygin said: "We sternly declare that the Soviet Union will not remain indifferent to the destiny of a brotherly socialist country, and is ready to give the Democratic Republic of Vietnam all necessary assistance if aggressors dare to encroach upon the independence and sovereignty of the DRVN." From Peking, the Chinese rulers declared that "650 million Chinese people will definitely not stand idly by." Thus, in effect, a small Viet Cong raid at Pleiku led two reluctant world leaders—Kosygin and Johnson—to a war neither wanted.

In Moscow, some two thousand demonstrators, led by Chinese and Vietnamese students, threw stones and ink bottles at the United States embassy. Two newsmen were injured, and Ambassador Foy D. Kohler protested "inadequate police protection." When the Kremlin called out Red Army units, Peking protested "police brutality."

On the day of the Pleiku raid, President Johnson gave the long-awaited order: all American dependents must leave Vietnam. The first of the 1,819 American women and children in South Vietnam left on February 9, and in a few days all were gone, on Pan American Airways charter flights. Some went to Japan, others to the Philippines or Hawaii, and many all the way back to the United States. Kitsy Westmoreland and the children were among the last to leave, departing on Valentine's Day for Hawaii. "We have no choice but to clear the decks," said President Johnson.

Just at dark on Wednesday, February 10, the Viet Cong struck again, this time at Qui Nhon, a good-sized coastal city at the eastern end of Route 19, from Pleiku. The guerrillas set off several bombs under the Viet Cuong Hotel, being used as a barracks for American enlisted men. The four-story structure collapsed, trapping many wounded in the rubble.

Viet Cong guerrillas blow up another American barracks, this one at Qui Nhon, on February 10, killing 23 Americans and injuring scores more. Here Sp5 Robert K. Marshall, who was trapped in the wreckage for three hours, tells U.S. Ambassador to Vietnam Maxwell Taylor and General William Westmoreland how he killed two VC before he went down with the four-story hotel. A few days earlier, the VC had staged a bloody raid on Pleiku, and President Johnson had ordered all American dependents out of South Vietnam.

Among them was Sp5 Robert K. Marshall of Premier, West Virginia. He heard gunfire and ran out on his third-floor balcony to see what it was. After spotting two Viet Cong running in the street, he killed them with his rifle. Then, hearing the first bomb explosion, he crawled under his cot, just in time to go down with the hotel. He was dug out three hours later.

Twenty-three Americans were killed, and more than a score seriously injured. One was saved, minus a leg, when a Korean surgeon, serving with a Republic of Korea medical detachment, crawled in the wreckage and performed an amputation in a space too small for American doctors. The death toll was the worst yet for Americans, and air reprisals came the next day.

This time the carrier *Ranger* joined the other two carriers in launching ninety-nine American planes against North Vietnamese barracks at Chanh Hoa, five miles above Dong Xoai, in monsoon weather—five-hundred-foot ceiling and one-mile visibility. South Vietnamese pilots, again with USAF fighter cover, hit other barracks and artillery sites nearby. Damage was moderate. Three Navy planes went down and two of the pilots were rescued. The third, Lt. Commander Robert H. Shumaker (USNA 1956), was captured and joined Lt. Alvarez in the North Vietnamese prison system for eight years of captivity. (In all, sixty-one Americans

U.S. NAVY CARRIERS IN VIETNAM SERVICE

No.	Name	Year Commissioned	Class
CVA 11	Intrepid	1943	Essex-M
CVS 12	Hornet	1943	Essex-M
CVA 14	Ticonderoga	1945	Hancock-M
CVA 19	Hancock	1944	Hancock-M
CVA 31	Bon Homme Richard	1944	Hancock-M
CVS 33	Kearsarge	1946	Essex-M
CVA 34	Oriskany	1950	Oriskany-M
CVS 38	Shangri-La	1944	Hancock-M
CVA 41	Midway	1945	Midway-M
CVA 42	Franklin D. Roosevelt	1945	Midway-M
CVA 43	Coral Sea	1947	Midway-M
CVA 59	Forrestal	1955	Forrestal
CVA 61	Ranger	1957	Forrestal
CVA 62	Independence	1959	Forrestal
CVA 64	Constellation	1961	Kitty Hawk
CVAN 65	Enterprise	1961	Enterprise (nuclear-powered, world's largest ship, 86,000 tons)

M – Modernized

became POWs during 1965. Thirty-five Air Force pilots, twenty-three Navy pilots, two Marines, and one civilian would come out alive in the February-March releases of 1973.)

At the command level, General Westmoreland discovered the full agonies of war by committee. In responding to the Qui Nhon attack, he first got an okay from the South Vietnamese command, then dispatched his plans to CINCPAC in Hawaii, which added its own consensus and sent the package on to Washington. After a welter of orders and counterorders, the approval for a counterstrike came through at dawn from the Commander in Chief, President Johnson. By that time all the pilots and crews, both American and South Vietnamese, were exhausted. They'd been up all night, at the ready.

Some of the red tape was eliminated in mid-February. The Strategic Air Command was allowed to move two B-52 squadrons from the United States out to Andersen Air Force Base, Guam. They would see no action until June, but in the meantime General Westmoreland finally received approval to use American aircraft within South Vietnam. The restrictions were severe. Westmoreland had to authorize each mission personally, and could do so only to deny the Viet Cong a "major" victory, or avoid "numbers" of Americans being killed or being on missions that were beyond the ability of the South Vietnamese Air Force. The general immediately sent twenty-four of his B-57 Canberra bombers against a Viet Cong Regiment in Phuoc Tuy Province (III 25), east of Saigon. An ARVN outfit had been mauled there. He also sent the bombers on February 19 against Viet Cong headquarters in Phuoc Long Province (III 18), near the Cambodian border. Three days later the

U.S. Marine choppers moved the ARVN's 1st Airborne Battalion into battle against the VC in the coastal paddies near Qui Nhon.

bombers were out again, rescuing a mixed U.S. Army/CIDG force being ambushed in the Mang Yang pass, on Route 19 east of Pleiku (II 8). This was a dangerous area, with a bad history. A crack French outfit, the Group Mobile 100 (The Centurions), had been destroyed here by the Viet Cong in 1954. Besides the Canberra bombers, Westmoreland ordered in F-100s, Huey gunships, and transport helicopters, and they brought out the force of 220 men safely. By fall, a great deal more would be heard from this area.

On February 13, President Johnson approved an operation code-named Rolling Thunder. It might more aptly have carried the code name Creeping Whisper. From the start it was severely limited, hemmed about with many restrictions. Johnson described it as "a program of measured and limited air action," and it was certainly that.

For the President, Rolling Thunder may have been a reluctant decision, but it was not a sudden one. The Joint Chiefs of Staff had been preparing options for the Commander in Chief since late 1964; it was plain to anyone who faced the situation squarely that a crisis was on the way. Someone would have to decide soon whether the United States should stay in Vietnam and at what strength. Remaining at present strength would mean certain defeat not far in the future. Taking over the war, beefing up, and winning it was another option. A third option, withdrawal, was then unthinkable.

As early as November 1964, the Joint Chiefs of Staff had completed a list of bombing targets in the North—ninety-four of them. If President Johnson wanted North Vietnam's industrial base obliterated, the chiefs said, that could be done in twelve days by rallying all American air power in the Pacific to the task. This would be "surgical" bombing, taking out only military objectives. (The United States never contemplated using in Vietnam the saturation bombing of World War II, such as the air campaigns that destroyed Dresden, Tokyo, Berlin, and other major cities of Europe and Japan. Public opinion would not countenance that, and anyway it was far too dangerous; all major powers now had nuclear weapons.)

Johnson gradually accepted the idea of bombing some targets in North Vietnam. Defense Secretary McNamara recommended starting the bombing slowly and gradually accelerating it, meanwhile watching the reactions in Hanoi, Moscow, and Peking. That appealed to Johnson; he approved Rolling Thunder, with no public announcement. It was a failure from the start.

The opening raid, Rolling Thunder 1, was laid on for February 20; it never came off because the South Vietnamese air force was busy at home quelling internal troubles. The Buddhists were unhappy again. On January 23 a mob in Hue had denounced Ambassador Taylor, stormed the United States Information Agency's library, set it afire, and pillaged it. There were demonstrations in Saigon also, and constant threats of coups and yet another military government in power. By mid-February, when the Khanh government fell, Westmoreland saw an opportunity (gone in a split second) for the United States to pull out of Vietnam with some honor, and let it all happen.

The bombing campaign finally got off the mark on March 2, with Rolling Thunder 5 (the intervening missions had been cancelled for various reasons), against an ammunition depot at Xom Bang, twenty miles above the DMZ, and a small naval base at Quang Khe, fifty miles above the DMZ. The attack, executed by one hundred and four USAF planes and nineteen South Vietnam planes, caused minor damage and carried no message to Hanoi.

But the USAF lost three planes to antiaircraft fire and learned some lessons:

- Better protection needed against antiaircraft artillery.
- Send fewer planes.
- Don't bunch or loiter over the target.
- Make only one pass over the target.

President Johnson finally approved United States air attacks on North Vietnam, but only in the south, near the DMZ. He called the operation "Rolling Thunder," and by April it had begun to take effect, with this steel railroad span dropped at Qui Vinh, near the city of Vinh (top), and a concrete span, the Dien Chau railroad bridge, disabled (above).

Rolling Thunder 6, after humiliating delays, finally took place on March 15. The targets were Hon Gio (Tiger Island), lying just twenty miles off the DMZ, and an ammunition depot near Phu Qui, one hundred seventy-five miles north of the DMZ. Results were hardly noticeable, but in the meantime President Johnson had faced up to Vietnam's most serious problem.

Westmoreland had been warning since early in the year that "we [were] headed for a Viet Cong takeover" in South Vietnam unless something was done. Specifically, he asked for American troops to save his three key air bases—Da Nang, Tan Son Nhut, and Bien Hoa; a Marine brigade (three battalions) to hold the city of Da Nang; and an Army outfit, probably the 173rd Airborne Brigade, to protect the Tan Son Nhut/Bien Hoa complex at Saigon. The moment Johnson dreaded had come; it was not to be all-out war, but it would be "American boys" fighting where "Asian boys" should be doing it. It was a hard decision for the Commander in Chief, but he made it. He approved Westmoreland's request.

The Marine Expeditionary Force, sixteen hundred strong, came ashore at Da Nang on the morning of March 8 in full battle dress. (As someone said, they seemed to believe they were "reenacting Iwo Jima.") Instead of the Viet Cong, they were welcomed by town officials, pretty girls in leis bearing flowers, and grinning U.S. Air Force and Army troops with cameras galore and a sign, "Welcome to the Gallant Marines."

Chosen to receive the flowers were Pfc. Robert Buckley of Theodore, Alabama; Pfc. Kenneth Lesnich of Buffalo, New York; and Navy Hospital Corpsman J. L. Brown of Jeanerette, Louisiana.

In Washington, Secretary of State Dean Rusk said of the Marines: "If they are shot at, they will shoot back."

General Taylor had opposed the introduction of American combat forces from the first day the question came up, contending "white-faced" troops could not adjust to the Oriental environment. His opposition did not decline when he saw that the Marines had brought with them tanks, self-propelled artillery, and other heavy weapons. The Marines had almost been forbidden to bring their eight-inch howitzers, because they were capable of firing atomic shells. But they had no such ammunition with them and, in any event, many American planes already had atomic capabilities.

But the name "Marine Expeditionary Force" had to go; General Westmoreland feared it might remind the Vietnamese of the hated French Expeditionary Corps, so it was changed to Marine Amphibious Force (MAF). Even as the Marines landed, two Army officers from Saigon were in Da Nang snapping up land to expand the airfield and build docks, warehouses, radar sites, all the myriad material things a modern military needs. In a few days they negotiated with eighteen hundred landowners and passed out $620,000 for land use rights. The golden flood of American money was starting—a monsoon of cash that would devastate the country as surely, and as dangerously, as iron bombs.

Da Nang, called Tourane by the French, is a good deep-water port, except during the winter monsoons, but early in 1965 it was run down and swollen by refugees to a population of some two hundred thousand. USAF planes, a Marine helicopter squadron, and the South Vietnamese air force were already using the airfield for raids across the DMZ, but five thousand or more Viet Cong were close by, and the field was clearly vulnerable. It was, in fact, ripe for the sabotage raids like the recent ones in Saigon, Bien Hoa, and Quang Tri. All bantering aside, this was hard-core Viet Cong territory, and had been for twenty years or more. The Marines, who had been at sea two months, made straight for the airfield, to secure it for the other half of the 9th Marines due by air from Okinawa at 11 A.M. The field was soon jammed and the airlift was not completed until March 12.

The Marines' mission was clearly defined in their orders: "To occupy and defend critical terrain features in order to secure the airfield and, as directed, communications facilities, U.S. supporting installations, port facilities, landing beaches, and other U.S. installations in the area against attack. The U.S. Marine force will not (repeat, not) engage in day to day actions against the Viet Cong."

Lest anyone get skittish at home, General Wheeler told Congress that in the face of growing Viet Cong activity "General Westmoreland recommended to us that we move a force of Marines into the Da Nang area to provide local security and to guarantee, in effect, that the place would not be overrun by a concentration of Viet Cong, our people killed and our aircraft destroyed." That seemed reasonable to

Da Nang harbor, as it looked just before the U.S. Marines landed March 8 to carve out a huge base, the bastion of the northern sector of South Vietnam. For those who remember, this is how the Bridge Complex looked "before."

115

some, but the media were already hinting that Army combat troops would not be far behind.

More Marine helicopters flew in from the USS *Princeton* (LPH-5) at sea, and two Hawk missile batteries that had arrived in February were also at the field. In line with basic Marine doctrine—"take the high ground"—combat teams moved into nearby hills on March 10, taking a thousand-foot hill west of the field, naming it the "hungry i," after Company I and a well-known San Francisco nightclub. Other Marines took a hill to the north, and also Monkey Mountain, at the harbor entrance, for the future Hawk base.

To the military eye, the Da Nang region was a shambles of old and crumbling French fortifications. The airfield itself, with one ten-thousand-foot concrete runway, was already jammed with mixed American and South Vietnamese units and surrounded by the city. On the west side of the airfield an area of sleazy bars and small shops became "Dog Patch" to the Americans. Bringing order and military security to the Da Nang base was obviously first priority. The anchor for I Corps, Da Nang was an area of about ten thousand square miles, a little larger than New Jersey, but longer and thinner. Both the 225-mile coastline of I Corps, and the uplands, with mountains of five thousand feet or more, belonged to the Viet Cong. So did much of South Vietnam.

A little before 11 A.M. on March 30, two men parked a Citroen alongside the United States embassy in downtown Saigon and began to walk away. A policeman called to them that they could not park there; they ran. The car, loaded with two hundred fifty pounds of explosives, blew up. Storekeeper 2/c Manolito W. Castillo, U.S. Navy, twenty-six, standing in the embassy doorway, was killed instantly, and inside, Barbara A. Robbins, twenty-one, of Denver, a secretary, died at her desk. On the fifth floor, Deputy U.S. Ambassador U. Alexis Johnson was cut on the face by flying glass. In all, seventeen persons were killed and one hundred eighty-three were wounded, including fifty-four Americans. In Washington, President Johnson said "outrages like this will only reinforce the determination of the American people and their government to continue and to strengthen their assistance and support for the people and government of Vietnam." (In a war full of irony, another attack, three years later, at the new American embassy nearby, would have exactly the opposite effect on "the American people and their government.")

Just six days earlier, on March 24, a new word had entered the American vocabulary. Faculty members and some two thousand students held a "teach-in" at the University of Michigan—a twelve-hour, all-night seminar protesting the Vietnam war. It was yet another of many "ins"—sleep-ins, sit-ins, etc.—to wrack the academic community. Secretary of State Dean Rusk said: "I sometimes wonder at the gullibility of educated men and the stubborn disregard of plain facts by men who are supposed to be helping our young to learn—especially to learn how to think."

At about the same time as Rolling Thunder was getting off, President Johnson called General Harold K. Johnson, the Army Chief of Staff, to the White House for a private breakfast. As they parted, one Johnson admonished the other Johnson, "You go out there and get things bubbling, General." The general spent March 5–

Mount Nui Ba Den, or Black Virgin Mountain to thousands of GIs, gets supplies courtesy of a U.S. Army Huey. The VC held the base of the 3,000-foot mountain 50 miles northwest of Saigon, but the Americans and South Vietnamese used the strategic peak throughout the war.

A U.S. Army Caribou transport, workhorse of the supply train, makes another ho-hum landing, this one in exactly 136 yards, stopping just short of the building at Xuyen Moc, near the seacoast east of Saigon.

12 in Saigon and found Westmoreland eager for action. The Viet Cong was threatening both Da Nang and Saigon, and the North Vietnamese 325th Division was gathering strength in the central highlands, probably preparing to cut South Vietnam in half by driving to the sea. Westmoreland told General Johnson he needed at least one American Army division to stop the North Vietnamese in the highlands, and other troops to break the siege of Saigon, particularly in the coastal area, the Bien Hoa/Vung Tau sector.

The time for critical American decisions was at hand, and those decisions were made at the so-called Honolulu Conference, convened April 20 by Secretary McNamara at the Pearl Harbor headquarters of Admiral Sharp, Commander in Chief, Pacific. This conference propelled the United States into the Vietnam war and set the course of American history for the next ten years.

The Secretary of Defense brought with him a large party from Washington, but it did not include the commander in chief, President Johnson. The military was present in force, headed by General Earle G. Wheeler, chairman of the Joint Chiefs of Staff. General Westmoreland outlined the Vietnamese situation in simple terms.

The United States could either stay in Vietnam or it could withdraw, Westmoreland said. If it stayed, it would need massive reinforcements quickly, or face defeat at the hands of the insurgents, powerfully backed by North Vietnam. The general said he would need thirteen American battalions immediately, and more to follow. Besides the Marines, he needed a full air-mobile division to hold the central highlands, and further troops in the Saigon sector. Westmoreland envisioned a war lasting several years and progressing from defense to buildup and then to the offensive. He was confident of victory, with full understanding that it could not be achieved overnight. It would demand the full military resources of the United States—land, sea, and air—and would require the building of a total military presence in a battle area that lacked nearly everything—ports, airfields, roads, communications, transport, housing, food, electricity, even drinking water.

McNamara and his party listened, asked questions, talked. When the conference ended, Westmoreland had assurances that the United States would stay in Vietnam, that he would get what he wanted, and that he should proceed at speed. McNamara's attitude was summed up in a phrase: "Just tell us what you need; we'll see that you get it."

General Westmoreland was promised seventeen more battalions, in addition to the three Marine battalions already in the north. He could have thirteen American Army battalions, three more Korean battalions, and one Australian. In addition, he got a half-promise of an American air-mobile division, for the Highlands, and enough Koreans to total a division. This would bring American strength in South Vietnam to 82,000 troops, and Allied strength to 7,250.

There was no public announcement of the Honolulu agreements until June 16, when McNamara disclosed that U.S. strength in South Vietnam would reach seventy-five thousand "in a few weeks," more than triple the January level. The doves at home made some noises, but when President Johnson asked for $700 million dollars to pay for the war, Congress quickly approved it—408 to 7 in the House, 88 to 3 in the Senate.

However, President Johnson's so-called credibility gap was beginning to show. Early in April, he had approved a request from General Westmoreland: Instead of a ten-mile, strictly defensive perimeter at Da Nang, the President agreed that the Marines could now take offensive action up to fifty miles from the air base. No public announcement was made, but the newsmen in South Vietnam could see it happening. In Washington, the media cornered Johnson. Did this mean an enlargement of the American offensive role?

"There has been no change . . ." Johnson intoned, but on the other hand, "General Westmoreland also has the authority . . . to employ these troops . . . in support of Vietnamese forces faced with aggressive attack . . ." Rusk put it more sharply on a TV show: "We don't expect these men to sit there like hypnotized rabbits waiting for the VC to strike."

The need in South Vietnam was indeed critical. In early May the Viet Cong struck Phuoc Binh (also called Song Be), the capital of Phuoc Long Province (III 18), sixty miles north of Saigon. Only intensive air support saved the ARVN defenders from decimation. In early July guerrillas hit the town of Ba Gia, only twenty miles south of the new Marine enclave at Chu Lai. They routed an ARVN battalion, smashed a rescue battalion and escaped with 200 American weapons, including ten 105-mm howitzers. Rebels also began a two-month siege of a Green Beret/CIDG camp at Duc Co, just west of Pleiku (II 8).

On June 10 the rebels struck closer to Saigon, in troubled Phuoc Long Province (III 18). They overran the Special Forces camp at Dong Xoai, ten miles south of their May attack at Phuoc Binh. They held Dong Xoai for two days, destroyed a rescuing ARVN battalion, and mauled two more relieving battalions. In the full-tilt battle for Dong Xoai, Second Lieutenant Charles Q. Williams of the 5th Special Forces Group won the Medal of Honor, the Army's second in Vietnam.

Help was on the way. On May 3, the crack 173rd Airborne Brigade (the "Sky Soldiers"), the Army's only "quick-reaction" unit in the Pacific, flew into Bien Hoa from Okinawa, the first major Army combat unit to reach South Vietnam. They immediately went to work in the combat area from Bien Hoa down Route 15 to the sea at Vung Tau. Westmoreland wanted the port of Vung Tau, but the Viet Cong units in the area were sharp and well armed; North Vietnam fed them the latest arms from the Soviet Union, by ship down the coast from Haiphong. The Navy would have to cut those sea lanes, and the U.S. Coast Guard would be called in, too. The real war had arrived around Saigon.

Four days later, on May 7, more Marines began landing in I Corps, in a place that would become known as Chu Lai. At the moment it was an unmarked stretch of sand and pines that somehow looked a lot like the North Carolina seacoast. Lieutenant General Victor H. Krulak had reconnoitered this area in 1964 when the possibility of an airfield south of Da Nang was under discussion in the field. When a name was needed, General Krulak simply used the Mandarin Chinese characters for his last name, which came out Chu Lai in English. Early in 1965 General Westmoreland had requested a second airfield for I Corps, and by late April approval came from the commander in chief himself, President Johnson.

By May 12, some six thousand Marines and Seabees had come ashore over the

More help arrives in May, with the crack U.S. 173rd Airborne Brigade (above) moving in to save the key American air base at Bien Hoa, near Saigon. More Marines arrive in the north to carve out a new base at Chu Lai (below). A sardonic sign of welcome is shown there, erected by the U.S. Army advisers who arrived a little sooner.

During his sixth trip to Vietnam in July 1965, Secretary McNamara talks in Saigon with Nguyen Van Thieu (left) and also meets with Nguyen Cao Ky (right). Thieu, now bearing the title "Chief of State," and Ky, a flamboyant "fly-boy" type, are emerging as the co-rulers of South Vietnam.

beach, and Chu Lai was under way. Once again there was a welcoming party, this time U.S. Army people with the ARVN 2nd Division. Their sign said: "Ahoy Marines!! Welcome Aboard. Area Secured. Courtesy Ly Tin District Army Advisors."

One more step remained to complete the transformation of the American role in Vietnam from advisory to combat. That step began July 16, when Defense Secretary McNamara arrived in Saigon on his first inspection trip in fourteen months. General Westmoreland was ready with his "shopping list." He wanted thirty-four more American battalions.

His overall plan called for three battalions to defend each major air base and two more for each minor base. The need was urgent, he said, at Tan Son Nhut, Bien Hoa, Da Nang, and Nha Trang, and by October he'd need new security battalions at Pleiku, Qui Nhon, Cam Ranh Bay, and Phan Rang, all in II Corps, and Binh Tuy, the big air base in the Mekong Delta near Can Tho (IV 37).

And the rest of the battalions? McNamara wanted to know. In I Corps they'd go to the Hue/Phu Bai base complex, and to the Da Nang and Chu Lai bases; in II Corps, they'd go to Qui Nhon and the vital Binh Khe/An Khe stretch of Route 19 leading up to Pleiku. Route 19 must be held at all costs, or the Communists could cut South Vietnam in half. Any forces left over could beef up the Cam Ranh Bay and Tan Son Nhut sectors.

Orders for these battalions emphasized the word "security," but added another seminal word, "offensive." Besides security, these units "will conduct *offensive* operations in the immediate vicinity to expand the TAOR (Tactical Area of Responsibility) around each base area" . . . and "the forces (over and above those required for security of the base) will be available to conduct *offensive* missions from the base area."

This time, President Johnson himself went to the nation with the news. On Wednesday, July 28, at noontime (critics said he chose an hour when the TV audience is small) he took a twofold message to the nation: Why we were in Vietnam, and what it might cost.

"Three times in my lifetime—in two world wars and in Korea—Americans have gone to far lands to fight for freedom. We have learned at a terrible and brutal cost that retreat does not bring safety, and weakness does not bring peace . . ." (That last phrase would come back to haunt him.)

"I have today ordered to Vietnam . . . forces which will raise our fighting strength from 75,000 to 125,000 men almost immediately. Additional forces will be needed later and they will be sent as requested. This will make it necessary to increase our active fighting forces by raising the monthly draft call from 17,000 over a period of time to 35,000 per month and for us to step up our campaign for voluntary enlistments."

There it was. America was at war.

8

Here Come the Troops 1965

RIGHT FROM the start, Vietnam was the strangest war the Marines had ever encountered—no halls of Montezuma here, no shores of Tripoli. From the first day ashore in Da Nang in early March 1965, the American troops discovered they were not in charge; they were guests in the house, and the house belonged to South Vietnam. The host was Major General Nguyen Chanh Thi, commander of I Corps, and nothing happened unless he gave permission.

His troops secured the beachheads as the Marines splashed ashore in Da Nang, and they also lined the route to the airfield. Then it was disclosed that the Marines were to secure only half the field, the western and northern perimeters. South Vietnamese troops would hold the eastern and southern perimeters; the eastern side led into the city and the southern into Viet Cong territory. General Thi was not sure the Marines were ready to meet the South Vietnamese people, and vice versa.

The Marines might look upon themselves as liberators, but the populace looked at the situation a little differently. They had been living with the Viet Cong for years, and many a family served with the Viet Cong. After all, they *were* Vietnamese. Now the Saigon government was allowing "white-faced" foreigners into the country. That would take some getting used to. After all, it had taken nearly a century to get rid of the last foreigners, the French. For many South Vietnamese it was better to face the devil they knew (the Viet Cong) than the devil they didn't ("Whitey").

For the Marines, Da Nang was no Iwo Jima, no Okinawa; there was no big offensive off the beach. For the first months the Marines were not allowed more than ten miles from the airfield. For the first ten months, through the rest of 1965, they had to fight for permission to fight; for concessions, both from Washington and from General Thi.

Just before 10 A.M. on March 8, Battalion Landing Team 3/9 (3d Battalion, 9th

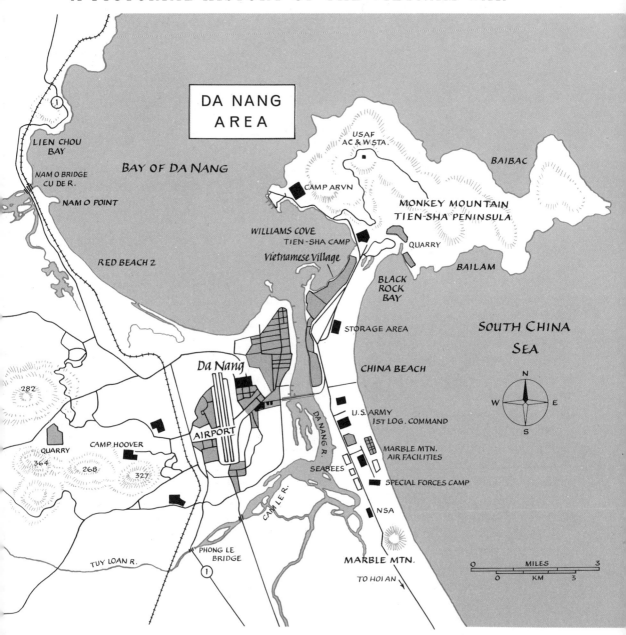

Regiment), with Lt. Col. Charles E. McPartlin, Jr., commanding, formed up on the beach and began a motor march from the beachhead to the southern end of the airfield, where it would be billeted. At the same time, leading elements of Battalion Landing Team 1/3 (1st Battalion, 3d Regiment), with Lt. Col. Herbert J. Bain commanding, were airborne from Okinawa. All of BLT 1/3 was due in by air that day, with landings to start at noon, but by then the field was jammed with men and equipment. On the first day, arrivals by air were cut off after thirteen landings. The

MAJOR UNITED STATES COMBAT UNITS IN SOUTH VIETNAM

Month of Arrival	Year	Unit
March/May	1965	3rd Marine Division
May	1965	173rd Airborne Brigade
July	1965	1st Brigade, 101st Airborne Division
September	1965	1st Cavalry Division (Air-mobile)
October	1965	1st Infantry Division
January/May	1966	1st Marine Division
March	1966	25th Infantry Division
August	1966	196th Infantry Brigade
August/December	1966	5th Marine Division (elements)
September	1966	4th Infantry Division
December	1966	1st and 2nd Brigades, 9th Infantry Division
December	1966	199th Infantry Brigade
September	1967	23rd Infantry Division (American) (formed in Vietnam of various units already present)
October	1967	198th Infantry Brigade
November	1967	2nd and 3rd Brigades, 101st Airborne Division
December	1967	11th Infantry Brigade
February	1968	3rd Brigade, 82nd Airborne Division
July	1968	1st Brigade, 5th Infantry Division
July	1969	3rd Brigade, 9th Infantry Division
December	1970	2nd Brigade, 25th Infantry Division (separate)

next day, the HMM-162 helicopters (Lieutenant Colonel Oliver W. Curtis commanding) began arriving from the USS *Princeton* offshore.

It was March 12 before the Marines completed their arrival at Da Nang, and on the same day General Thi had a garden party for the top Marine officers, complete with hors d'oeuvres and orchestra. By that time Brig. Gen. Frederick J. Karch, commanding general of the 9th Marine Expeditionary Brigade (MEB), and every Marine down to the troop level could tell that Vietnam was not your usual Marine operation. In fact, the orders from General Westmoreland in Saigon said the 9th MEB "will not (repeat not) engage in day-to-day actions against the Viet Cong." The Army general said that overall defense of the Da Nang area "remains a RVNAF [Republic of Vietnam Armed Forces] responsibility." From the first day, the Marines began to dislike Vietnam; this was not their style of war.

125

Their real war began on the last day of March 1965, when twenty-five Marine helicopters joined up with ten U.S. Army helicopters, doing strike and resupply duty for South Vietnamese forces in a dust-up with the Viet Cong twenty-five miles south of Da Nang. In a short and sharp encounter, two Marines were killed, seventeen more wounded, and nineteen helicopters destroyed or damaged. Marine infantry, meantime, had moved out to the west of the field and occupied Hills 268 and 327, some four miles and two miles, respectively, from the runway. It was during these days that the first Marines were killed in ground combat. One Marine shot and killed two of his buddies, in the dark, by mistake.

There was plenty of housekeeping work to be done at the base, and the Marines quickly discovered that heat and humidity were also enemies. Heat prostration became a problem to deal with, just as "immersion foot" would in a few weeks, as the Marines deployed into the rice paddies. Wet feet could swell up and within hours become puffy and painful, knocking a man out of duty for days. As to the heat, no heavy work could be done during the middle hours of the day except with double squads, working thirty minutes on and thirty minutes off. As Noël Coward had said, only "mad dogs and Englishmen go out in the noonday sun."

The Marines opened their enclave at Chu Lai with a second unopposed landing on May 7. Chu Lai had been chosen as the site for a SATS (Short Airfield for Tactical Support), which usually meant an airstrip of three thousand feet or less. In this case the NMCB 10 (Navy Mobile Construction Battalion 10, or Seabees) was being put ashore to build an eight-thousand-foot airstrip, taxiways, hardstands, and facilities for three jet squadrons. No Viet Cong appeared, though they were nearby; intelligence was estimating the guerrillas could mass two thousand troops in twenty-four hours, and another two thousand in three days.

Two BLTs (battalion landing teams) landed the first day, quickly secured the beaches, and moved inland to Route 1, where they united with elements of the ARVN 2nd Division. The main enemy at Chu Lai was the beach sand, as white and fine as powdered talc, and almost as bad as quicksand. In the first hours, four Marines went down with heat prostration, and trucks simply could not move in the sand. Tons of pierced aluminum matting for the airstrip had to be wrestled ashore by hand, and unloading was finally completed on May 12. Chu Lai was established, and with it the 9th MEB disappeared, to be replaced by III MAF (Marine Amphibious Force), Major General William R. ("Rip") Collins commanding. With the forces still pouring in, General Collins had some ten thousand Marines under his command in I Corps, complete with infantry, artillery, engineers, and air power. It was a time for building.

The Marines soon opened a third enclave in I Corps, at Phu Bai, fifty miles north of Da Nang. They had opposed setting up there but General Westmoreland had insisted, so BLT 3/4 arrived by air on April 14 from Da Nang, and more Marines came by landing craft. They disembarked at Hue to the music of an ARVN band, five hundred cheering Vietnamese, and a large banner, "Welcome U.S. Marines." Then they were trucked five miles south to Phu Bai, where ten UH-34D helicopters had just arrived. One of the main jobs was to guard the Army's 8th RRU (radio

By the summer of 1965 the U.S. Marines are swarming over I Corps, first building
the bases, at Chu Lai (above) and at Da Nang (below).

research unit), a hush-hush listening post that Westmoreland considered vital to Intelligence.

There were other reasons for Phu Bai. It had an airfield, and it established an American presence north of the Hai Van Pass. The pass carried Route 1 and the railroad into the two northernmost provinces of South Vietnam, Quang Tri and Thua Thien, and to the important cities of Quang Tri and Hue. The Annamite Mountains cut right across South Vietnam from Laos to the sea at Hai Van, and the pass had to be held if Quang Tri and Thua Thien were to be defended. Ho Chi Minh had fought hard at Geneva to get these two provinces included in North Vietnam. He lost then, but would certainly try again, by force this time.

General Westmoreland had another critical problem: holding Qui Nhon until the 1st Cavalry Division could get there to seize and hold the whole Central Highlands. The division was being assembled in the United States, but could not arrive before September. Westmoreland, with support from Admiral Sharp, decided to use the Seventh Fleet's SLF (Special Landing Force) made up of a battalion of Marine infantry (BLT 3/7, Lieutenant Colonel Charles H. Bodley commanding) and supporting helicopters (HMM-163, Lieutenant Colonel Norman G. Ewer commanding). The SLF was quickly loaded at Okinawa, arrived off Qui Nhon on June 30, and landed the next day. General Westmoreland was waiting for them on shore and directed them to high ground south of the city. Once more the Marines were working for the Army.

All pieces were now in place, and the war began the next morning, but at Da Nang. An assault force of some eighty-five Viet Cong and thirteen North Vietnamese sappers, heavily armed and specially trained, crossed the Cau Do River, penetrated two wire fences, and burst upon the airfield at about 1:30 A.M. The attack came at the southern edge of the field, where the South Vietnamese Army had command, and caught them by surprise.

Within minutes, heavy fire broke out from small arms, automatic weapons, and mortars up to 81 mm. In the confusion, the sappers, experts from the 3rd Battalion, 18th Regiment, North Vietnamese Army, ran among the U.S. Air Force and Marine aircraft, hurling satchel charges on the F-102s and C-130s. Counterfire came from all sides, but the attackers were already withdrawing and were soon gone into the night. One Marine was killed and three wounded; six planes were destroyed and three others damaged. It was all over in thirty minutes.

The raid had little tactical significance, but profound military and political consequences. The media coverage was instantaneous, spectacular, and worldwide. Major General Lewis W. Walt, the III MAF commander, had been sleeping in his night command post, an amphibian tractor in a rice paddy west of the airfield. Within the next two hours he had telephone calls from General Westmoreland's headquarters in Saigon, Admiral Sharp's headquarters in Hawaii, Marine Corps headquarters, Defense Secretary McNamara's office in the Pentagon, the Secretary of the Navy, and the watch officer in the situation room at the White House.

General Walt was to recall later: "All of them wanted to know all about the attack and what I was doing about it. This points out one of the hazards for a commander of having present-day instantaneous communications to the battlefield, all over the world."

The incident was typical of Vietnam, and heralded fundamental changes in military practice. From the Da Nang raid on, the war was fought in the glare of media publicity never before imagined. No battlefield was safe anymore from a blizzard of queries and "advice" from the highest quarters in Washington, both military and political. For the military it presented problems never dreamed of by Clausewitz, and opened new realms of study at military colleges around the world.

In this specific instance, the Da Nang raid had salutary effects. It illustrated once again an age-old axiom of war: a passive defense is an invitation to disaster. The Marines had known this, of course, and attack had always been basic doctrine to the corps. Perhaps now the Washington politicians and bureaucrats would give back to the field commander the authority that meant life and death for him and his men.

General Westmoreland had tried to unleash the Marines as early as mid-April, when he gave them the order to go over to the offensive. But General Thi refused to allow them outside the perimeter. "This is enemy country," he said, "and you are not ready to operate out there." But that was nonsense; the Marines were already running into the Viet Cong. The first clash came April 22, nine miles southwest of Da Nang, and another followed two days later, a mile south of Phu Bai. The Marines had to move into the field, and they did. Patrol action began, and it grew every day until it was a major feature of the war, a horror chronicle of thousands, and hundreds of thousands, of *patrols,* a ceaseless bleeding of the infantry.

The other war—the war of *battles,* or engagements, the larger set pieces—began in August, south of Chu Lai. The 1st Viet Cong Regiment had been on the prowl there for some weeks. A month earlier they had given the ARVN a bloody nose at Ba Gia. Around mid-August the Marines found the Viet Cong concentrated, some fifteen hundred strong, near the Phuoc Thuan Peninsula, twelve miles south of Chu Lai. They were vulnerable from land and sea, an opportunity the Marines had been dreaming of. They called it Operation Starlite.

Early on August 18 the Marines dropped in by helicopter at three LZs (Landing Zones Red, White, and Blue) and began pushing the VC toward the coast. Amphibious forces came ashore at the southern end of Phase Line Banana, and the ships offshore laid on gunfire as needed. The Marines rolled out everything they had— choppers, tanks, flamethrowers, artillery, ship's fire—everything they'd been itching to use. By August 24th it was over: 614 Viet Cong counted dead, 9 prisoners, 42 suspects, and 109 weapons. The Marines lost 45 dead and 203 wounded, and won two Medals of Honor. Lance Corporal Joe E. Paul gave his life for his medal; Corporal Robert E. O'Malley was wounded three times for his, but was a one-man hurricane.

The media, as starved for action as the Marines were, provided news coverage approximating the Normandy landings and thus hurt South Vietnamese sensibilities. No ARVN forces had taken part, and they weren't even informed in advance, except for General Thi and the local commander, Brigadier General Hoang Xuan

The U.S. Marines move out, into the rice paddies during Operation Harvest Moon (above), and resupply ammo for the Marine howtars (combination howitzer-mortars) during Operation Starlite (right).

Lam. Thereafter, the South Vietnamese were brought in on all operations, despite American fears of leaks to the Viet Cong; well-founded fears, it turned out.

Starlite had destroyed the 60th and 80th Battalions, it was said, but the 1st Viet Cong Regiment would have to be "destroyed" two more times in 1965. The second engagement (Operation Piranha) came September 7–10, when the Marines trapped the regiment again, this time on Batangan Peninsula, eight miles south of the Starlite battlefield. The Marines took two South Vietnamese battalions in with them this time, and opened the operation with a first for the "Daisy Cutters." These were 250- and 500-pound air-dropped bombs with a nose probe several feet long. As the end of the probe hit the ground, the bomb went off with a devastating shrapnel effect, chest-high for yards around.

In three days Piranha was over, with 178 Viet Cong counted dead, including 66 blown up in a cave. They refused to surrender, so the attackers grenaded them. Some 360 Vietnamese were captured, along with twenty weapons, but the bulk of the 1st Regiment again escaped; they had melted away less than twenty-four hours before the battle.

The final engagement of 1965 with the 1st Viet Cong Regiment opened December 8, this time ten miles north of Chu Lai. The regiment had been rebuilt with three battalions—the 60th, 80th, and 90th—and had circled inland and around Chu Lai, now threatening Route 1 at Tam Ky, on the road to Da Nang. It was a bitter four-day battle, in mountainous country, with a well-armed and wily Viet Cong in home territory.

This time the B-52 bombers swung the balance. Westmoreland offered them to the Marines and they accepted. General Walt was a thousand feet up in a helicopter when the giant bombers came in from Guam on December 12 and carpeted the jungle with tons of iron bombs. They did it twice again, on successive days, and General Walt was a convert. Said he, "The timing was precise, the bombing accurate, and the overall effort awesome to behold." Operation Harvest Moon ended on December 20, with 407 Viet Cong counted dead and 33 captured, along with many weapons and much food. The Marines paid with 45 killed and 218 men wounded, while the ARVN lost 90 killed and 141 wounded.

It was building, not combat, that held center stage in Vietnam for most of 1965. When General Westmoreland flew back to Saigon from the Honolulu conference, he had full authority for the American buildup, and his planning was already far advanced.

The U.S. Army's 1st Logistical Command, working out of temporary quarters near Tan Son Nhut, had decided on a massive port and airfield development at Cam Ranh Bay, one hundred seventy-five miles northeast of Saigon; a major expansion of the port of Qui Nhon, one hundred thirty miles north of Cam Ranh Bay, and at Vung Tau, forty miles southeast of Saigon. These three ports would be the main gateways for the Army hordes already getting duty orders for II and III Corps. The Navy and Marines, working from Da Nang, would handle I Corps in the north.

The Army Engineers began arriving in Saigon by early May, and the Army hoped to have 2,300 engineer troops at work by the end of the month. Even before that, Saigon had sent a single lieutenant up to Cam Ranh Bay to look over the ground. There was little there, except some units of the Vietnamese Army and Marines, and a fine sand that no one who walked in it, lived in it, or ate it would ever forget. There were also some Viet Cong, on the mainland, directly across from the peninsula that formed the harbor. Everybody walked softly, quite happy to leave the Viet Cong alone if the latter would reciprocate. It was far too early to pick a fight.

The 35th Engineer Group, the first major outfit to arrive, hit Cam Ranh on June 9 after a twenty-seven-day voyage from San Francisco. Crammed into the USNS *General LeRoy Eltinge,* a World War II Liberty ship, were two construction battalions and four support companies, equipment, and parts of outfits, including officers who had never met their opposite numbers, or even half their own units. The *Eltinge* broke down in mid-Pacific and had to be towed five hundred miles to Midway Island. The 35th waited for days, then transferred to the USNS *Barrett,* which finally deposited them on the shores of Cam Ranh Bay, a seventeen-mile peninsula then containing one unpaved road, one narrow pier, and an eight-hundred-foot airstrip left by the French.

The 35th was not intimidated. It welcomed a challenge, and Cam Ranh was certainly that. On this desolate shore, the Army would build a base to rival any in Engineer history, and to hell with sand that could grind your teeth to stubs, the Viet Cong who never quit, and heat over one hundred degrees and humidity nearly as high.

For the first month, the 35th provided its own perimeter defense, night and day, until a battalion of the 1st Infantry (Big Red One Division) came in. Finally, in October, Korean troops—2nd Marine Brigade (Dragon), Republic of Korea—took over defense. In the meantime, the 35th began its real job, building a major base. Everything was in short supply, so they used what they could find, including Philippine mahogany plywood for concrete forms. "Nothing's too good for us, boys," was the understanding.

No water? The 35th Engineer Group found some mineral springs, used trapped surface water from the monsoons, and eventually drilled enough deep wells for a huge port complex. Too hot to work at midday? The 35th went on two shifts: 3 P.M. to 1 A.M., and 1 A.M. to 11 A.M.

By July 1965, Cam Ranh Bay was a tent and sandbag city, roaring with priority construction: the airfield—a major jetport; roads, storage areas, piers, and fuel-tank farms not seen since World War II.

But Cam Ranh was not the only task. The 35th barely unloaded their machinery before some elements were transshipped to Qui Nhon and Vung Tau, to become the cadres for other engineering miracles. Since this was a modern war, one priority near the top was the automatic data processing center, to be housed in a reinforced concrete building. By the end of 1965 it was well under way, and seven thousand Army engineers were working feverishly. Vietnam was the kind of building challenge that rallied the best in Americans. There was plenty of work for everybody, and little time to ask questions or hear the negative vibrations just beginning in the United States.

Construction in South Vietnam was a joint effort of the military and private contractors. The Army and Marines sent in their construction and combat engineers; the Navy sent in thousands of Seabees; and the Air Force fielded six Red Horse squadrons (Rapid Engineer Deployable Heavy Operational Repair Squadron, Engineering), five in Vietnam and one in Thailand. The private consortiums, mainly RMK (for Raymond International, Morrison-Knudsen) and BRJ (for Brown & Root, and J. A. Jones) pitched in on the major projects with thousands of American engineers, field supervisors, and foremen, and a peak work force of more than fifty thousand laborers—men, women, and children—from South Vietnam, Korea, the Philippines, and other corners of the world. Together they built seven seaports, eight major jetports, hundreds of airstrips and heliports, hospitals, warehouses, barracks, roads, and bridges, supplying these temporary cities with water, electricity, air conditioning, tennis courts, swimming pools, movies, and television. This war went first-class.

The first Army combat unit in South Vietnam was the 173rd Airborne Brigade, the "Sky Soldiers," flying into III Corps on May 7, 1965. Two infantry battalions and an artillery battalion came in from Okinawa on urgent call to put down the Viet Cong menace in the Army's rear, from Vung Tau on the coast to the Saigon/ Bien Hoa complex. The 173rd moved directly into the helicopter era, a new style of warfare. The helicopter was the only feasible method of movement in Vietnam, a land of few roads but more than enough jungle, rivers, rice paddies, mountains, and swamps. Learning to use the helicopter had to be on-the-job training, with few essentials like how to get out of a helicopter and into the woods without wasting a second or, just as important, how to run for a helicopter and get aboard before the enemy fire crawled right up your back. Unexpected problem: Vietnamese are much smaller than Americans, and it soon became apparent that many of them could not get up the steps into the choppers, particularly under heavy pack. The solution was to modify the steps for the Vietnamese.

The troops also learned how to fight under helicopter gunships, and not to be frightened by the noise, or expended cartridges falling all around, or the gunships firing on their flanks and in front of them. The helicopters are your friends: point out the target for them and they'll blast it for you.

In June, the 1st Battalion of the Royal Australian Regiment joined the 173rd, followed shortly by a field artillery battery from New Zealand. By late June the Allied forces seemed ready for a field operation, and on June 28 the 173rd, the Aussies, and the ARVN units moved out for a three-day foray into Zone D, which the Viet Cong had "owned" for nine years.

Seventy-seven Army transport helicopters lifted four battalions of Vietnamese infantry into the heart of Zone D, northeast of Saigon. Four more battalions, including the Aussies, moved in from the perimeter to close a trap. Most of the VC slipped away into the jungle during the three-day action, but twenty-five were killed, more than fifty were wounded, and some rice and weapons were captured.

Six days later the 173rd went back to War Zone D, with about the same mix of forces, and did it all over again. This time fifty-six Viet Cong were killed, twenty-eight prisoners were taken, and a huge cache of documents was seized.

Neither of these actions was spectacular, but they did set a pattern: strike, punish the enemy, and withdraw, then strike again. It was a pattern that the United States command would develop, orchestrate, and polish over the next few years until they made it their own. Americans had not fought a war like this since the nineteenth-century Indian wars in the West. But this time the "cavalry" came in helicopters.

At the post-operation critiques, the command felt good about these first brushes with the enemy. The helicopters—both gunships and transports—had flown nearly fifteen hundred sorties in the second operation, performing superbly, and the artillery had been a pleasant surprise, firing nearly five thousand rounds of 105-mm in four days, stunning and killing the Viet Cong, or driving him from the field. As one battalion commander said, ". . . the artillery lent dignity to what otherwise would have been a vulgar brawl . . ."

There were things to learn, of course; for example, clearing LZs (landing zones) in the jungle. Axes and machetes could do some of the work, but the C-4 plastic explosives weren't being used right. "They took the bark off the trees and made a few splinters, but that was about it," the critique showed. Thereafter, better charges and chain saws, bulldozers and other special tools would have to do the job.

But the helicopters were magnificent. When it came time to withdraw, "we took three thousand troops out of three different landing zones in three hours and ten minutes," said Brigadier General Ellis W. Williamson, the 173rd's commanding officer; and it was done with style. As the troops moved in toward the evacuation points, the helicopter gunships formed a protective ring around the contracting circles. At the same time, the transport helicopters were coming in under the artillery fire, picking up another load, and returning to base. With all this going on in three adjoining LZs, things were "just a little hairy," but the maneuver worked. These men were writing the first draft of a textbook for war, Vietnamese style. "We could not have done that a few weeks ago," said General Williamson.

The 173rd's artillery (3rd Battalion, 319th Artillery) led the way, and other artillery units quickly followed. By year's end, the Army had twenty-three battalions firing everything from 105 mm up to the self-propelled 175 mm, an awesome gun that could throw a shell over twenty miles. By war's end, nearly one hundred battalions of artillery served in Vietnam.

Early in July, the 1st Brigade of the 101st Airborne Division began moving out from Fort Campbell, Kentucky, for Vietnam. An advance party flew into Cam Ranh Bay late in July, but the main body of thirty-six hundred troops, jammed into the now repaired *Gen. LeRoy Eltinge,* was treated to a twenty-one-day cruise across the Pacific to Qui Nhon. From there, the brigade launched Operation Highland on August 22 to open up the An Khe area for the 1st Cavalry Division (Air-mobile), due in early October.

By fall 1965, the U.S. Army is arriving in force in the Central Highlands. Here the 2nd Brigade, 1st Cavalry Division, moves inland from the coast near Qui Nhon (top), and troops of the 101st Airborne wade a flooding stream as they advance up Route 19 toward Pleiku (above).

The brigade, using air drops and ground troops, fought its way forty miles up Route 19 from Qui Nhon to the An Khe plateau, clearing the Viet Cong out of An Khe pass and establishing strongpoints along the highway. Movement was only by armed convoy, with tactical air cover. Once on the highland, the brigade cleared the division headquarters' area in a series of air-mobile assaults and ground actions. All in all, the operation killed nearly seven hundred Viet Cong, at a cost to the brigade of twenty-one lives. It was just a day's work for the brigade, almost a nonevent in military history, like hundreds of other Vietnam days.

It wasn't spectacular enough for television or newspaper headlines, not nearly as exciting as a Buddhist monk burning himself to death to stir outrage in American homes; but it bought a base for the 1st Cavalry Division, a base that would dominate the Central Highlands and prevent the enemy from cutting South Vietnam in half.

The 1st Cavalry arrived early in October—nearly sixteen thousand men, with over sixteen hundred vehicles and four hundred aircraft. Staging out of Mobile, Alabama, and Jacksonville, Florida, most of the planes, vehicles, and other hardware sailed east through the Suez Canal in the Navy's escort carrier USS *Boxer*. Most of the men went west in merchant vessels.

Halfway across the Pacific the division got radio orders to be prepared to fight its way ashore; but it had no weapons, planes, or vehicles, no landing aircraft, not even any cargo nets. Furthermore, the master of the convoy did not know his destination yet; he thought it might be Korea. It turned out to be Qui Nhon. There was no enemy present, and the troops were finally ferried ashore. It was October 3 by the time the full division reached An Khe, and then it was quickly split up.

With responsibility for a square area about one hundred fifty miles on each side, authority was split up this way: the 1st Brigade drew Pleiku Province (II 8); the 2nd Brigade took Kontum Province (II 6); and the 3rd Brigade got Binh Dinh Province (II 7), along the densely populated coast. Many a name in this vital zone would enter military history: Dak To, Plei Me, and the Chu Pong Mountains.

The 1st Cavalry's blooding was quick and violent. On October 19 an enemy band overran the Special Forces' camp at Plei Me, twenty-five miles southwest of Pleiku. It looked like a routine raid, but it turned out to be three regiments of North Vietnamese regulars—the 32nd, 33rd, and 66th. The battle lasted a month, earning itself a name, the Battle of the Ia Drang Valley (Silver Bayonet), and in time involved almost every unit of the entire 1st Cavalry Division plus units of the ARVN. The Americans, at first stunned by the intensity of the fighting, learned many lessons very quickly. The enemy was tough, professional, and vicious. He could surround you, "bear hug" you, and disappear into the bush before you knew he was there and before reinforcements could arrive. He was a tough soldier, but so were the Americans.

The American soldiers adjusted quickly, learned to use all their equipment to best advantage—rifles, machine guns, rockets, helicopters, artillery—and gradually got the upper hand. In thirty-five days of battle, the enemy regiments were shattered and scattered. By November 26 it was over, and the enemy's counted dead totaled 1,771. Silver Bayonet was the official name of the battle, and we find this designation in military records.

During the battle, the B-52s were called in for the first big backup of Army ground forces, opening with a 344-ton bomb-drop on November 14. From then on, the bombers came in daily, proving especially effective when the infantry discovered a secret North Vietnamese base at the foot of the Chu Pong Mountains. In a few days, the B-52s put in nearly eighteen hundred tons of bombs, routing the Communist forces. The troops were delighted, and so was Westmoreland. He said the Americans had met the enemy and "demonstrated beyond any possible doubt" that they could "defeat the best troops the enemy could put on the field of battle."

Back in October, help had arrived for the critical Saigon area. In came the 1st Infantry Division, the famed "Big Red One" of World War II, nearly twenty thousand strong, to join with the 173rd Airborne Brigade. The orders were simple: Help the ARVN clean out the Viet Cong in III Corps, the enemy's strongest positions. The 1st Division would spend the rest of the war doing just that, expending blood and heroism, achieving precarious domination, but always threatened by a determined foe.

McNamara was back in Saigon again on November 25 and was upset by the confusion he saw; it offended his computer-like mind. Westmoreland tried to explain that this was a revolution in progress and there were shortages of everything

In the Central Highlands, a mother and her children flee bombs from U.S. planes raining on her village, a stronghold for Viet Cong snipers. The giant B-52 bombers were first used in 1965 as tactical support for ground troops, and the heavy bomb loads devastated the enemy.

—time, men, materials, money. McNamara exploded; he'd seen scores of ships anchored offshore waiting to unload; couldn't we get those ports going? he demanded. Yes, the general replied, but it would take a lot of money. How much to get those ports open at Da Nang, Chu Lai, Nha Trang, Cam Ranh Bay, and Vinh Long? Westmoreland gave him a figure the next morning: $8 million, for openers; $40 million to follow. "Don't worry about it," said McNamara. "Go. I'll get the money for you." This was money to buy pile drivers, dredges, pavers, quarry equipment, tugboats, and other hardware; and it was in addition to the money already going out, at a rate that was up to $40 million per month in October.

McNamara and Westmoreland also talked troops, and when McNamara got back to Washington he was talking in terms of "force levels" reaching four hundred thousand by the end of 1966, and possibly six hundred thousand by the end of 1967. These figures were not being announced, of course, but they could not be kept secret either. Senator Mike Mansfield, a loyal Democrat but no friend of this war, went out to Vietnam to see for himself in November and came back with his own estimate: five hundred thousand. Frank McCulloch, *Time* magazine's Saigon chief, was reporting that the generals were thinking in terms of a force of 640,000 Americans, but his editors didn't believe that; they regularly cut his figures before they got into print. McCulloch knew what he was talking about; he was very close to the military and was already preparing *Time*'s "Man of the Year" cover story. For 1965 that man was General William Childs Westmoreland.

The big numbers worried many of the media. Stanley Karnow, reporting for the

Mike Mansfield, U.S. Senate majority leader, talks with South Vietnamese Chief of State Thieu in late 1965 in Saigon and returns with unhappy news for the commander in chief, President Johnson; half a million American troops may soon be needed in Vietnam, the senator believes.

Washington *Post,* was uneasy because he felt "this was akin to crossing the 38th parallel in Korea." Newscaster Sander Vanocur got McNamara on NBC-TV and said he was "depressed" because Vietnam looked like a bottomless pit. "Every pit has its bottom, Mr. Vanocur," NcNamara replied.

The big machine roared on. Chu Lai had launched its first tactical air strikes in June, and by mid-October the main runway at Cam Ranh Bay was ready. An army of nearly twenty-five thousand workers, more than half of them Vietnamese women, had paved the ten-thousand-foot runway and countless square yards of taxiways, shops, and aprons. Most of the work had to be done at night, to avoid the hundred-degrees-plus daytime temperatures, and the "tiger ladies" were amazing. They didn't weigh a hundred pounds (many of them were war widows), but they could work like men. They learned quickly, and many were soon expert at handling the heavy equipment: bulldozers, trucks, pavers. They finished the main runway in fifty days from start. Cam Ranh's first good drinking water, from a deep well, came in at the end of October, and the planes began coming in the next day. The first six

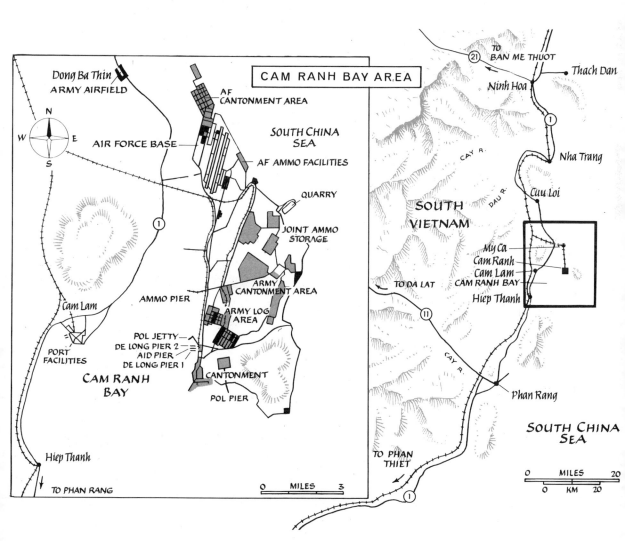

The sea war intensifies in Vietnam. Here the supply ship USS Mars *(AFS-1) moves in to service one of the big American carriers prowling the long Vietnamese coastline (above). A typical South Vietnamese junkman sailor (right) is shown with appropriate tattoo—"Kill the Cong."*

F-4s of the Air Force flew their first combat mission November 2; a year later the field was handling eighteen thousand takeoffs and landings per month. This was Cam Ranh, which Bob Hope had nicknamed "the world's biggest sand trap."

The building boom reached all the way around into the Gulf of Siam, where RMK built a Navy base at An Thoi, on the tip of Phu Quoc Island. (An Thoi means "peaceful stink," and was the home of the famous, or infamous, *nuoc mam*, the strong fish sauce endemic to South Vietnam.) This base was to keep an eye on Sihanoukville and other Cambodian ports being used by Russian and Communist bloc vessels to supply the tools of war smuggled in by South Vietnam's back door. Like Haiphong, these ports were off limits to American air power. McNamara was dead set against letting the war get outside the borders of South Vietnam, but the munitions coming through these ports were already killing Americans. Seventy-six Communist ships unloaded tanks, artillery, SAMs (surface-to-air missiles), and other munitions at Haiphong in 1965, with total impunity, and the number would jump to 122 ships in 1966 and zoom to 433 in 1967.

The air war against North Vietnam began in earnest in the spring of 1965, with both the Air Force and the Navy eager for it. They had the pilots, the planes, and the weapons to mount a powerful campaign. Both the Air Force and the carrier pilots were of high quality, with thousands of hours of experience, and esprit was excellent. Here was a chance to prove what air power could do. Alas, it was not to be all-out war.

From the start, the military and the politicians in Washington parted company on how to use air power against North Vietnam. The Joint Chiefs of Staff believed that the war would most likely be concluded at the negotiating table. Since the Communists responded only to one thing—force—the best way to force them to negotiate was to punish them, and the sooner the better. Heavy air power should be applied quickly, especially to the Hanoi/Haiphong area. Military targets in that area—where all war material arrived from the Soviet Union and China by rail and ship—should be bombed decisively, and Haiphong harbor should be closed by mines. That was elementary military doctrine—destroy the enemy's supplies before they can reach the front—and it could be done with minimum risk to the civilian population. It would shorten the war and thus be the most humane solution for both sides, or so the military argued.

The political and civilian sector saw it differently. Heavy bombing would raise opposition in the United States and among allies overseas. It might also escalate the war to world proportions by bringing in rising Soviet and Chinese forces, both in weapons and manpower. Was the United States ready to face the Communist hordes of Russia and China on the Asian land mass?

The ultimate decision had to be made by President Johnson, and he chose to compromise. The President opted for a "limited" war, somewhere between withdrawal and all-out war. It satisfied neither side, but it lasted as long as Johnson did. Operation Rolling Thunder was his answer; it was not what the military wanted, but it went to work within the limitations set by the commander in chief.

Rolling Thunder began with every move being called from Washington. Targets had to be approved individually and on a daily basis; if an attack had to be aborted because of weather, a new approval was needed. Washington specified the types of planes and munitions that could be used, the number of sorties, and the timing of the attack. No attacks could be made above the 20th parallel, which meant that the enemy's main ports, power plants, industries, and rail lines were off limits.

Below the 20th parallel, populated areas must be avoided. The enemy soon realized that he could use the main towns and villages in southern North Vietnam as sanctuaries and supply depots. Every day the streets were jammed with parked trucks and the sidewalks piled high with fuel drums, ammunition, food, and weapons of all kinds. At night the convoys moved south, taking refuge before dawn in the streets of another village. It was frustrating to the American pilots, but Johnson told his associates: "They can't even bomb an outhouse without my approval."

The targets left in southern North Vietnam were barracks, rail lines, oil and ammunition dumps, radar sites, and any military equipment that could be found in the open, away from towns and villages. Among the targets was the Ham Rung (Dragon's Jaw) rail and road bridge near the city of Thanh Hoa, just south of the 20th parallel. The French had built a bridge there, spanning the Song Ma River, but the Viet Minh rebels had destroyed it in 1945 with a crude but effective weapon; they loaded two locomotives with explosives and crashed them together in mid-river: no more bridge.

Ho Chi Minh's forces, aided by the Chinese, had built a new bridge and dedicated it in 1964 as a national monument to the revolution. Dragon's Jaw was 540 feet long and carried the main rail line to the south, plus a roadway on either side of the rail line. The central pier in mid-river was a block of reinforced concrete sixteen feet thick. It was a tantalizing target to the U.S. Air Force, and they went after it April 3.

Sixty-nine planes from bases in Thailand and South Vietnam rendezvoused near the DMZ, refueled from ten KC-135 tankers, and were off for the target, heavy with missiles, bombs, and cannons. The weather was fine, and hopes were high.

Exactly on time (1400 hours), they roared in from the Gulf of Tonkin. The attack echelon, thirty-one F-105D Thunderchiefs, laid thirty-two Bullpup missiles and one hundred twenty 750-pound general-purpose bombs on the target. Two cover planes were lost to enemy fire, an F-100 flak suppressor and an RF-101 recon plane. The remaining sixty-seven planes rallied over the gulf and returned to bases via friendly territory in the south.

When all the reports were in, results were disappointing. No serious damage to the bridge. One roadway was closed but could be repaired quickly. The other roadway and the rail line sustained minor damage.

The planes went back the next morning, but with a different configuration: no Bullpups; those missiles had bounced off the concrete abutments like hail off a roof. This time it was forty-eight F-105 "Thuds," each with eight 750-pound bombs. The raid went perfectly, with probably three hundred bombs hitting on target, and this time the damage was serious. Large chunks of concrete had been blown out of each

With American air power severely
restricted by President Johnson, U.S.
air forces chased mostly small game
in 1965, such as a disguised railroad
car (left) and a crudely camouflaged
train (below).

roadway, and the railroad deck was pierced. One of the two spans was sagging, but did not go down. The railroad could be put back in service, but the roadways would never be the same.

Three F-105s were lost. Captain Smitty Harris, first man down the chute, was tagged by ground fire. He bailed out as the plane disintegrated, but landed among angry peasants and spent seven years as a prisoner of war. The other two planes were lost to MIG-17s in the first MIG attack of the war, and neither pilot was recovered. There was one other ominous note. For the first time, the North Vietnamese used 57-mm AA guns, in addition to the usual 30-mm weapons.

There were two pluses: the 750-pounders destroyed the Thanh Hoa power plant, and cover planes bagged a locomotive and twenty-two freight cars, setting a nice fire with their 20-mm cannons. The U.S. Air Force went back to Thanh Hoa two more times, on May 7 and May 30. Each time they found the bridge in use again, and put it out of commission for a couple more weeks. The Dragon's Jaw refused to go down!

There was another surprise. Early in April a U-2 on a high-altitude reconnaissance flight over North Vietnam picked up a picture of what looked like a SAM site fifteen miles southeast of Hanoi. A few days later an RF-8A from the aircraft carrier *Coral Sea* confirmed that it was a surface-to-air missile site. The commander of Task Force 77 flew to Saigon immediately and conferred with his opposite number, Commander Seventh Air Force. They felt the base should be destroyed immediately, and sent a request up the chain of command. Early in May, a second SAM site was discovered, and by summer several more.

The Russian-built SA-2, officially called Guideline and nicknamed "the flying telephone pole," was definitely coming to North Vietnam. The SA-2 was a two-stage rocket, thirty-five feet long, with a 350-pound warhead and a range of sixty thousand feet. There was still no reply from Washington on attacking SAM sites, but countermeasures were prepared. American planes mounted jamming pods on their wings to knock out "Fan Song," the radar emissions needed to aim the missiles. They also began dropping "chaff," thousands of tiny squares of metal foil, to clog enemy radar, and using "pop-up" bombing tactics. This meant going in low, under the radar, and steeply climbing to bombing altitude at the target.

The electronic warfare planes also began to come into the theater, for the carriers and the Air Force. The Air Force's first was the EB-66 (Destroyer), while the Navy used EF-10Bs, both old models eventually to be replaced. (The EF-10B was a modified twin-jet night fighter which the Marines insulted with the reverse acronym DRUT, but it got the job done.)

On June 1, the Navy took over responsibility for the Thanh Hoa area from the Air Force, including the Dragon's Jaw bridge, and kept pecking away at it. (As it turned out, the Air Force would not get another crack at that bridge until 1972, and it was still in use then, even though at a low order.) The Navy also won the honor of bagging the first MIGs. On June 17, Secretary of the Navy Paul Nitze, who was aboard the *Midway*, announced that the carrier's F-4B Phantoms had shot down two MIG-17s with Sparrow missiles. Three days later, the Navy got another one,

Russian-built SAMs, surface-to-air missiles, are first spotted in April 1965, by U.S.
reconnaissance planes. This composite photo shows in upper left inset a closeup of the
Soviet-made SA-2, nicknamed the "flying telephone pole," and a typical base with
several missiles visible, bamboo matting to camouflage service roads, and the radar
guidance equipment at upper right.

this time with a twist! While the MIG-17 was maneuvering to escape a Phantom jet,
a prop plane, an A-1 Skyraider from the *Midway,* caught the jet with a burst of
gunfire and put it away. It was July 10 before the Air Force got its first jets, a pair of
MIG-17s. Four F-4Cs, flying escort on a bombing mission over the southern provinces of North Vietnam, drew the MIGs into combat and in four minutes of high-
speed aerobatics bagged both of them with heat-seeking Sidewinder missiles up the
tailpipe. The MIGs were painted light gray and carried the Chinese Communist red
star on the wings.

Two weeks later, on July 24, the first American plane was lost to a SAM. A
group of F-4s, flying MIG–Cap (top cover against the Russian-built jets), heard the
SAM warnings from an EB-66 monitoring the enemy's radar. Within seconds, one

145

of the F-4s was hit and disintegrated, as fellow pilots watched the SAM climb nearly straight up at Mach 1 speed. All the other F-4s were damaged by the original burst, but escaped with violent evasive action. The enemy now had a three-ply answer to American air intruders—AAA, MIGs, and SAMs.

Permission finally granted, the Air Force went after the SAM sites with a strike by the Thunderchiefs, results not known. The Navy quickly joined in, and from then on evading SAMs in flight, or destroying the bases, became routine procedure. The pilots discovered that the SA-2 could be fooled by a sharp turn at the last second, just before the hit. A steep dive would leave the SAM hurtling into space, and the pilot shaken, but alive.

Not all of them made it. The Navy lost its first plane to a SAM in August, an A-4 from the *Midway,* and launched a special operation, Iron Hand, against the missile sites. By fall, the Navy was keeping five carriers on station at all times, to General Westmoreland's delight. Dixie Station, off the Mekong Delta, was used to warm up new pilots by strafing and bombing runs against the Viet Cong in South Vietnam. Then the carriers rotated up to Yankee Station, off the Da Nang area, for action over North Vietnam, which carried with it not only the threat of death but of capture and torture in the North Vietnamese prison system.

By year's end, the Air Force had made over ten thousand sorties over the north and delivered better than eighty thousand tons of bombs. The Navy counted over fifty thousand sorties, and over one hundred aircraft lost. In combat, some thirty-five thousand Communists and VC were killed in a year, and six thousand were captured in the south. Result: The Communists were stronger than ever. They had raised their combat strength to 220,000, and seemed determined to keep fighting.

But Westmoreland could see his grand plan beginning to take shape. His forces had jumped nearly 160,000 and would total 181,000 by year's end. The end of Phase I was in sight: "to halt the losing trend." If Westmoreland got what he was asking (and he had McNamara's assurance that he would), he would better than double his forces in 1966 and be well into Phase II: "to take the offensive in high priority areas, destroy the enemy, and reinstitute pacification programs." Somewhere beyond that lay Phase III: "to destroy the enemy if he persists in his efforts to take over South Vietnam."

Late in the year, as the holiday season approached, talk rose in Washington of another bombing pause. President Johnson had tried one, May 12 to May 18, and it had been a failure. Hanoi sneered at it, and used the time to infiltrate men and munitions into South Vietnam. Johnson also found that the pause hurt him two ways at home: the hawks were angry when he halted the bombing; the doves furious when he resumed it.

Nonetheless, McNamara began talking up a new bombing pause in November, and he had strong support. At the crucial meeting in the White House on December 18, the President opened discussion by saying, "The military says a month's pause would undo all we've done." McNamara quickly said, "That's baloney." The discussion lasted nearly five hours, and Johnson left the meeting still undecided.

As it turned out, the President ordered the pause and it lasted thirty-six days,

BOMBING HALTS OVER NORTH VIETNAM

PRESIDENT JOHNSON'S ADMINISTRATION*

Date	Duration	Type
May 12–18, 1965	5 days, 20 hrs.	Complete
Dec. 24, 1965–Jan. 31, 1966	36 days, 15 hrs.	Complete
Dec. 23, 1966–Mar. 1, 1967	78 days	Within 10 miles of center of Hanoi
Dec. 24–26, 1966	2 days	Complete
Dec. 31, 1966–Jan. 2, 1967	2 days	Complete
Feb. 8–12, 1967	5 days, 18 hrs.	Complete
May 22–June 9, 1967	18 days	Within 10 miles of center of Hanoi
May 23–24, 1967	24 hrs.	Complete
June 11–Aug. 9, 1967	59 days	Within 10 miles of center of Hanoi
Aug. 24–Oct. 23, 1967	60 days	Within 10 miles of center of Hanoi
Dec. 24–25, 1967	24 hrs.	Complete
Dec. 31, 1967–Jan. 2, 1968	36 hrs.	Complete
Jan. 3–Mar. 31, 1968	88 days	Within 5 miles of center of Hanoi
Jan. 16–Mar. 31, 1968	75 days	Within 5 miles of center of Haiphong
Mar. 31–Nov. 1, 1968	214 days	North of 20th parallel
Nov. 1, 1968–Jan. 20, 1969	81 days	Complete

*Source: *The Vantage Point: Perspectives of the Presidency, 1963-69,* by Lyndon B. Johnson. Holt, Rinehart & Winston, New York, 1971.

PRESIDENT NIXON'S ADMINISTRATION

There were no formal bombing halts during Nixon's administration. U.S. air power was used as a military weapon with all vigor against the enemy in South Vietnam and across the borders into Cambodia, Laos, and southern North Vietnam. In 1972 Nixon applied the full power directly against North Vietnam. U.S. Navy planes closed all enemy ports with mines, and together with the U.S. Air Force attacked military targets all the way to the Chinese border. In mid-December, as peace talks lagged, the B-52s were unleashed for the first time against the enemy's industrial/military complex along the Hanoi-Haiphong axis. Within two weeks North Vietnam signaled surrender. Cease-fire followed in January 1973.

from December 24, 1965, to January 31, 1966. During that period, President Johnson mounted a diplomatic peace offensive, sending a message to the Communists through the United Nations, the Vatican, Moscow, and key embassies around the world. In his State of the Union message on January 12, 1966, Johnson told the world:

"For twenty days now, we and our Vietnamese allies have dropped no bombs in North Vietnam . . . We have talked to more than a hundred governments . . . We have talked to the United Nations and we have called upon all of its members to make any contribution they can toward helping to obtain peace . . . We have also made it clear—from Hanoi to New York—that there are no arbitrary limits to our search for peace . . . We have said all this . . . and we have waited for a response . . . So far, we have received no response . . ."

He got a response on January 28, via Hanoi Radio. Ho Chi Minh had written a letter to some heads of government denouncing the United States and its "so-called search for peace." He said the United States had been "deceitful" and "hypocritical" and there could be no peace until the United States withdrew all its forces from Vietnam and recognized his government as "the sole genuine representative of the people of South Vietnam."

President Johnson received his copy of Ho's letter on January 31, 1966, and on the same day he ordered the bombing of North Vietnam resumed.

9

Year of Hope 1966

IN GENERAL Westmoreland's grand scheme, the "fire brigade" phase had ended with 1965, and 1966 was the year to go over to the offensive. He seized the initiative on New Year's Day, sending the 173rd Airborne Brigade into the Plain of Reeds, southwest of Saigon. Moving by land and air, the brigade jumped the Oriental River into the Bao Trai airstrip, the first American force ever to operate west of the river.

At the same time, the 1st Battalion, Royal Australian Regiment, established a position on the east side of the river, by aerial assault, and the river was now cut off to the Viet Cong. The Viet Cong reacted angrily and in force. The Americans called in artillery, helicopter gunships, and tactical air support, and in seven days of heavy fighting decimated the 267th Viet Cong Battalion and the headquarters of the 506th Viet Cong Battalion (Operation Marauder). The enemy left over one hundred dead in the field and much equipment, and the 173rd learned some valuable lessons in the jungle and marsh. It learned how to maneuver all elements in coordination— troops, artillery, air cover—and punish the enemy with minimum losses.

Marauder went so smoothly that the 173rd quickly moved to Binh Duong Province, north of Saigon, and did it all over again (Operation Crimp). This time the brigade put in six hard days of fighting in the Ho Bo woods, looking for the headquarters of Viet Cong Military Region 4. It was found and destroyed, along with a network of tunnels and bunkers, and a huge quantity of documents and weapons was captured. The 173rd had established a pattern of offense that many another American outfit would use throughout the war.

But the heaviest fighting of the war thus far broke out in mid-January 1966, along the key coastal region between Chu Lai and Qui Nhon. Search-and-destroy missions by both the Marines and the 1st Cavalry Division uncovered heavy enemy concentrations in the area where I and II Corps met. This was a heavily populated

AMERICANS FIGHT—1966
I CORPS

The Marines move in to lift a 105-mm howitzer (left) and take out a shot-down helicopter for repairs so it can fight another day (above).

(Below) Marine reinforcements are on a hot LZ (landing zone). (Bottom) A flying crane lifts out a damaged CH-46 Sea Knight.

Early in 1966 the U.S. Navy beefs up its Naval Support Activity in Da Nang, and Rear Admiral Thomas R. Weschler, second from right, takes command. With him are, from left: Rear Admiral Edwin B. Hooper, Commander, Service Forces, Pacific Fleet; Captain Kenneth P. Huff, chief of staff at the Da Nang supply facility; and Major General Lewis Walt, commanding officer of Marines in northern South Vietnam.

Marines look over a captured souvenir, paid for in blood: a Soviet 12.7-mm heavy machine gun, Chinese Communist type 54 (above right). The U.S. Navy hospital at Da Nang swells to meet the rising casualty cost (below).

area and an important rice producer, astride Route 1, South Vietnam's main north-south highway.

On January 24 the 1st Cavalry Division, operating with South Vietnamese and Korean troops, launched Operation Masher, working north in Binh Dinh Province. At the same time the Marines began pressing south in Quang Ngai Province in Operation Double Eagle. Caught between them were the 1st and 2nd Viet Cong regiments, and the 19th and 98th North Vietnamese regiments, in an area of swamps and rice paddies.

In six weeks of hard fighting, the enemy was routed and scattered from an area he had controlled for years. There were 2,389 counted bodies left behind. During the fighting, the Americans and their allies had harassed the enemy day and night, on the ground and from the air. The Air Force, Navy, Marines, and the Vietnamese threw in over 1,100 combat air support missions by day, and the C-47 gunships took the field at night with flare attacks that gave the enemy no rest. Masher was an encouraging display of what Americans could do under difficult conditions. (History may show this as Operation White Wing; President Johnson felt the word Masher would inflame the doves at home, so it was changed to White Wing, New York City's old name for its white-garbed street sweepers with broom and shovel and can on wheels.)

Masher/White Wing set the style for part of the Vietnam experience for the next two years—the style of the larger set pieces, involving battalions, regiments, and brigades, backed up with flocks of helicopters, multiple artillery units, heavy tactical air support by fighters, fighter-bombers, and the awesome B-52s. These operations, big enough to bear names that would appear in the record books, piled on the power all through 1966 and 1967, with clear, evolving purpose—drive the enemy out of his coastal strongholds, up into the highlands, and steadily westward, out of South Vietnam into Cambodia and Laos, meantime holding the dike at the DMZ, to cut off incursion from the north. It was a difficult style of war, because it was forbidden to attack the enemy at his source of power, the Hanoi-Haiphong axis. Under President Johnson, American military power could not cross a national border, except for severely limited aerial assault into a few areas of enemy country.

The other war—the little war of thousands of foot patrols—went on throughout South Vietnam daily, nightly, ceaselessly, without names, or even numbers to catalog them. They would never be remembered, except by the men who could never forget them. But they went on relentlessly; every night the company clerks toted up the little numbers of dead and maimed, with nothing to show on the other side of the ledger—objectives captured, advances made, goals achieved, victories.

There was progress, of course; good, solid progress in routing the enemy from the coast, in driving him into the uplands, westward, ever westward; but it wasn't spectacular, or exciting. At home you couldn't follow this war, like the wars that had gone before. There were no lines across the map, no pushpins, no names you could remember. Every night the same film clips were shown on television—the burst of bombs, the splash of napalm fires, the whirring of choppers, the rattle of fighter-plane fire, and the people, the pitiful people, so poor in their tattered clothes, without any shoes. They were so bewildered, so helpless, so alien; and some so deadly—the old crones, the children, the women, the old men, who could set punji stakes, land mines, or triggered grenades so cleverly, to blow you apart or into a bloody, quivering mass that might live or might not, that might walk again or might not, or cause you to wear a plastic face for the rest of your life.

But this was Vietnam, and for 1966 at least it looked as though the American plan might work. The troops were mostly fresh and well trained, many of them regulars, thinking they saw a job to be done and ready to do it. Esprit was high as they ran through the big operations. For the Marines in I Corps, now nearly two full divisions, the 1st and 3rd, some sixty thousand strong, it was the task of working out from three strong bases—Hue, Da Nang, and Chu Lai—and knitting them into a secure zone of twenty-seven hundred square miles and two million people. It was the time of the big offensive sweeps, with the names, the dates, the places, and the counted dead—like Hastings/Deckhouse II, July 7–August 3, 882 enemy killed; Prairie, August 3–January 31, 1967, 1,397 enemy killed; Colorado, August 6–21, 647 enemy killed.

Meanwhile, in II Corps, the Army was pouring it on—Paul Revere, Hawthorne, Paul Revere II, Byrd, Irving, Paul Revere IV, Thayer II—some engagements a few days, some a few weeks, some a few months—531 enemy dead counted in this one, 809 in that one, 977 in that one, and 1,757 in Thayer II, October 25–February 12, 1967. That one was mainly the 1st Cavalry Division in Binh Dinh Province, still slugging away on the coast and pushing the enemy westward. Plus, there were thousands of deadly, anonymous patrols.

In III Corps it was the Army, gradually getting the upper hand around Saigon, and pushing toward Cambodia—El Paso II, the Big Red One in Binh Long (III 22) Province, around An Loc, June 2–July 13, 855 enemy bodies found; Attleboro, September 14–November 24, in Tay Ninh Province (III 21), the biggest operation to date, cleaning out War Zone C, 1,106 enemy bodies; and Fairfax, November 20 through 1967, working over the Saigon area with elements of three U.S. divisions (the 1st, 4th and 25th), 1,043 enemy bodies counted. As in II Corps, thousands of deadly, anonymous patrols took place in III Corps.

In IV Corps, the Mekong Delta still belonged to Charlie and would have to wait until next year.

Progress? Yes, on a broad front, but as a war on television it was a dud. One jungle shot looked pretty much like any other, with all the little brown people in black pajamas, with bad teeth—sometimes smiling, sometimes terrified, always in-scrutable, always dangerous, and above all alien. The media, the ever-growing horde of press, radio, and television, could never seem to put it together for the home audience. There was no name to catch, to remember, to mark the place of victory, defeat, advance, retreat—no Château Thierry, Ardennes, Stalingrad, Tarawa, Inchon, Midway, Verdun, Anzio, Remagen.

But the fighting grew, and the casualties, and the Americans poured in by the thousands—more than two hundred thousand of them in 1966, cascading in by battalions, regiments, brigades like the 196th Infantry (Light) and the 199th Infan-

153

AMERICANS FIGHT—1966

II CORPS

The Army's 1st Cavalry Division sweated all year along the central coast, here shown digging out the VC from rice paddies at Bong Son, north of Qui Nhon (above), and on drier ground inland, in heavy chopper actions (below).

Using an old Viet Cong trench, troops of the crack 101st Airborne Division (Co. A, 2nd Bn., 502nd Bde.) push the enemy back toward the Ho Chi Minh trail, high in Kontum province (left). Northeast of An Khe, a captured VC points out where his unit went, to 1st Cavalry Division troops, 2nd Bn., 5th Reg., 2nd Bde. (below).

A deadly American weapon, the famed (or infamous) Claymore mine, that sprays shrapnel forward when the trip wire is pulled.

try (Light), divisions like the 1st Marine Division and the Army's 4th, 9th and 25th Divisions, and dozens of support outfits including trucks, signal, port, and maintenance equipment, police, even dogs. Thirty-six dogs were killed in action and one hundred fifty-three wounded smelling out the Viet Cong, patrolling thousands of yards of wire fences in "rear" areas.

Plus, there were new wrinkles, like rotation, and R & R. When General Westmoreland arrived in Vietnam in 1964, he found that the rule was one year's duty in Vietnam and then home, back to the "real world," the United States. He thought it was a good rule, for morale reasons and for health reasons, and he kept it. It took some adjustments. The Marines came in 1965 by units, their customary rotation method. So in the summer of 1965 they went through Operation Mixmaster, shifting to individual rotation. The Army began to experience rotation problems in 1966. When midsummer came, nine thousand officers and men of the 1st Cavalry Division—more than half its strength—were eligible for rotation and went home, taking with them years of experience and eroding unit identification.

This became a pattern in Vietnam, and many will argue that it cost too much in unit pride and spirit. Increasing numbers of new men coming in were draftees, not career men. The quality of American fighting units began a steady decline, aggravated by many other problems: opposition to the war, the black revolution, unfair draft rules, the youth rebellion. Looking back, it is easy to see that American fighting effectiveness peaked out in 1966–67. After that it was downhill, leading to a breakdown in morale and discipline unprecedented in American military history.

R & R, Vietnam style, was a first in American military history. Rest and Recuperation (or "rape and run," as some called it) was the plan under which qualifying combat soldiers got five days off during their service year, usually around the halfway point. Plucked from the battlefronts, the troops were quickly assembled and jetted off (by Pan American charter flights) to pleasure spots in the real world —Australia, Singapore, Bangkok, Tokyo, Hong Kong, Taipei, and Hawaii, for starters. Uncle Sam paid the round-trip fare. (The government bill to Pan Am in 1967 was $23.5 million, and worth every penny to the frontline grunt.) The GIs were stuffed with combat pay; and, as the service developed, loved ones from America could join in at reduced fares for happy reunions on the beach at Waikiki or wherever.

R & R, the next best thing to going home, became wildly popular. Pan Am carried over a hundred thousand troops in 1966 and planned for 375,000 in 1967. For other thousands of troops who did not qualify for R & R, there were consolations nearer the battlefield—a three-day pass to special resort beaches at Da Nang and Vung Tau. War ain't all hell.

———————◆———————

In February 1966, President Johnson met the war halfway; he flew to Honolulu for one of the regular military conferences. This was a double surprise to General Westmoreland; he hadn't expected the President, and certainly hadn't expected the

President would bring along the general's daughter, Stevie, sixteen, on holiday from boarding school. Westmoreland took along the flamboyant Air Marshal Nguyen Cao Ky, by now Prime Minister of the military clique ruling South Vietnam, General Nguyen Van Thieu, head of the armed forces, and Minister of Defense Nguyen Huu Co. None had ever met President Johnson. They were enthralled by Johnson's sheer size, the ebullient Texas manner he loved to put on, and certainly by his country speech. He baffled them completely when he declared that the time had come to "nail the coonskins to the wall."

To Westmoreland, President Johnson seemed "intense, perturbed," and "torn by the magnitude" of the Vietnam problem. The President asked Westmoreland many times how long the war would last, and each time the general told him "several years." Westmoreland repeated that at a news conference, winding up the meeting. "There comes a time in every war," he said, "when both sides become discouraged by the seemingly endless requirement for more effort, more resources, and more faith. At this point, the side which presses on with renewed vigor is the one to win." In the eye of history, that was prophetic.

Westmoreland asked for thirty-one more battalions, some combat but mostly service units, to bring his year-end strength to 429,000 troops. He was mindful, and reiterated, that it required about ten men behind the lines to keep one at the fighting front. The general didn't get any answer at the conference, and this time the free and easy attitude of 1965 ("Just ask for what you want and you'll get it") was receding. By negotiation between McNamara and the Joint Chiefs, the authorized 1966 year-end figure for American strength came down to 385,000.

A good deal of the Honolulu conference was given over to politics. Johnson was not satisfied with the Saigon government's progress. He pressed Thieu and Ky hard. The President wanted their military dictatorship replaced by a constitution and a freely elected assembly. The best he could get was a promise that all of this would happen "in the months ahead," as stated in the Declaration of Honolulu.

As it turned out, South Vietnam was in for three months of internal upheaval, centered in I Corps. The principal figures were the I Corps commander, General Thi, and Prime Minister Ky (pronounced Tea and Key). The doughty Thi was, in Saigon's view, guilty of insubordination, "warlordism," and separatism. As Saigon saw it, there was even the possibility that Thi would go over to Hanoi's side, and take the northern half of South Vietnam with him.

On March 10, Ky summoned Thi to a meeting of the military clique at Tan Son Nhut and informed him that he (Thi) was going on "vacation" for his "health," but first would go back to I Corps and calm the people. Thi promised to do so, but in fact went back to I Corps and aroused the Buddhists to the point that by the end of the month thousands were parading and rioting in both Hue and Da Nang. The American forces, caught in the middle, did what they could to stay out of the way.

By early April, both Ky and the United States were being denounced publicly, both in I Corps and in Saigon. Ky first sent four thousand South Vietnamese marines to Da Nang, labeling the insurgents as Communists, then went north himself to take command and put down the revolt. He was forced to announce that

AMERICANS FIGHT—1966
III Corps

The Army, working all year to blast the Viet Cong out of the Saigon area, found heavy going to the northwest. Troops of the 25th Infantry Division (Co. B, 1st Bn; 27th Reg.) fight out of hedgerow near Cu Chi (above), and comrades get ready to move out (below).

The 196th Light Infantry Brigade cleans out the VC west of Tay Ninh, near the Cambodian border (above), while the 173rd Airborne Brigade works near the coast in Phuoc Tuy province, east of Saigon (below).

national elections would be held September 11 to pick an assembly to draft a constitution, after which the military junta would resign.

But unrest continued and even grew until the middle of May, when Ky had to fly in twenty-four hundred more South Vietnamese troops. They seized the Da Nang city hall, the radio station, and the market place, and began pressing the Buddhists into small pockets. On two occasions, the U.S. Marine Commander, General Walt, intervened to prevent major bloodshed between warring factions of the ARVN. On May 18, there was a showdown on the Da Nang River bridge, a vital crossing that connected U.S. Marine installations at the airfield to installations on the eastern peninsula, including a huge ammunition dump. Vietnam Marines loyal to Ky held the western end of the bridge, and anti-government ARVN forces loyal to Thi held the eastern end. The rebels declared that the bridge was mined and that they would blow it sky-high if a single Vietnamese marine put foot on it.

At this time General Walt felt he had to act. He and Colonel John R. Chaisson walked to the center of the bridge to meet an ARVN warrant officer advancing from the eastern end. They argued a long time at mid-river, and finally Walt said, "Well, I'm going to stay right here and send for a platoon of Marines." The warrant officer said, "General, we will die together." He raised his arm and brought it down sharply. Nothing happened, and Walt said later, "I shall never forget the expression on his face when his signal did not blow up the bridge and us with it." The Vietnamese marines crossed the bridge, and ARVN engineers disarmed the demolition charges.

There followed some very tense days. The rebels still held the Marine ammunition dump and threatened to blow it up, with grave consequences for Da Nang. For two days Lieutenant Colonel Paul X. Kelley negotiated with the rebels at the dump, relaying progress reports to General Walt while the rival sides tried to outface each other. Even the Vietnamese Air Force got into this one, firing on U.S. Marine aircraft. General Walt warned the rebels, then put four Marine A-4s over the rebel planes. The rebels put four more Skyraiders over the Marine planes, and Walt put four more A-4s over *them*. One false move, Walt declared, and every Vietnamese plane would be blasted from the sky.

Finally, early on the morning of May 23, the rebels capitulated and Da Nang fell quiet. General Thi had been defeated, but Hue was still aflame with Buddhist revolt, behind a revered monk, Tri Quang, forty-two, considered an extremist. On the morning of May 29, a Buddhist nun sat down in the street in front of a pagoda, sprinkled gasoline on her robe, and burned herself to death. That night, another nun immolated herself in Saigon at the Buddhist Institute, and on the last day of May a third nun died in flames in Da Lat, a city in Tuyen Duc Province (II 14), fifty miles inland from Cam Ranh Bay. Tri Quang went on a hunger strike, declaring President Johnson was responsible for the national revolution.

On June 1, a mob of eight hundred Vietnamese attacked the United States consulate in Hue, set it afire with barrels of gasoline, and also fired the buildings next door, which contained the U.S. Information Service Library. Within a week, more Buddhists, both men and women, had immolated themselves. On June 10, Ky flew in more paratroopers and riot police, bringing government strength to four thousand. These troops moved through the streets of Hue very cautiously, trying to pacify the dissidents. The Buddhists finally surrendered on June 19, in both Hue and Quang Tri city, as well as other cities around the country. Tri Quang ended his hunger strike, and civil war had been averted. It had been a narrow escape for the Americans. Colonel Chaisson, for one, said he felt that had there been American casualties "the U.S. government would probably have pulled out of the war right then and there."

President Johnson's "stand-down" in the air war against North Vietnam, the so-called "bombing pause" that lasted thirty-six days, from December 24, 1965, to January 31, 1966, was a political decision made entirely in Washington, without advice from or the knowledge of Admiral Sharp, General Westmoreland, or Ambassador Lodge. As disclosed when the "Pentagon Papers" were published in 1971, Secretary of Defense McNamara strongly favored the pause, while Secretary of State Rusk just as strongly opposed it. In any event, the pause was a failure, advantageous only to North Vietnam. During the stand-down, General Westmoreland twice specifically asked Washington to resume bombing north of the DMZ, and in mid-January Admiral Sharp sent a similar plea to the Joint Chiefs.

The bombing must be resumed, Admiral Sharp said, and this time "destruction of resources within North Vietnam should begin with POL [petroleum-oil lubricants]. Every known POL facility and distribution activity should be destroyed and harassed until the war is concluded. Denial of electric power facilities should begin at an early date and continue until all plants are out of action. All large military facilities should be destroyed in northern North Vietnam as they have been in the southern area."

In essence, he stated three objectives for the air war: Destroy all military material as it enters North Vietnam, destroy such material already in North Vietnam, and destroy such material moving south.

"The alternative," he said, "appears to be a long and costly counterinsurgency . . . costly to United States and South Vietnamese lives and material resources." Writing after the war, Sharp said he believed this course of action "would have ended the war possibly by the end of 1966, and surely by the end of 1967."

Thus, the admiral was shocked and dismayed when a limited order to resume the air war came on the last day of January. Rolling Thunder 48, the first new operation, permitted only armed reconnaissance south of the Hanoi/Haiphong area, and prohibited attacking even SAM sites north of the 21st parallel. "We were starting 1966 with heavier restrictions than we had had in late 1965!" Sharp said. The military continued to press its battle in Washington, but it would be late June before any meaningful concessions were won.

In the meantime, there was good news for the troops in South Vietnam: The "Big Belly" B-52s began to phase in. The new models could carry sixty thousand pounds of bombs, instead of twenty-seven thousand—a total of 108 bombs in each basket.

Even more important, the big bombers (185-foot wingspan) began coming through with radar capable of ground-directed bombing, and a camouflage paint job to confuse hostile ground fire. The B-52 had become a formidable tactical weapon. It could deliver a heavy bomb load in almost any weather with great accuracy.

The bombers, still making that long haul from the Guam bases, became a terror to the enemy. They attacked from above 30,000 feet, and the Viet Cong could neither see nor hear them. The jungle was no longer a sanctuary. Special USAF ground teams, using radar, could direct bomb drops on targets as much as a hundred miles away, with pinpoint accuracy. The first of these ground stations, "Combat Skyspot," opened in March and was followed by six more, with a range that gradually increased to two hundred miles. By July, a "quick reaction force" of six B-52s could respond within hours to a ground call for bombs, and saturate an area of 1×2 kilometers with "flying artillery." The bombers could be diverted in flight if fatter targets came up, and could accept any target three kilometers or more from friendly forces.

The infantry loved the B-52s, and Westmoreland kept calling for more. Starting at three hundred sorties in April, the rate was slowly doubled to six hundred sorties per month by November, as field conditions and ammunition supply permitted. Almost all B-52 sorties were over the battlefields in South Vietnam. A few raids were tried against the Mu Gia Pass, a bottleneck in the Ho Chi Minh trail on the Laos–North Vietnam border, sixty miles northwest of the DMZ. A few raids were also made over southern North Vietnam, near the DMZ, but they were not as effective as the tactical fighter raids. Only in late 1972, under President Nixon, were the B-52s allowed anywhere near Hanoi-Haiphong.

The first thaw in the air war freeze came in April 1966, when President Johnson approved a total of nine hundred sorties against the roads, railroads, and bridges in northeast North Vietnam. Most of Hanoi and Haiphong were still off limits, and so were most POL targets. At this point, the Air Force and the Navy divided up North Vietnam into six zones, or "Route Packages," to avoid accidents and over-lapping.

Area 1, directly above the DMZ, came under Westmoreland's command, as a "hot pursuit" area for all tactical planes in the war zone, Air Force, Navy, Marine, or Army. The Navy was assigned Areas 2, 3, 4, and 6B, and the Air Force Areas 5 and 6A. Hanoi and Haiphong were divided into prohibited zones, a ten-mile circle from center city, and restricted zones, a thirty-five-mile circle.

Despite restrictions, both the Air Force and the Navy welcomed the April relaxation and turned to the permitted targets with a will. The fattest targets were just outside the Hanoi and Haiphong prohibited areas, with the Air Force taking the former (Route Package 6A) and the Navy the latter (RP 6B). The Air Force attacked a power plant and cement factory in Hanoi, road and rail bridges northwest of the city, and a radar facility at Kep, thirty miles northeast of Hanoi.

But it was the Navy's newest weapon, the A-6 Intruder, that really stung the Communists. The A-6, an ugly-looking twin jet crammed with radar and computers, could attack in any weather without visual contact. On the night of April

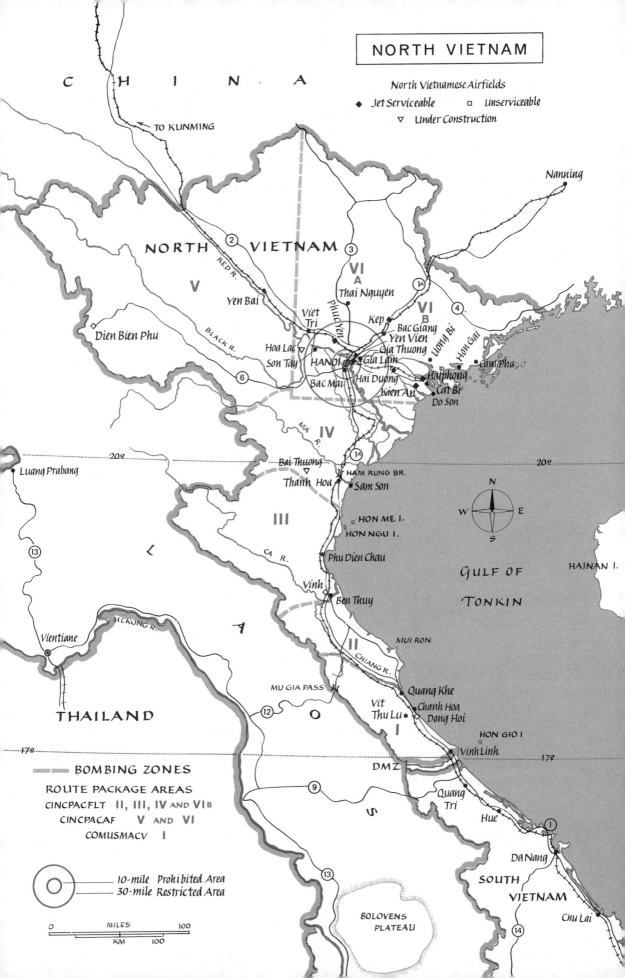

NORTH VIETNAM

North Vietnamese Airfields
♦ Jet Serviceable   □ Unserviceable
▽ Under Construction

C H I N A

TO KUNMING

NORTH VIETNAM

Nanning

② RED R.

V

Yen Bai

Dien Bien Phu

BLACK R.

Hoa Lac
Son Tay

⑥

③

VI A

Thai Nguyen

Viet Tri

Phuc Yen

Kep

④

VI B

Bac Giang
Yen Vien
Gia Thuong

Uong Bi

Hon Gai

HANOI
Gia Lam
Bac Mai
Hai Duong
Kien An

Haiphong
Cat Bi
Do Son

Cam Pha

①④

MA R.

IV

20°

Luang Prabang

Bai Thuong
Thanh Hoa

HAM RUNG BR.
Sam Son

20°

①④

III

CA R.

HON ME I.

HON NGU I.

Phu Dien Chau

GULF OF
TONKIN

HAINAN I.

Vinh
Ben Thuy

N
W   E
S

17°

L

A

O

S

Vientiane

MEKONG R.

THAILAND

⑬

⑫

II

CHIANG R.

MU GIA PASS

MUI RON

Quang Khe

Vit
Thu Lu

Chanh Hoa
Dong Hoi

HON GIO I.

Vinh Linh

17°

DMZ

⑨

Quang
Tri

BOMBING ZONES
ROUTE PACKAGE AREAS
CINCPACFLT II, III, IV AND VI B
CINCPACAF   V AND VI
COMUSMACV   I

Hue

①

Da Nang

10-mile Prohibited Area
30-mile Restricted Area

⑬

SOUTH
VIETNAM

0   MILES   100

KM   100

BOLOVENS
PLATEAU

Chu Lai

⑭

The first Russian-built jet fighters to be found in North Vietnam were MIG-17s such as these two, photographed by American reconnaissance planes at Phuc Yen air base, 20 miles northwest of Hanoi.

18, two A-6s from the carrier *Kitty Hawk*'s "Black Falcon" squadron, went after the power plant at Uong Bi, twenty-five miles north of Haiphong. The plant, supplying most of Haiphong's power and one third of Hanoi's, had been struck four months earlier with little effect. This time the Intruders, each carrying thirteen thousand pounds of bombs, came in under the enemy radar, hit within seconds of each other, and were gone without a shot being fired at them. All twenty-six one-thousand-pound bombs hit the target, smashing the complex and enraging Hanoi.

In late June, President Johnson finally gives American planes the go-ahead to bomb petroleum supply targets in enemy territory, with almost immediate results at this depot outside Hanoi.

For days afterward, Radio Hanoi blared that the United States was using B-52s against heavily populated areas.

As early as April 19, Navy planes went after Cam Pha, North Vietnam's third largest port, northeast of Haiphong and only thirty-five miles from China. Twenty-four planes from the *Kitty Hawk* attacked the port and no planes were lost, but a diplomatic incident shook world capitals. A Polish merchant ship was unloading war goods at Cam Pha, and the Communists claimed a bomb had nearly hit the

165

ship. The Chinese radio shouted of border violations by the "United States imperialists." The raids continued.

It is not certain which American downed the first MIG-21, but the Navy thinks it did, on April 26, when two of the Russian planes, new to the Asian theater, came after three Phantoms covering a reconnaissance mission. One of the Phantoms fired two Sidewinders at one of the MIG-21s, and the pilot was seen to eject, but no kill was claimed. The Navy's first *confirmed* kill came October 9, when Commander Richard Bellinger off the *Oriskany* put a MIG-21 away with a Sidewinder. Bellinger, age forty-two, fighting his third war for the United States, said, "I've waited twenty years for something like this."

The big breakthrough came June 23, when President Johnson secretly approved POL targets in North Vietnam, surrounded with myriad restrictions and exhortations. The "secret" was promptly leaked in Washington, infuriating Admiral Sharp, who said it made the future raids "many, many times more hazardous for our *own* [his italics] pilots." The approval was abruptly canceled June 25 but reinstated June 28, and the first raids got off on June 29.

Two squadrons of Navy A-4Cs went after oil storage areas in the Haiphong/Do Son area, laying on nineteen tons of bombs and Zuni rockets. The Air Force sent seventy planes from Thailand bases against a thirty-two-tank storage farm four miles from Hanoi, setting off spectacular fires. The next day, Secretary McNamara told a news conference the raids had been approved because of "mounting reliance by North Vietnam on the use of trucks and powered junks to facilitate the infiltration of men and equipment from North Vietnam into South Vietnam." This wasn't exactly news to American military leaders, who had been urging such raids for well over a year. McNamara concluded that the opening raids had "inflicted heavy damage on three of North Vietnam's petroleum facilities."

Only one plane was lost, an Air Force F-105, but there was another price to pay. In Hanoi, on July 6, prison guards assembled fifty-two American POWs who thought, and hoped, they were to be repatriated. Instead they were paraded through downtown Hanoi streets lined with hysterical crowds. Many raced into the streets to attack the shackled POWs. Even the prison guards were terrified, but the battered POWs finally reached a stadium and the doors were shut behind them. Guards told them anyone who would "follow the way of Fulbright, Morse, and Mansfield" (i.e., condemn American participation) would receive lenient treatment; others would be turned over to the mob.

The trip back to prison was a horror. The POWs were gagged, beaten, run into concrete steps or stone arches, and kicked in the testicles. Bleeding, reeling, or unconscious, the lucky ones made it back to the "safety" of their cells. Major Fred V. Cherry, USAF, the first black POW, had his own ordeal. He could not parade because he was in hospital having his infected wounds opened and scraped down to the bone, with no anesthesia. Cherry did not cry out, and was returned to the care of his cellmate, Lieutenant (JG) Porter Halyburton, a white Southerner. These two men had long since discovered that torture and pain are color-blind.

Nearly a hundred Americans were in prison camps by the end of 1966, but a few

166

The Communists staged their infamous parade of American POWs through Hanoi streets on July 6. This picture of unidentified Americans came out of North Vietnam through Japanese sources.

were escaping that fate, by luck, heroism, and SAR (Search-and-Rescue) tactics. For example, Lieutenant Commander Thomas Tucker, flying recon off the *Oriskany,* bailed out in Haiphong harbor on August 31, one hundred fifty yards from shore, in plain view of junks and sampans. (By this time the bounty on his head was $200, a fortune for anyone who captured him.) A Sea King helicopter came out from the carrier *Kearsarge,* hovered at thirty feet in heavy gunfire from shore, picked up Tucker and delivered him, unhurt, to his own carrier.

Lieutenant (JG) Robert Adams, from the *Oriskany,* was saved twice. On July 12 he was plucked from the sea, and in October from the Laotian jungle. The second time he called in the choppers with his hand radio, guided the sling down by voice, and first saw his saviors when he emerged above the jungle trees.

Lieutenant (JG) Dieter Dengler, from the *Ranger,* was one of the few Americans who escaped from captivity. In February he was shot down over Laos and captured by the Pathet Lao. He wound up in a jungle camp with other POWs, some of whom were already in their second year of captivity. In June, Dengler and others escaped into the jungle after killing six guards. Only Dengler made it to freedom. He walked into American lines July 21, weighing ninety-eight pounds. The others had wan-

167

dered apart and Dengler had watched one, an Air Force lieutenant, being slashed to death with a machete by pursuers.

———————

The first of three big aircraft carrier fires occurred October 26, when a blaze broke out in a flare locker on the *Oriskany*. (Carriers are potential volcanoes because of the jet fuel and armament they must carry. The *Oriskany* fire was possibly caused by carelessness in handling flares.) The fire burned through four decks of the carrier, killing forty-four crewmen, including several pilots just back from missions over North Vietnam. They were trapped in their cabins.

———————

As promised by Ky at the Honolulu meeting in February, the election of a 117-member Constituent Assembly to draft a constitution for South Vietnam took place on September 11. The Buddhists had urged the people to boycott the election, and the Viet Cong had tried to prevent it by terror. But over five million South Vietnamese registered to vote, and 81 percent actually went to the polls. The New York *Times* reported that "foreign observers who roamed freely on election day generally agreed there were few irregularities."

Early in October, McNamara was back in Saigon, on his eighth visit to the country. He was clearly unhappy with the way the war was going. He felt that the time had come for the United States to level off its military support. The air war against the north was failing, he believed, and should be curtailed. The United States should build a barrier across the 17th parallel, from the South China Sea all the way into Laos, and retire behind it. This was what came to be known as McNamara's Wall. It was a failure from the start, and it marked the beginning of the end for McNamara. His split with the military, though not yet apparent to the public, had begun.

The barrier idea had originated early in 1966 with Project Jason, an elite group of scientists, thinkers, and engineers, somewhat akin to Dr. Vannevar Bush's World War II group that perfected radar, the atomic bomb, and sulfa drugs. The idea was that a belt of electronic sensors, connected to explosive charges and controlled by computers, could cut off infiltration from the north. McNamara was enthusiastic, but the military was skeptical. The barrier project was activated in September as Joint Task Force 728, headed by Lieutenant General Alfred Starbird, and General Westmoreland was summoned to Manila to learn of it from General Starbird. Westmoreland said he thought it a "noble idea" but "highly theoretical." He said later that "some of the people promoting it, if not McNamara himself, saw it as a cure for infiltration that would justify stopping the bombing of North Vietnam."

The barrier project died aborning, perhaps the first victim of McNamara's growing disenchantment. He never seriously pushed it. The pessimism of McNamara's report on his return from Saigon gave the Joint Chiefs of Staff great concern. This was set forth in a Joint Chiefs of Staff report to McNamara that stated bluntly, "The Joint Chiefs of Staff do not concur in your recommendation that there should be no increase in the level of bombing effort and no modification in areas and targets subject to air attack." They also recommended no further bombing pauses or peace offensives such as the thirty-six-day halt of December 1965–January 1966. They also included this sentence: "The Joint Chiefs of Staff request that their views as set forth above be provided to the President." This reflected a growing view in the military that McNamara was becoming a filter, not a conduit, between them and the Commander in Chief.

As to President Johnson himself, he was still most chary about Vietnam; to some he seemed reluctant to go there. He had a perfect opportunity at the Manila Conference in October. Called by President Ferdinand Marcos of the Philippines, the meeting brought together high officials of South Vietnam, Thailand, South Korea, Australia, New Zealand, the Philippines, and the United States. It was a political meeting and, for Johnson, a political trip resulting in a broad declaration denouncing communism and supporting democracy.

Johnson visited the capitals of all the participating countries and traveled 31,500 miles in seventeen days. For Vietnam, he allotted just over one hour. The trip was not even on his official agenda, and the Army barely knew he was there. He flew from Manila in the morning, arrived at Cam Ranh Bay in time for lunch, decorated five soldiers, spoke to a few grunts in the hospital, and was gone, back to Manila the same evening. On the rest of his trip he made over forty speeches, gave huge Texas-style parties, received two kangaroos and an albino turtle, and was also picketed by antiwar groups. The message Johnson left at Cam Ranh Bay said: "I could not come to this part of the world and not come to see you. We shall never let you down, nor your fighting comrades, nor the fifteen million people of South Vietnam, nor the hundreds of millions of Asians who are counting on us to show here in Vietnam that aggression does not pay and that aggression cannot succeed . . . We believe in you. We know you are going to get the job done." In Seoul, Korea, more than a million people saw President Johnson; in Vietnam, a handful.

Just before Christmas the President summed up 1966 as the year the tide had turned in Vietnam, but he warned that "long and difficult days" lay ahead. McNamara said that during the year "progress [had] exceeded our expectations." He warned that additional American forces were destined for the war front, but hoped that draft calls might be halved in 1967. At their last meeting, Westmoreland had asked McNamara for a 30 percent troop increase, to round off the American strength in Vietnam at around a half million. He had asked McNamara to keep about three divisions as a ready reserve in the United States, to be called forward if and when needed.

By year-end, United States strength in South Vietnam had grown by over two hundred thousand to a total of 385,000. The South Vietnamese forces had also grown, from 565,000 to 617,000, half of them regulars. The total Allied forces stood at fifty-two thousand, mostly Koreans, who were proving to be hard fighters. But the enemy had grown too, despite losses of some fifty thousand killed in battle. Infiltration was increasing, and North Vietnamese regulars in South Vietnam jumped during the year from eleven thousand to about fifty thousand.

President Johnson made his first visit to South Vietnam in October, a stay of just over an hour, during which he met with the South Vietnamese Chief of State, Lieutenant General Nguyen Van Thieu (top), visited American wounded and decorated five GI's at Cam Ranh Bay (above). Here Captain John Nolan of the 21st Trans. Bn., USAF, receives the Bronze Star.

American losses jumped, too. During 1966, 5,008 Americans were killed in action, more than triple the total of 1,636 killed in the previous five years altogether, 1961–65. It was true the enemy was losing about ten men to one American, but the price did not seem to bother North Vietnam. Even though Moscow was pressing Hanoi to compromise, Ho Chi Minh was adamant. He never wavered in his belief that the United States would crack.

On Christmas Eve, 1966, an extraordinary event occurred—a professional American journalist, Harrison E. Salisbury of the New York *Times,* arrived in Hanoi, the capital of a country with which the United States was warring. Salisbury, then fifty-eight, had been chief of the *Times* bureau in Moscow for five years in the early 1950s, and had won the Pulitzer Prize for international reporting in 1951. He was not the first foreign correspondent into Hanoi (others from Britain, France, and the Communist countries had preceded him in 1965 and 1966). Nor was he the first American—a year earlier Tom Hayden, a young radical and organizer of the SDS (Students for a Democratic Society), had visited Hanoi with Herbert Aptheker, a leader of the American Communists.

Salisbury's dispatches from Hanoi electrified the world, angered the American administration, and caused anguish in the homes of thousands of Americans then serving in South Vietnam. Salisbury, who spoke no Vietnamese, toured the countryside around Hanoi with Communist interpreters and guides. He was shown the set pieces other visitors had seen before him—the bombed church or school, the obliterated town "with no military targets," the maimed women and children, the victims of "aggressor American pilots" who "deliberately" bombed residences, schools, and other forbidden targets. The picture emerging from his dispatches was quite clear—United States military might was being used to destroy the people of North Vietnam, not the military forces.

That was hard reading, especially hard at Christmas time for Americans whose sons and husbands were dying in the war; and it was infuriating to the administration, from President Johnson down, because Salisbury committed errors of fact, which elementary rules of American journalism would normally have prevented.

The Nam Dinh story provided an example: On December 26, 1965, Salisbury's second day in the enemy's country, he was taken to Nam Dinh, a city fifty miles south of Hanoi. He reported that U.S. Navy pilots of the Seventh Fleet had destroyed the city, which contained few, if any, military targets; had killed mostly women and children; and had kept the entire campaign secret. Fact: North Vietnam's main railway and highway, Route 1, passed through the city, which also contained railroad yards, naval facilities, petroleum dumps, and many rocket and anti-aircraft sites. The Nam Dinh raids had been reported at the time in three official American communiqués, and U.S. correspondents had been briefed regularly at U.S. military headquarters in Saigon. (When Salisbury's book *Behind the Lines—Hanoi* was published in 1967, he included this line in his discussion of Nam Dinh: "It was not correct to say it [the city] had not been mentioned as a United States target.")

The New York *Times,* by Salisbury's own account, had planned in advance to capitalize on its "coup" of getting its correspondent into Hanoi. Salisbury himself had hoped for a second Pulitzer Prize, and he almost got it. The editorial jury voted it to him but was overridden by both the Pulitzer advisory board and the Columbia University trustees—in each case, as Salisbury himself pointed out, "by a one-vote margin."

Salisbury had hoped to interview Ho Chi Minh, but the Communists did not permit this. Salisbury did, however, talk with Prime Minister Pham Van Dong, who at one point said: "And how long do you Americans want to fight, Mr. Salisbury? . . . One year, two years, three years, five years, ten years, twenty years? We will be glad to accommodate you."

10

Year of Doubt
1967

T HE IRON Triangle, they called it, and it had been Viet Cong country for twenty years, but not for much longer. It was a heavily jungled area lying twenty miles or so north of Saigon, between the Saigon River and Route 13. Charlie used it as the center for communications, supply, planning, assembly, and attack against the capital area of South Vietnam. Inside the triangle were villages, rice paddies, abandoned and overgrown rubber plantations—ideal country for guerrillas. It was time for the Americans to smash this sanctuary.

Operation Cedar Falls began January 8, with twenty-five thousand troops involved, the largest action in the war to date. Elements of the U.S. Army's 25th Division crossed the Saigon River at the southern end of the triangle, and the 173rd Airborne, the 11th Armored Cavalry, and ARVN troops pushed in from the east. Together they formed the anvil. The 1st Division, the Big Red One, was the hammer, pounding down from the north.

The B-52s flew 102 bomb sorties, tactical air added 1,113 close support missions, and thirty batteries of artillery fired almost constantly. On the ground, the infantry closed in relentlessly, in hard, steady, night and day patrolling. In eighteen days Phase I was over, and Phase II followed right on. In came the bulldozers and the Rome plows, tearing down the triangle, cleaning out the jungle, leveling villages, destroying towns, moving out thousands of refugees, crushing bunkers, tunnels, redoubts—erasing the home base of Viet Cong Region 4. From now on, the Iron Triangle was a "free-fire zone"—anything moving in it was presumed hostile and would be destroyed immediately.

Nobody knows how many guerrillas were killed in Operation Cedar Falls— probably several thousand—but if the Viet Cong wanted the Iron Triangle back they'd have to pay for it. In the cleansing, the Americans captured thousands of weapons, enough rice to feed thirteen thousand Viet Cong for a year, and a treasury

173

Civilians are moved out as American infantry moves in to penetrate the Iron Triangle, north and west of Saigon, where the Viet Cong has held power for years. Operation Cedar Falls opened January 8, with several crack American outfits and ARVN units in action.

of Communist documents, some half million pages of them, a veritable history of insurgency running back to 1962.

A month later, the same treatment was applied to War Zone C in Tay Ninh Province (III 21), up against the Cambodian border. Twenty-two American battalions, spearheaded by 1st Division outfits, plus four ARVN battalions—over thirty thousand troops—moved forward in Operation Junction City. This time the ground forces formed a horseshoe, and the 173rd Airborne, in its first combat jump of the war, parachuted to close the open end of the shoe.

The B-52s came in from Guam again, this time laying twelve thousand tons of bombs, and artillery and air (five thousand tactical sorties) added thousands of tons more. In eighty-three days of fighting, ending in mid-May, Charlie was killed by the thousands, or ran for the border. The Americans captured over six hundred big

First came the B-52s, the "flying artillery" (left), whose bombs left craters like this (below).

weapons (crew-served), eight hundred tons of rice, and vast amounts of medical supplies, ammunition, and field equipment.

This pattern raised serious problems in Hanoi. That spring advisers flew in from Communist Cuba, China, and North Korea to confer with General Giap, the North Vietnamese commanding general. He had beaten the French at Dien Bien Phu in

175

1954, but he hadn't won a battle in South Vietnam in two years. Viet Cong cadres in South Vietnam were becoming demoralized, and desertion was rising both in the Viet Cong and among the North Vietnamese regulars. Then Giap flew to Moscow and tried to put on the best face he could. What was happening, he explained, was a consequence of his strategy—to lure the Americans out of the cities into the countryside and, at the proper time, the guerrillas and his regulars would attack and capture the heavily populated areas—Saigon, Da Nang, and other cities. For that, he said, he would need more money and more weapons. The Russians listened, and decided the time had come to raise the ante. Moscow agreed to send "even more planes, high-altitude missiles, artillery, and infantry weapons, together with factories, means of transportation, petroleum products, iron and steel and nonferrous metal equipment, food and fertilizer." It would take many months, they agreed, but the grand attack should be ready to go in 1968.

The Americans could not have known the whole scheme at this time, but they watched it develop all during 1967. The clearest sign of impending trouble was the huge increase in ships unloading in Haiphong and its sister ports, Hon Gai and Cam Pha, and in Sihanoukville, in the Cambodian refuge. In the Haiphong area alone, 433 Communist ships unloaded in 1967, as against 122 the year before.

The Communist ships had full sanctuary—by American decree no bomb could fall near them, and the Haiphong docks worked day and night. For the rest of the year, the highest American war councils, right up to the Commander in Chief, wrestled with this problem—to bomb the northern ports or not to bomb, to cut off the weapons at the source or face the consequences. On this decision rested the outcome of the war, and the lives of thousands of Americans.

Militarily, South Vietnam exploded in battle in 1967, in all four corps areas. In the north, heavy fighting erupted in March as General Giap began sending his regulars south through and around the DMZ. The Marines moved the 3rd Division up to Hue to meet the challenge, and brought the 1st Division up from Chu Lai to fill the gap at Da Nang. The Army in turn took over responsibility for the southern part of I Corps, bringing up Task Force Oregon for the job, and using elements of the 25th Division, the 101st Airborne Division, and the 196th Infantry Brigade, with headquarters at Chu Lai. By April, the Marines in the north were into the First Battle of Khe Sanh (April 24–May 12), in the northwest corner of South Vietnam, close to Laos and the DMZ, to be followed by Operation Hickory (May 18–28), a surprise attack on half a dozen enemy battalions lurking south of the DMZ.

The action at Khe Sanh, a name later to be known to the world, began with a single Marine rifle company running into North Vietnamese forces five miles northwest of the base. The first encounter was sharp, and in succeeding days both sides threw in reinforcements. The Marines added a battalion from the Dong Ha area, and a second one, SLF Bravo, which had been fighting along the Quang Tri coast. (SLFs, Special Landing Forces, were shipboard-based Marine units, usually about battalion-strength, that could be called into action wherever needed.) They also called in the 1st Marine Airwing, helicopters and artillery. By May 12, the Marines

1st Division GIs move out from their helicopters in War Zone C (left), and 11th Cavalry troops send captured rice to the rear (right).

Marines scramble into action from choppers near Tam Ky, north of Chu Lai (right), while the Army's 4th Division units fire M-79 grenades into a village in Quang Ngai province on a search-and-destroy mission (below).

Hawk missiles stand guard at Quang Trang, ten miles north of Saigon.

had driven the Communists off Hill 861 and Hills 881 North and 881 South, out of the Khe Sanh area. The Communists lost at least 940 killed, many falling to air attacks, with the Marines flying over a thousand sorties and dropping fifteen hundred tons of bombs. Marines losses were 105 killed.

In Hickory, the North Vietnamese were caught by Marines and ARVN forces driving north, and an SLF coming in from the side. SLF Alpha (a battalion of Marines) came ashore at the very top of I Corps, under cover fire by five destroyers and two cruisers, and drove west along the DMZ, threatening to cut off the Communists' forces loitering below the DMZ. Fighting was heavy for a few days, but the Communists withdrew, leaving 815 dead—445 killed by the Marines and 370 by ARVN forces. During the battle, South Vietnamese forces, using trucks, amtracs, and helicopters, removed thirteen thousand civilians from the battle area to new refugee housing at Cam Lo.

During 1967, the Marines in I Corps fought more than 110 major engagements (battalion-size or larger) and 456,000 small unit operations—those patrols, from squad-size to company-size. Enemy deaths in ground fighting were estimated at eighteen thousand, plus another eight thousand credited to General Hoang Xuan Lam's ARVN forces. Marine planes had flown a record numbers of sorties—sixty-three thousand in direct troop support, ten thousand more in Allied support, and eleven thousand strike sorties into North Vietnam. The ordnance totals were 134,000 tons of bombs, 166,000 rockets, and over two million rounds of 20-mm fire. Marine helicopters made 490,000 sorties and lifted 723,000 troops.

By year's end, Allied strength in I Corps totaled seventy-one battalions: twenty-one U.S. Marines, thirty-one ARVN, fifteen U.S. Army, and four Korean Marines.

Taking the hills around Khe Sanh, Marines go over the top on Hill 881 (above), welcome chopper supplies on a wooden-topped landing zone (right), receive a 6-ton 155-mm howitzer (below left), and watch the Army's 175-mm field piece blow smoke rings (below right).

The long summer of 1967 finds the 9th Cavalry beating the bushes along the coast in II Corps (above left), Republic of Korea troops slogging through a river near Cam Ranh Bay (left), and the 1st Cavalry Division still trying to rout the VC along the coast near Bong Son (above right; below left). Late in December the 11th Light Infantry Brigade debarks at Qui Nhon to head out into the Central Highlands (below right).

U.S. Marine strength alone was about seventy-eight thousand men. Total forces were two hundred thousand.

The same bloody drama was being worked out in the other three Corps. In the II Corps area, the vital Central Highlands, the U.S. 4th Division operated from Pleiku city right through the summer, driving against North Vietnamese Army elements spilling across the Cambodian border. The Americans built roads, cleaned out the jungle, and established strongpoints. At the same time, the 1st Cavalry Division worked over the enemy in the coastal province of Binh Dinh in Operation Thayer II (1,757 enemy killed) and Operation Pershing, a year-long offensive that counted 5,401 enemy killed. Elements of the 4th and 25th Divisions, fighting in Pleiku and Kontum provinces, counted 733 enemy bodies in Operation Sam Houston. The 4th Division claimed 1,203 killed in Operation Francis Marion in western Pleiku, and started Operation MacArthur in October, an operation that would last all through 1968 and tally 5,731 enemy dead.

The climax in the Central Highlands came late in 1967 around Dak To, a Green Beret camp in Kontum Province (II 6). At least five North Vietnamese regiments gathered at the Cambodian border, and early in November an enemy prisoner declared that Dak To was the objective. Elements of the 4th Division, plus three ARVN battalions, were rushed into the area, and the 173rd Airborne Brigade was alerted. The town of Dak To itself lay in a valley surrounded by peaks up to six thousand feet high. The Americans put artillery on the high ground, called in the B-52s for the "flying artillery" strikes, and otherwise prepared for the storm.

It broke November 17, and for the rest of the month the fighting in the mountains was vicious, particularly around Hills 875 and 823. Sixteen American and ARVN battalions were involved, and by early December the Communists had been thrown back into Cambodia. They never got out of the mountains into the Dak To valley, and they left behind at least 1,400 dead. It was the biggest battle in this area since the Ia Drang valley campaign two years earlier. American units lost two hundred eighty-nine killed, and the South Vietnamese seventy-three killed, but they closed out the II Corps campaign that year on a solid victory. Captured documents indicated that all the enemy forays from Cambodia in the three northern corps areas, I, II, and III, were really rehearsals for a larger offensive by all of Giap's forces. It was the strategy he had outlined in Moscow.

The Riverine campaign, designed to take the Mekong Delta away from Charlie, finally got under way in 1967. IV Corps was South Vietnam's "breadbasket," a huge area of rivers and canals, the country's largest producer of rice and tropical vegetables and fruits. The United States had not fought a campaign like this since Grant's Mississippi River operations in the Civil War. To do the job, it welded a team from elements of the U.S. Army and Navy, Vietnamese Army and Marines, U.S. and Vietnamese air units, and even a brief thrust by a U.S. Marine Special Landing Force. Mostly the job was done by the 2nd and 3rd Brigades of the 9th Infantry Division, aided by a fleet of watercraft improvised for the job—barracks

In the fall monsoons, American forces take Hill 875 and finally throw the enemy out of the Central Highlands, back into Cambodia (left). In a photo that won the Pulitzer Prize, entitled "Dreams of a Better Life," an unsung GI sleeps in the rain (below).

ships, monitors, floating artillery and helicopter pads, barges, dredges, tugboats, minesweepers, rubber rafts, plastic assault boats, and hovercraft.

The 9th Division troops spent the early months of 1967 training in the Vung Tau area and then cleaning out the RSSZ (Rung Sat Special Zone), a swampy area southeast of Saigon. This was where the guerrillas lurked along the Saigon River, a

Once a sand dune, Chu Lai by 1967 is a roaring military base (left), and booty from the enemy flows back in many forms: Russian flamethrowers (below left), Communist weapons in great variety (below right), 407,000 piasters captured from a VC paymaster (bottom left), and 560 tons of enemy rice, "liberated" 18 miles from Da Nang (bottom right).

menace to shipping. But by May the 9th Division was moving into its new head-quarters at Dong Tam, an island created by the Army engineers and personally named by General Westmoreland with words meaning "united hearts and minds." Dong Tam, a square mile of sand, was one of the few spots in the delta that stood above the flood plain. It was a tribute to the engineers, who pumped sand for months while fighting off the Viet Cong, giving up two dredges sunk by the enemy and a third blown up when it sucked in live ammunition.

The Riverine Force had a tangled command of Navy and Army brass, but it worked. In the first year, the MRF (Mobile Riverine Force) fought five major engagements, killed over a thousand Viet Cong, and crafted a style of warfare the guerrillas could not stand up to. It consisted of locating the enemy, usually by intelligence; throwing a net around him by blocking roads and waterways, then drawing the strings of the net. The key to success was speed—place the blocks at night and close the net beginning at first light, as quickly as possible. Otherwise the Viet Cong wriggled through the holes in the net, a few minnows at a time. The "catch" was frequently only a few enemy, dead or alive, but a good haul of weapons, supplies, and documents. Tactical air was available on call, but the MRF counted more on its own floating artillery and aerial gunships.

In July, MRF moved some thirty-nine hundred troops of the 9th and 25th Divisions into Dong Tam and began clearing the enemy out of the north bank of the My Tho river, the northernmost of the Mekong's four main mouths. By year-end these operations, Coronado I through IX, had pushed westward into Kien Phong Province (IV 30). American casualties were running lower than expected, and the MRF was well positioned to go on full offensive in 1968.

In the air war, the U.S. Navy introduced during 1967 the first of the "smart" bombs, the Walleye Glide Bomb. This was a thousand-pound bomb with a TV camera in the nose. The camera focused on a high-contrast aim point at the target. When the bomb was released it would usually hit the aim point with perfect accuracy.

There was great excitement on the first raid on March 11, as pilots of air squadron VA-212 took off from carrier *Bon Homme Richard* to try out Walleye against military barracks and small bridges at Sam Son, just south of Thanh Hoa. Results were spectacular, and it was decided to have another shot, the very next day, at the Dragon's Jaw bridge at Thanh Hoa.

Specialists on the carriers decided that 1412 hours (2:12 P.M.) would be the optimum time for the raid, with the sun providing high contrast aim points. Three A-4 Skyhawks took off, each carrying one Walleye and covered against MIG attack by two F-8 Crusaders. The raid went perfectly and the three smart bombs impacted the target within five feet of each other, but the bridge still stood! Even thousand-pounders were not enough, but three-thousand-pounders were coming. (Alas, the U.S. bombing halt was also coming, and it would be 1972 before the monster smart bombs would get a chance at any targets above the 19th parallel.)

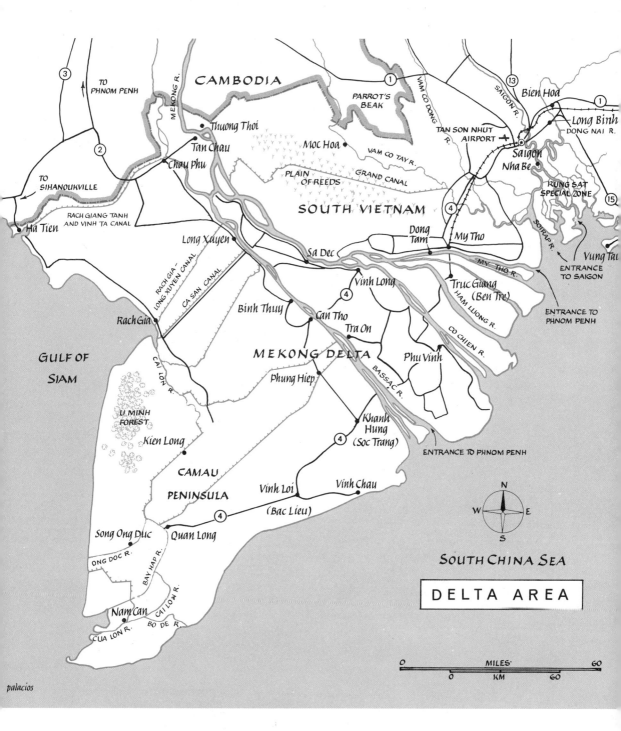

For the rest of 1967, the Navy used the Walleye sixty-eight more times, with a fantastic sixty-five hits, against North Vietnamese bridges, barracks, power plants, and other military targets. The smart bomb could only get smarter.

Navy planes didn't forget the Dragon's Jaw, either, dropping over two hundred tons of bombs in passing during the rest of the year. The bridge was not really

The U.S. Army and Navy team up in 1967 as the Mobile Riverine Force to root out the Viet Cong from the Mekong Delta. The 9th Infantry Division troops wade yet another river in IV Corps, in the vast river plains (above left). A Navy ATC (armored troop carrier) sweeps for VC mines in a Mekong tributary (above right). A Navy minesweeper keeps the Long Tau River clear of mines south of Saigon (below left). Navy brass get together for strategy talks (left to right): Captain Wade C. Wells, commander MRF; Admiral Ulysses S. Grant Sharp, Commander in Chief, Pacific; and Rear Admiral Kenneth L. Veth, Commander, U.S. Naval Forces, Vietnam.

usable, since rail lines at either end were constantly torn up. The enemy was forced to expend huge amounts of labor and time trying to keep the artery open, but Thanh Hoa stood as a symbol of North Vietnam's national pride. The world's richest and strongest nation could not destroy it!

The Air Force had no smart bombs until after the long bombing halt, but did achieve an important breakthrough. In April, Thailand granted permission for the B-52s to use U Tapao, the huge, American-built airbase at Sattahip, on the Gulf of Siam, fifty miles south of Bangkok. This was a great improvement over the long bomber flights from Guam, and by July more than half the B-52 missions in support of the ground troops were being flown from Thailand. The whole of South Vietnam was now within a five-hundred-mile radius of the B-52s, to the joy of the American infantry.

The sortie rate for the big bombers rose steadily to a thousand a month by November, when McNamara approved a rate of twelve hundred sorties per month, effective in February 1968. No B-52 flights were permitted over North Vietnam, however.

In Operation Neutralize, in September and October, the combination of B-52s, ground artillery, and tactical aircraft was used in continuous SLAM operations (Seek, Locate, Annihilate, Monitor). The Marines at Con Thien, Dong Ha, and Camp Carroll fire bases felt enemy pressure decrease markedly in November and beyond. Westmoreland called it "a Dien Bien Phu in reverse."

In one November mission near Con Thien, a B-52 accidentally dropped its bombs within fifteen hundred yards of Marine lines, with spectacular results. Secondary explosions of ammunition revealed a new tactic—the enemy was "hugging" Marine positions to avoid the aerial bombing. B-52 tactics were quickly adjusted to take advantage of this, as the enemy would soon learn.

In the campaign against North Vietnamese targets, the Air Force opened 1967 with a new tactic, Bolo. The MIGs had been in the habit of jumping laden F-105s to make them jettison their bombs before reaching the target. On January 2, Colonel Robin Olds used the F-105s as bait, and, when the MIGs charged in, the colonel's 8th Tactical Fighter Wing was there with the crack F-4s. In the largest air battle to date, they destroyed seven MIGs in twelve minutes without losing a plane. Four days later Bolo worked again, shooting down two more MIGs, and the enemy fell back to consider his problem. No longer could the MIGs attack the fighter/bombers and then run. The Air Force had another good day on May 13, when Bolo bagged seven more MIG-17s.

The Navy finally got permission to mine small rivers in southern North Vietnam, and promptly mined the Song Ca and South Giang rivers, near Vinh. The big rivers and ports farther north were still prohibited to mines or bombing, which irked the Navy. The port of Cam Pha, for example, could not be bombed if there was a foreign ship in port. Naturally, Cam Pha was never without a foreign freighter. As the coal piles mounted, one carrier pilot suggested a dose of napalm could set off

An A-4E Skyhawk clears the runway at Chu Lai (above left). Ordnance men load up the A-6A Intruder, a workhorse plane that can bomb around the clock (above right; below left). The legendary F-4B Phantom makes a business call (below right).

the world's largest barbecue; but the pilots could not even fire back at antiaircraft fire.

The Navy destroyed a total of seventeen MIGs in air combat in 1967, but the Air Force had done much better. After an investigation, the Navy opened a school for training in "old-fashioned dogfighting with new-fashioned weapons." Navy plane losses were also comparatively heavy, with sixteen planes lost in August alone. On one day, August 21, eighty SAMs were fired at Navy planes. Hanoi was now the most heavily defended city in the history of air warfare. It had fifteen SAM sites, six hundred antiaircraft batteries, and the MIGs.

On July 29 the Navy suffered another blow, the second big aircraft carrier fire, this time on the *Forrestal.* The carrier had been on Yankee Station just four days when, at 11 A.M., a Zuni rocket on a parked F-4 at the stern discharged and hit the fuel tank of an A-4. The flight deck went up in flames, and planes and ordnance exploded everywhere. The fire on the flight deck was controlled within an hour but it took another twelve hours to extinguish the blazes below decks. In all, 134 men were killed, twenty-one planes destroyed, and forty-three more damaged. The *Forrestal* limped off for Norfolk and $72 million worth of repairs.

In July, a new Rolling Thunder target list came out, easing up on targets within the restricted areas of Hanoi and Haiphong. One target on the list for the first time was the Paul Doumer rail bridge just north of Hanoi. It was the most important rail target in North Vietnam, since it carried all rail traffic coming in from China. Six of the targets on the Rolling Thunder 57 list were within ten miles of Hanoi, and the pilots chortled, "We're going downtown."

The date to go after the Doumer bridge was August 11. The bridge itself was just over a mile long, with nineteen spans, and the Air Force tapped three fighter wings to get them, one each from the Thailand air bases at Takli, Korat, and Ubon. Thirty-six strike aircraft dropped ninety-four tons of bombs, cutting both rail and road spans and stopping twenty-six trains per day. The pilots turned for home, no planes lost, and radioed ahead, "giraffe, giraffe," the code word for success. Twenty-one F-105s went back on October 25 and closed the bridge again, and also on December 14 and 18.

On August 22, the Air Force had gone after another key rail bridge, the Canal des Rapides bridge just northeast of Hanoi, where the northeast rail line came in from China. For the rest of the year, all rail bridges, lines, and marshalling yards in North Vietnam were fair game, right up to within thirty-five miles of the Chinese border.

The year 1967 also was a key one in "the other war," the war on the American home front. Most Americans watched it from ringside seats at the TV—the mobs looting and burning in American cities, the nation's campuses erupting with riots and demonstrations. The great outpouring of unrest embraced race relations, the draft, and Vietnam; but almost any excuse for protest would do, and "the Establishment" ran for cover. Public officials had to look to their own safety, and that of

Fire on the USS Forrestal, *one of four serious aircraft carrier fires in Vietnam waters. This one claimed 134 lives and destroyed or damaged 64 planes in late July, 1967.*

their children, as the disaffected burned them in effigy and even threatened real fire against their persons. Bags of blood were hurled, and bags of human excrement; public and private buildings were assaulted, bombed, burned, and defaced; and innocent people were killed. There was a great rage in the land, and Vietnam was certainly part of it.

The key military decisions for Vietnam were being made in Washington during 1967, and these decisions would shatter the Johnson administration and cut the ground from under a half million American troops in Vietnam. The process began early in the year, when General Westmoreland was asked to submit his views on fighting the war into 1968. He replied that the war could be won either quickly (using optimum force) or slowly (using minimum essential force). He recommended the former as the best way to save American lives and money. His specific options were:

1. *Optimum force.* This would commit two hundred thousand more American troops, for a 1968 total of 670,000 men. (The new forces would comprise four and one third combat divisions, support troops, and ten tactical fighter squadrons.)
2. *Minimum essential force.* This would give Westmoreland 80,500 additional troops and raise the total American force to 550,000. (The new forces would comprise two and one third divisions and five tactical fighter squadrons.)

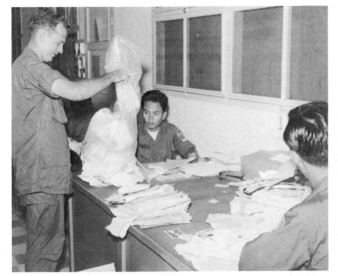 

Intelligence is also a weapon, and so all captured Viet Cong papers are translated and assessed at this special center near Tan Son Nhut for use against the enemy (left). The people-sniffer (right) is also a weapon, though not always reliable; it couldn't distinguish between human smells and animals smells, and thus saw limited use.

In April, the Commander in Chief summoned Westmoreland home, the first of three trips the general would make to Washington in 1967. President Johnson's purpose in calling the general home was mainly public relations: to have Westmoreland help the President stem the rising discontent with the war. The forum was the annual meeting of the Associated Press, at the Waldorf-Astoria hotel in New York City, with Westmoreland as the main speaker. As the general arrived at the hotel on the morning of April 24, he had the emotional experience of watching himself being burned in effigy at the door. (A few weeks earlier, his daughter Stevie had watched her father's effigy being burned at Harvard.)

General Westmoreland's theme was that the war in Vietnam was going well, though "the end is not in sight," and a warning that Hanoi's strategy and hope was to "win politically that which [it] cannot accomplish militarily." As an ad lib to his prepared speech, the general said that his troops in Vietnam were "dismayed, and so am I, by recent unpatriotic acts here at home." He had in mind the burning of the American flag at an antiwar rally in Central Park. His offhand remark was, of course, the next day's headlines.

The military business took place three days later at two sessions in the White House, with President Johnson, Secretary McNamara, Secretary of State Rusk, General Wheeler, and other important advisers present. Toward the end of the long day, McNamara began to press for an estimate of how long the war would last. Westmoreland did not like such questions, but he finally answered.

McNamara's ninth, and final, trip to Saigon was not a happy one; he and the military quarreled bitterly and the Secretary of Defense was on the way out. As the meeting opens, McNamara is greeted by U.S. Ambassador Ellsworth Bunker (left) and General Westmoreland (center).

"With the optimum force, about three years; with the minimum force, at least five." This was assuming, he said, that the air war against North Vietnam would continue. All those present knew that, even then, McNamara opposed the bombing and wanted it stopped.

The showdown between the military leaders and McNamara came early in July, at a Saigon meeting. Secretary McNamara was coming in for his ninth (and his last, as it turned out) visit to Vietnam, and was bringing with him the first team of advisers from the Defense and State departments, plus the chairman of the Joint Chiefs of Staff, General Wheeler. All military commanders in the Pacific would attend. Admiral Sharp, sensing the vital nature of the meeting, flew from Hawaii to Saigon a week ahead of time to set up the military presentation.

The meeting opened July 7, and it was quickly apparent that the principal question of substance was the bombing of North Vietnam. McNamara urged that it be stopped, or at least curtailed. The military opposed him, to a man. So tense was the atmosphere that McNamara finally cut Admiral Sharp dead. When Sharp mentioned this to General Wheeler, he said Wheeler told him McNamara "was furious at you." The breach between McNamara and the military was now complete.

By coincidence, Act 2 of this drama was played out within days. General Westmoreland's mother had died as the Saigon meeting ended, and the general flew home to attend her funeral on July 12. The same day McNamara was reporting to President Johnson on the Saigon meeting. Johnson's memoirs say that McNamara told him that Westmoreland "had accepted a troop increase somewhat smaller than the 'minimum essential force' he had proposed."

Westmoreland got word at the funeral that the President would like to see him. ("One of the few messages President Johnson ever sent me directly," Westmoreland later said.) Westmoreland was at the White House the next day, and it was then that Johnson "informed me he had decided on the lesser of my two troop packages." Actually, it was worse than that. The general soon discovered that his "minimum" request for 80,500 troops had been "cut almost in half." He would get only 47,000 troops and a new ceiling of 525,000. "I was extremely disappointed . . ." the general wrote later. Johnson publicly announced the new figures the next day at a news conference as a "meeting of the minds"—but, Westmoreland appended: "I made clear to him privately that I reserved the right to request more troops if required. War is too unpredictable to do otherwise."

Other things were happening. Johnson was thinking of retiring, and so was McNamara. Johnson put it this way in his memoirs: "When I nominated him [McNamara] to the Presidency of the World Bank late in 1967 the story circulated that I had fired him because of a disagreement over Vietnam. The fact is that he knew in the summer of 1967 that I was seriously considering retiring from office at the end of the current term." Johnson goes on to say he told McNamara he had served well and was entitled to any job the President could give him.

The fact also is that there *was* a disagreement over Vietnam. It came to a head late in the year when Johnson had to make a decision on the bombing program. He decided against McNamara and in favor of the military. Even before that, McNamara had suffered other blows. The Preparedness Subcommittee of the Senate Armed Services Committee (Senator John C. Stennis, chairman) held secret hearings on the war in August. The first witness was Admiral Sharp, who found the committee members "a most sympathetic audience" for his plea not only to continue bombing North Vietnam but to increase the pressure. (The very day he testified, Sharp noted, more targets were approved for bombing; this was not a coincidence, he says, just McNamara trying to "spike my guns.")

McNamara was the final witness, and the subcommittee's report gave him no comfort. The report castigated "the administration's conduct of the bombing campaign," and called for even greater effort.

Westmoreland had gone back to the battlefield, and on August 8 had moved into "Pentagon East," the new, $25 million U.S. headquarters complex at Tan Son Nhut airport. It looked like the American military was in Vietnam to stay.

In November, General Westmoreland was back in Washington, once again summoned by Johnson on a public relations mission. Just a few weeks earlier, more than 50,000 people demonstrated at the Lincoln Memorial, and several thousand marched on the Pentagon. The 82nd Airborne Division, which had been called in on standby, was even now camped across the Potomac at Bolling Air Force Base. (Ironically, the 82nd's 3rd Brigade would be rushing to Vietnam within three months to protect another "American" capital, Saigon.)

Westmoreland made some speeches to rally support for the war, attended a football game, visited Camp David, and had the rare experience of breakfasting with the President in the White House. (Johnson was in his bathrobe, lying in bed with three television sets blaring, the phone ringing constantly.)

It was late Monday night, November 20, when Westmoreland got the real news from the President. After a busy day for both men, the White House was finally quieting down and the two sat alone in the presidental family living room. Then it came out quickly. McNamara was resigning as Secretary of Defense, the President said, and would be replaced by Clark Clifford, a highly regarded lawyer who had been working in Washington circles for years.

Then came the real shocker: The President asked Westmoreland what the troops in Vietnam would think if he, Johnson, failed to run for reelection in 1968. Would they think the Commander in Chief was letting them down? Johnson said his health was "not good," and his family had been urging him not to run. The questions were many, and the talk lasted until nearly midnight. There was really little doubt that Johnson would not run again. "He had obviously made up his mind," Westmoreland wrote. The general also knew that he himself was not long for Vietnam; his successor, General Creighton Abrams, was already in place in Saigon.

Only a handful of men knew what was going on at the highest levels in Washington. (Westmoreland did not even tell his wife: Johnson had said his disclosures were "sensitive.") As far as the world could see, it had been a year of advances for the Allies in South Vietnam. The first national election had come off on September 3; the people had voted in true democratic style and Thieu was a legitimate president, Ky vice-president. This was so despite Viet Cong terrorism, a wave of torture and killing that wiped out at least three hundred thirty-five village officials.

The fighting had been heavy and American casualties had risen sharply, but troop morale was high. The bases were secure and the ports were booming, with a million tons of supplies per month coming through. The ratio of enemy losses to ours was nearly ten to one, to be sure, but American POWs were paying a special price. They had to listen to tapes of Harrison Salisbury's dispatches to the New York *Times,* with statements like "One can see the United States planes are dropping an enormous weight of explosives on purely civilian targets"; or of the Reverend Martin Luther King, Jr., declaiming that the war was "blasphemy against all that America stands for"; or Dr. Benjamin Spock, a pediatrician, comparing American actions to Hitler's holocaust of the Jews. These were cutting words for men under torture and terror.

For many an American POW, the treatment in enemy prisons was truly cruel and unusual. Ensign Ralph E. Gaither, Jr., a pilot off the carrier *Independence,* was chained to the Hanoi power plant for three months, a sure victim if the plant was bombed. Lieutenant William F. Metzger, Jr., a *Bon Homme Richard* pilot, was kept naked in his cell for two months. Lieutenant Commander John S. McCain II, the so-called Crown Prince, was captured October 26. "Your father is a big admiral," the North Vietnamese shouted as they beat him so badly he could not walk or feed himself. Some POWs simply disappeared. Air Force Major Norman Schmidt was taken from his cell August 31, exactly one year after his capture, and was never seen again.

In the final three months of the year, the North Vietnamese were clearly up to something big. All the trails leading south were seething with movement. At the fronts, enemy troops were building roads, preparing artillery sites, massing ammunition and supplies, probing American lines. There was going to be a major offensive; that was clear to everyone.

Westmoreland asked for more troops, and got them. Two outfits scheduled for 1968 were moved in quickly. The 2nd and 3rd Brigades of the crack 101st Airborne Division, the famed "Screaming Eagles" of Normandy, arrived November 19 and immediately joined the shield around Saigon. The 11th Infantry Brigade flew in a month later from Schofield Barracks in Hawaii on an emergency basis. (The 11th would become part of the Americal Division and would be heard from later, at a place called My Lai.)

Just before Christmas, the Commander in Chief paid his second, and last, visit to the Vietnam war. Once again he flew into Cam Ranh Bay, stayed an hour or so, and was off for Rome to see Pope Paul VI. Bob Hope came in right behind him and entertained the troops for Christmas. The year went out in one of those thirty-six-hour truces, a false calm before a very real storm.

President Johnson greets GIs as he makes his second, and last, brief visit to Cam Ranh Bay on December 23, 1967. Three months later he would shock the nation, and the world, by declining to run for reelection.

195

Victory into Defeat
1968

T̲HE T̲ET offensive of 1968 was no surprise to the American and South Vietnamese troops. Anyone near the front had seen the evidence, or heard the rumors: Charlie was gathering for a big one. The exact date could not be known, but it would be soon. As early as January 5, the 4th Division troops around Pleiku had discovered "Urgent Combat Order No. 1" in a batch of captured enemy documents. It was the plan to attack Pleiku "before the Tet holidays." On January 15, the 4th's artillery opened up on the enemy, and the B-52s began to work over the assembly areas along the Cambodian border.

On January 20, a North Vietnamese lieutenant surrendered near Khe Sanh and said that an attack was coming in that area. Again the B-52s were set loose, this time on the Laotian border areas. In III Corps, the enemy could be seen shifting in the Cambodian jungle, moving closer to the border, aiming toward Saigon. In I Corps, near the DMZ, the build-up was so obvious that the Marines called for reinforcements. Westmoreland ordered elements of the 1st Cavalry and American divisions from the coastal areas to move north into Thua Thien Province, around Hue.

The big question was, would the enemy attack in force before Tet, during Tet, or after Tet? Westmoreland concluded the attack would come before Tet; his intelligence chief, Brigadier General Phillip B. Davidson, thought it would come after Tet. Neither believed it would come during Tet; that was such a sacred holiday that the enemy would not interrupt it and thus incur the wrath of the South Vietnamese, the very people the Viet Cong hoped would arise and fight *with* them.

Official Washington had been fully alerted—by Admiral Sharp and General Westmoreland through military channels, by Ambassador Bunker through diplomatic channels. Only the American people seemed surprised. President Johnson put it this way in his memoirs: "Looking back on early 1968, I am convinced I made a

As the fighting raged in Saigon in early 1968, the bodies of Communists littered the streets near the Old French Cemetery (top), in the Cholon section of town (above), and in the city's center. In one of the most spectacular photographs of the war (right), the South Vietnam National Police Chief, Brigadier General Nguyen Ngoc Loan, encounters a Viet Cong officer and shoots him dead near the Quảng pagoda.

mistake by not saying more about Vietnam in my State of the Union report on January 17. In that address I underscored how intensely our will was being tested by the struggle in Vietnam, but I did not go into details concerning the build-up of enemy forces or warn of the early major combat I believed was in the offing. I relied instead on the 'background' briefings that my advisers and I, as well as the State and Defense departments, had provided members of the press corps for many weeks. In these briefings we had stressed that heavy action could be expected soon."

At this time, Saigon was crawling with a media corps approaching one thousand people and reflecting every shade of world opinion. It is still not clear today why this "secret" never seeped out of Saigon, a city where nothing was secret for very long. To some it would seem the American media was acting out a self-fulfilling prophecy—the Americans had lost the war, and only the last battle remained; when it came, they would trumpet it for what it would be, defeat. In any event, that is what happened.

Tet fell at a very convenient time in 1968; convenient for the enemy, that is. The Year of the Monkey, the lunar New Year, would actually start on Tuesday, January 30. In order to extend the holiday time, the South Vietnamese government decreed that Tet would fall on Monday, making Sunday New Year's Eve, the start of a three-day celebration. It was customary for the South Vietnamese military to return to their home areas to celebrate the holidays.

Westmoreland was so concerned he took the matter to President Thieu, who finally agreed to cut the customary cease-fire to thirty-six hours; Westmoreland had wanted it shortened to twenty-four hours. Fifty percent of all ARVN troops were supposed to be on full alert. Westmoreland could not give orders to Vietnamese troops, but for American forces he canceled the cease-fire entirely in the two provinces nearest the DMZ.

The enemy offense opened early on Tuesday morning, January 30. Not in one stroke, but in a ragged action, almost as if the orders had been scrambled in the North Vietnamese attacks. Before dawn on Tuesday, the Communists attacked in three areas. In I Corps the action came at Da Nang and at Hoi An, also on the coast, ten miles south of Da Nang. In II Corps the firing began at the important coastal cities (and U.S. bases) of Qui Nhon and Nha Trang, and in the three most important provinces of the Central Highlands—Kontum (6), Pleiku (8), and Darlac (11). All three provincial capitals came under attack—Kontum, Pleiku, and Ban Me Thuot, the capital and chief city of Darlac Province. In addition a district capital, Tan Canh, near Dak To, twenty-five miles north of Kontum City, was attacked and captured. At Pentagon East, General Davidson looked at the push-pins in his map and said to Westmoreland, "This is going to happen in the rest of the country, tonight or tomorrow morning."

It did. By dawn on Wednesday at least eighty thousand North Vietnamese and Viet Cong forces were on the attack against a hundred cities and towns from the DMZ to the Mekong Delta. The Americans were ready everywhere and sprang into action. This was what the United States command had hoped for—a frontal attack, in the open, by an enemy whose entire strategy had been built on guerrilla tactics.

He was giving away the strongest weapons he had—stealth, surprise, and disengagement. For Westmoreland and company it was a dream come true. All the stops were pulled out—American mobility, armor, artillery, and air power were unleashed.

The assault began before dawn in Saigon, the grand prize for the enemy. General Westmoreland's phone rang about 3 A.M.; the United States embassy was under attack, although there was no military advantage in it. A special squad of Viet Cong sappers placed a satchel charge against the outside of the compound wall, detonated it, and quickly scrambled through the hole onto the embassy grounds. The first two sappers through the hole were killed by two military police, who also died in the exchange of fire.

Then the firing inside the compound became general and rattled on until dawn, when U.S. airborne troops landed on the roof of the chancery. By that time all fifteen sappers had been killed; not one had gotten inside the embassy. Five Americans and four Vietnamese were also dead. The military battle of the embassy was

The Tet 1968 offensive was the Communists' supreme bid for victory, and the U.S. embassy in Saigon was a key target. Before dawn on January 30, a special squad of Viet Cong blasted a hole in the compound wall at the U.S. embassy (left) and rushed the embassy building. All 15 Communists were killed, including these two (below), and none penetrated the embassy building.

South Vietnamese regulars sweep a still burning Saigon sector (above); the U.S. 9th Division's "Pink Pussy Cat" personnel carrier works a Saigon suburb (left), and Vietnamese pick the rubble (below).

over; the political battle had just begun. For reasons which psychologists are still probing, the Battle of the Embassy assumed, in American media minds, something of the proportions of a combined Battle of the Bulge and Dien Bien Phu.

Actually, the battle for Saigon, carefully planned by the Viet Cong, went badly for the enemy right from the start. Besides the failure at the embassy, there was disappointment everywhere. By careful infiltration in the days before Tet, the Viet Cong had placed about forty-five hundred troops inside the city. They had strolled in dressed as peasants or ridden in on bicycles, produce carts, trucks, or vans. Many had entered the city in coffins, along with their weapons, in what seemed a sudden rush of funerals.

By whatever means, they had arrived, and at the outbreak of hostilities—so the plan went—the natives in Saigon would arise and join them for the slaughter of the Americans. It never happened. There was fierce fighting, including mortar and rocket attacks from the outskirts of the city, but nothing seemed to succeed for the Viet Cong. They could not capture the police headquarters, the radio station, or any other vital spots. The people did not rise to support them; in fact, many civilians were butchered in their homes by the supposed "comrades."

The Thieu government quickly rallied its seven thousand troops, and the Americans threw in four thousand more from nearby bases. "We have come to liberate Saigon," many of the Viet Cong shouted as they called for help. But it was no good. Their command post in the An Quan pagoda fell to South Vietnamese marines, and quiet—the quiet of martial law—fell over the city. All bars, theaters, and public places were closed, and the streets were littered with the bodies of civilian dead, garbage, and the wreckage of burned and shattered buildings and vehicles. With the hyperbole common in the American press, one newsman referred to the city as "Stalingrad with palm trees."

Of far greater importance was the fact that the Tet offensive was a failure for the enemy. The South Vietnamese—both military and civilian—performed well. Nowhere did the Viet Cong succeed, except in Hue and a few small towns. There was no uprising, except to fight off the Viet Cong. Only a few American bases came under attack. There was heavy fighting around Tan Son Nhut and Bien Hoa, but there and throughout the country the enemy was quickly beaten off. Within days, most battles were over, with two exceptions: at Hue, the nation's third city, and at an outpost called Khe Sanh, in the northwest corner of South Vietnam.

In multi-battalion raids on the Tan Son Nhut and Bien Hoa airfields on the night of January 31, the enemy was severely mauled by American and Vietnamese defenders. The raiders struck Bien Hoa at 3 A.M., but were thrown back with 139 killed and 25 captured as against the loss of 4 Americans killed and 26 wounded. Only two planes were destroyed in the assault, and seventeen damaged.

The enemy losses were even higher when the Communists hit Tan Son Nhut field at 3:20 A.M., with 157 enemy killed and 9 captured, for a loss of 23 Americans killed and 86 wounded. The South Vietnamese lost 30 killed and 89 wounded, but not a single plane was destroyed, although thirteen were damaged. These were, by far, the largest air base raids of the war. The enemy threw in large forces and learned a very costly lesson.

Mortars got this F-100 Supersabre at Bien Hoa, but the VC never cracked its perimeter (top), nor did they do so at the big American base at Long Binh (center) or Khe Sanh, here with smoke screen protecting the northern perimeter (bottom).

The enemy never got near the main prize at Da Nang during Tet '68, but lost a mountain of weapons (above). Meanwhile Da Nang's Bridge Ramp piers kept working (below).

The major attack against an American base was that against Long Binh, fifteen miles northeast of Saigon, near Bien Hoa, a huge base for command, supply, and combat forces. When a Viet Cong regiment attacked the base perimeter, it found itself up against Colonel Frederick E. Davison's 199th Infantry Brigade. The guerrillas were soon surrounded and crushed. (Davison was later promoted to become the Army's first black general officer since World War II.)

American civilians were also victims of the Tet offensive. In the highlands around Ban Me Thuot, Michael Benge found himself ringed by men pointing AK-47s at him. "Surrender; humane treatment," they called out. With those machine guns, Benge had little choice. His career as a farming adviser for the U.S. Agency for International Development (AID) was at an end; a new career, POW, was beginning.

Within days Benge watched "trials" for many of the young men he had been teaching. Then the AK-47 boys slaughtered all the South Vietnamese they had captured. Benge was taken away, along with two other Americans who had been working in the area—Betty Ann Olsen, a nurse at the leprosarium in Ban Me Thuot for the Christian Missionary Alliance, and Henry F. Blood, who had been translating the Bible into Montagnard as a missionary with the Summer Institute of Linguistics. Miss Olsen knew seven missionaries of her group had been murdered, and Blood had been torn away from his wife and three children.

All spring and all summer, Benge, Blood, and the nurse were on the trail with their captors, first into Cambodia, then aimlessly, going nowhere, and steadily weakening from bad food and bad treatment. Blood, the oldest at fifty-three, died first, probably of pneumonia and malnutrition. The other two buried him, somewhere in the jungle. Then Betty Ann, thirty-three, died, toward summer's end. The leeches were terrible near the end, dropping off the trees and sucking her blood. Mike Benge tended her carefully, but he could not save her. He buried her by the trail, in some secluded spot. Mike went on, into the final hell of a Hanoi prison, and the final miracle of 1973, release, and back home to Oregon.

Hue was mainly a Vietnamese tragedy. The city had been taken easily, by stealth, early on January 31, and when the populace arose the Viet Cong flag was flying above the Citadel, a walled portion of the city on the Perfume River. The only Americans in the city were a small advisory group of MACV and a few Army people assigned to the ARVN 1st Division. Most of them were rescued the first day by a U.S. Marine battalion, but it took twenty-five more days of fighting before the city of 140,000 was recaptured.

Only then was the Viet Cong's bestiality exposed. The guerrillas had entered the city well prepared with death lists—their own countrymen they planned to kill. Some observers watched in horror as the Viet Cong went from street to street with clipboards containing the names of those scheduled for death. In all, nearly three thousand residents of Hue were massacred, including nuns, women and children, whole families, many of them buried alive. When the mass graves were opened, many innocent civilians were found sitting upright where the bulldozers had piled sand over them. Among the victims at Hue were a half dozen American civilians, two French priests, a German doctor and his wife, and several Filipinos.

Members of the U.S. 101st Airborne Division honor their dead near Hue as the enemy forces retreat in defeat and disarray.

Three U.S. Marine battalions helped in the relief of Hue, alongside eleven ARVN battalions. The Marines suffered 142 killed; the South Vietnamese lost 384. Over five thousand of the enemy were slain in the city, another three thousand in the outskirts by Allied forces that included the 1st Cavalry Division. The Viet Cong flag came down on February 25, and the South Vietnamese flag went up.

By the end of February the main thrust of the Tet offensive was over. The enemy had been crushed in one of the most disastrous campaigns of military history. He had thrown a force of about eighty-five thousand troops against thirty-six of the nation's forty-four provincial capitals, five of its six autonomous cities, and sixty-four of the two hundred forty-two district capitals. He had suffered defeat everywhere, and had paid the price of at least thirty-seven thousand killed in battle. Americans killed to this point totaled 1,001, and South Vietnamese dead 2,082.

There remained one other battle, at Khe Sanh, a U.S. Marine outpost less than ten miles east of the Laotian border. It had started early on the evening of January 2, when a Marine guard dog sniffed danger and barked. A Marine patrol found a party of six men and opened fire, killing five of them. They were all North Vietnamese officers, up to regimental commander.

In the next few days further probes disclosed that elements of two North Vietnamese divisions were nearby, the 325C and 304th divisions. The Marine Command immediately doubled the Khe Sanh defense force to four battalions, three from the 26th Regiment and one from the 9th Regiment. An ARVN Ranger battalion was also added, and one CIDG company, for a total force of about six thousand.

General Westmoreland decided to hold Khe Sanh. It was a roadblock protecting

205

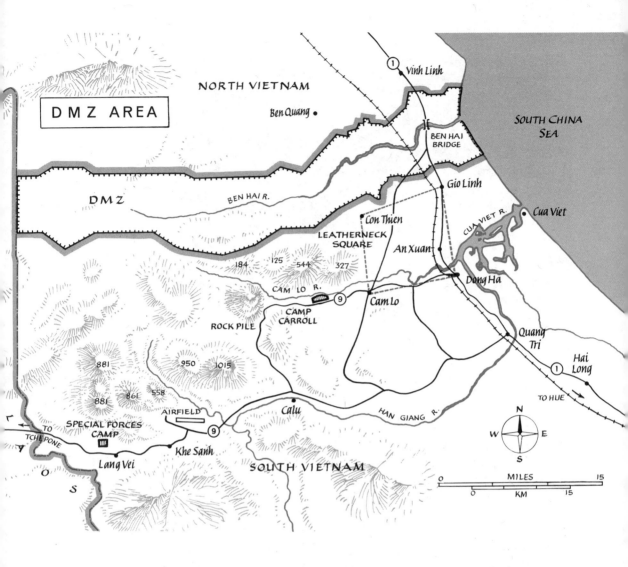

the entire coastal plain; if the enemy came through he could cut off Allied forces holding the DMZ and could flood into the coastal cities. Furthermore, Khe Sanh offered an ideal site from the American military viewpoint. The defenders could be supplied by ground, or by air if necessary, and could call on overpowering artillery and air support. Meanwhile, the two massed enemy divisions would give the Americans just the target they wanted. The enemy could be hammered to death on the anvil of Khe Sanh. That's the way it happened.

But Westmoreland had not figured on a third force, the American media. Within days Khe Sanh was turned into a "siege," then a "desperate siege," then "another Dien Bien Phu." It was never any of those things. It was, without question, a severe and testing battle, with fury and noise enough to frighten some Americans at home, including President Johnson. There were stories that he roamed the White House corridors in the early hours, in slippers and bathrobe, and haunted the "situation room" in the basement, seeking the latest word from the battlefront. Friends said he

206

Tet '68 is over and American forces have never been stronger, as attested by the U.S. military headquarters for Vietnam, nicknamed Pentagon East, at Tan Son Nhut (top); the Pleiku switchboard, manned by 43rd Signal Bn. (above left); and the Christmas Tree heliport at Camp Holloway, in the Central Highlands (above right).

looked haggard and his voice was hoarse. There were reports that at one point he summoned the generals and admirals and wanted them to "sign in blood" that Khe Sanh would not fall.

Westmoreland had a plan, and it was working: Pinpoint the enemy and then hit him with artillery and bombs. The pinpointing was done by Marine patrols, air reconnaissance, radio intercepts, radar, and the use of hundreds of ground sensors, transplanted from the abandoned McNamara's Wall. Once the enemy was located, the weight of iron that could be placed on him was terrifying. The Marines used 105s and 155s, plus mortars and 106-mm recoilless rifles. The Army added sixteen tubes of 175-mm guns, hurling seven-inch shells 20 miles.

From mid-February on, tactical air added three hundred sorties daily, and the B-52s made 2,602 sorties, with devastating effects.

The B-52s, guided by the most sophisticated battlefield electronics seen until that time, laid down thousands of tons of bombs with incredible precision, to within a thousand yards of Marine lines. The artillery, firing fifteen hundred rounds daily, blanketed the area to within four hundred yards of the Marine perimeter. The Marines on the ground handled the rest. With fences, dogs, grenades, small arms, and courage, they held the perimeter. In the ultimate hand-to-hand fighting they fell on the North Vietnamese in trench and bunker with fury rarely seen, even in Marine annals.

Even the old noncoms were surprised. They had wondered how the young and untested Marines would hold up. They needn't have worried. For the entire battle the Marines held the airstrip, the Khe Sanh plateau, and all the surrounding hills. Esprit was at its highest, and it never faltered. By late March the jungle had been torn to shreds, and so had the enemy. He fell back into Laos. Tet was over, and North Vietnam was so badly beaten it could not launch another major offensive for four years.

General Westmoreland immediately went over to the offensive. There was heavy fighting ahead for the rest of the year. The enemy forces that had been scattered at Tet, both Viet Cong and North Vietnamese, must now be rounded up, annihilated, or chased back across the borders. But even as the troops were winning the ultimate battle in the field, they were losing it in the supreme headquarters, the White House.

President Johnson, who hated to make decisions, was being forced to make them. He had to decide what to do about Vietnam. Johnson was losing ground in the political polls; he was losing ground in his own political party, and he was losing ground in his own administration. In late February, Johnson sent General Wheeler to Saigon, on yet another mission.

Wheeler arrived there, covered with Washington gloom, and found Westmoreland full of hope and plans. The Americans were at top strength, the enemy was being severely wounded, and now was the time to take the offensive. Westmoreland even began planning to pursue the enemy into his sanctuaries in Cambodia and Laos. He thought, perhaps naïvely, that many Americans could now see victory ahead, as he did. Even the South Vietnamese seemed to smell victory. Tet had been

In this photo, captured in War Zone D, Viet Cong act out their chants and slogans to show their "high degree of ideological awareness" (left). On the battlefield, however, they give up Soviet-made 37-mm AAA gun (center left), thousands of rounds of ammo (center right), hand grenades made with old soda cans (bottom left), and a 107-mm rocket launcher (bottom right).

(Left) During the Tet offensive, General Westmoreland confers with Ambassador Bunker and General Wheeler, chairman of the U.S. Joint Chiefs of Staff, who is in from Washington at Tan Son Nhut. (Right) In June, Westmoreland turns over command in South Vietnam to General Creighton W. Abrams.

a great morale builder for the South Vietnamese troops. The Viet Cong offensive had not only failed, it had backfired. The ARVN felt the Viet Cong had betrayed their own country. For the first time, the people saw the North Vietnamese as intruders, and the Viet Cong as traitors.

Westmoreland went right back to his Optimum Force plan of 1967. Of the two hundred thousand troops discussed then, he wanted about half, some one hundred and eight thousand, in the coming months. The other half could be held in the United States, to be called forward in 1969, if needed. Wheeler took the tidings back to Washington and went through a grueling series of meetings. The answer came on March 4, at the end of a long meeting in the White House. The President turned to Wheeler and said: "Tell him [Westmoreland] to forget the one hundred thousand. Tell him twenty-two thousand is all we can give him at the moment."

The war had peaked out. Westmoreland never got the additional twenty-two thousand; he got half that number. The next Sunday, the New York *Times* headline read: "Westmoreland Requests 206,000 More Men, Stirring Debate in Administration." The *Times* had it only partly right; Johnson had finally made two decisions: No more troops for Vietnam, and he was bailing out.

This was an extremely low point for Johnson. He had lost control of the Vietnam problem; his health was declining; and deficits and inflation were plaguing his administration. Worst of all, 1968 was a presidential election year, and Bobby Kennedy was threatening to run against him. What could he do now? It was time for

Johnson's nationwide television address, which he had been planning for at least six weeks. At 9 P.M. on Sunday night, March 31, the President reported to the people on Vietnam and other national problems. He also had a surprise. Johnson had alerted American diplomats in all major capitals of the world to arrange to listen by radio. At the last minute the President asked General Wheeler to telephone General Westmoreland in Saigon with a message: The President was about to act on "the matter I had informed him of last November." Only a few friends in the White House learned the secret, and then only minutes before air time. The President, looking drawn and tired, droned through his text for forty minutes, and wound up with two surprises. The first was the bombing halt. After months of debate within the administration, he had made a decision, once again a compromise, a partial bombing halt.

"Tonight I have ordered our aircraft and our naval vessels to make no attacks on North Vietnam, except in the area north of the demilitarized zone, where the continuing enemy buildup directly threatens Allied forward positions and where the movements of their troops and supplies are clearly related to that threat."

Then came the biggest surprise, as the President read the words that he had filed into the teleprompter just before nine o'clock:

"With America's sons in the fields far away, with America's future under challenge right here at home, with our hopes and the world's hopes for peace in the balance every day, I do not believe that I should devote an hour or a day of my time to any personal partisan causes or to any duties other than the awesome duties of this office—the presidency of your country.

"Accordingly, I shall not seek, and I will not accept, the nomination of my party for another term as your President.

"But let men everywhere know, however, that a strong, a confident, and a vigilant America stands ready tonight to seek an honorable peace—and stands ready tonight to defend an honored cause—whatever the price, whatever the burden, whatever the sacrifice that duty may require.

"Thank you for listening. Good night and God bless all of you."

Johnson had laid down the burden. "It was all over and I felt better," he wrote in his memoirs. Just before the broadcast he had told Walt Rostow, a trusted adviser, what was coming. Rostow made no comment until Johnson prodded him, then he said "that as lame ducks it would be hard for us to get all the things done that we would like to do, but that we would give it a good try."

The American POWs—nearly five hundred were now in North Vietnamese torture prisons—heard about the President's speech very quickly. Their guards began taunting them that Johnson was being driven from office and Westmoreland had been pulled out of Vietnam in disgrace. (He had just been named Army Chief of Staff.) The Communists were winning the war, said the jailers, and the antiwar party now held power in the United States. The President's decision was a blow to the POWs, but some struggled to keep hope alive. The real answer, some believed, was that Johnson and the Communists had come to some kind of an agreement. The war would soon be over and they'd be going home.

211

Communist supplies are flooding into North Vietnam, as shown by this photo of a Chinese freighter unloading in Haiphong harbor in April, even as President Johnson orders a halt to the bombing of the country.

Hanoi announces on July 18 that it will free these three U.S. Air Force pilots: (from left) Major Fred N. Thompson, Major James F. Low, and Captain Joe V. Carpenter. Hundreds of other American POWs suffered in enemy prisons until the war ended, and at least 72 Americans died in the prisons as a result of brutal treatment.

Within weeks, that hope faded and the POWs began rooting for Nixon. So were the North Vietnamese. They believed their chances of a good settlement would be better under a new administration. The Americans were losing hope, and decided to just wait it out. Curiously enough, the South Vietnamese government felt the same way. Thieu and Ky crossed off Johnson and were content to wait for the American election. They were sure Nixon would win.

The "peace talks" did open in May, in Paris, but it was quickly apparent they were going nowhere. The delegations argued for weeks over the shape of the conference table, and who could sit at it. All parties concerned were clearly waiting for the American elections; nothing substantive would happen until the new regime came to power in 1969. Until then, America was a ship with no one on the bridge. The new commander in chief would not even be named until November, and could not take the helm until January 1969.

Now the nation could forget the war that everybody hated. But what about the half million Americans in the field?

They must keep on fighting, and dying, but the nation could turn to other things. When it came time for the newspaper editors of the country to vote on the Associated Press' Top Ten Stories of 1968, the Vietnam war had dropped to number seven position. In 1966 and 1967 it had been number one. Vietnam had been upstaged by Apollo 8, by President Johnson's withdrawal and the campaign for his successor, by the double assassinations—the Reverend Martin Luther King, Jr., in April, and Senator Robert F. Kennedy in June—and by the Russian invasion of Czechoslovakia.

But the war in Vietnam was like a juggernaut that could not be stopped. The battle for Khe Sanh had ended as undramatically as it had begun. Toward the end of March the enemy had begun disengaging, thoroughly whipped. The relief of the

213

American-built bases in Thailand come into full use in 1968. A B-52 takes off from U-Tapao (top), and an F-4E Phantom lands at Korat (above).

Marine garrison was also low-key, nothing like Chinese Gordon and the relief of Khartoum.

As the enemy ebbed away, General Westmoreland organized twenty-one battalions of troops (seventeen American and four ARVN), spearheaded by the 1st Cavalry Division and the Marines, into Operation Pegasus. This force marched into and through the Khe Sanh area cleaning out enemy remnants as it went. There was

All through 1968 it was nothing but mud and water through the Delta for U.S. troops. A 9th Infantry Division Unit fords yet another stream in Operation Coronado V near Cam Son (above left) and waits in mud for the artillery near My Tho (above right). A unit of the 199th Light Infantry Brigade pushes west across the paddies and marshes (below).

An Army crane helicopter delivers a new bridge, by air, in I Corps (left); an M-577 keeps communications open for the Big Red One in III Corps (below left); and a 9th Division gunner sights a .50-caliber machine gun at Dong Tam base in the Delta (below right).

great joy at Khe Sanh, and throughout the U.S. forces in I Corps. The North Vietnamese had been slaughtered. Said Colonel David E. Lownds, the Marine commander at Khe Sanh: "My kids will be very happy to get out of here."

But at home, the media paid little attention. Walter Cronkite had given up the fight as early as February 27, when he said on the evening news that he had been "too often disappointed by the optimism of American leaders." A few days later, newscaster Frank McGee of NBC declared that "the war is being lost."

Other commentators ranged from humor to vitriol.

Art Buchwald had said in his column of February 6:

"General George Armstrong Custer said today in an exclusive interview with this correspondent that the battle of Little Big Horn had just turned the corner and

216

he could now see the light at the end of the tunnel. 'We have the Sioux on the run,' General Custer told me. 'Of course we will have some cleaning up to do, but the Redskins are hurting badly and it will only be a matter of time before they give in.' "

Arthur Schlesinger, Jr., the historian, succumbed to the "field marshal" psychosis that raged among the intelligentsia. He declared that Khe Sanh should have been abandoned promptly. In a letter to the Washington *Post* on March 22, he said the Americans were kept there "because Khe Sanh is the bastion, not of the American military position, but of General Westmoreland's military strategy—his 'war of attrition' which has been so tragic and spectacular a failure."

The 1st Cavalry Division did not have time to read its press notices. Without stopping at Khe Sanh it turned south into the A Shau valley for Operation Delaware, April 19–May 17. It joined the 101st Airborne Division, elements of the 196th Infantry Brigade, the ARVN 1st Division, and other South Vietnamese troops in cleaning out the uplands behind the coastal cities of Hue and Da Nang.

All in all, Tet was a great military victory for the Americans and the South Vietnamese. Lieutenant General Robert E. Cushman, Jr., the Marine commander in I Corps, estimated the enemy lost 33,500 killed, the equivalent of seventy-four battalions, in his command area in the first three months of 1968. Tet and its aftermath, by the best estimates, cost General Giap about a hundred thousand troops killed in action. By the end of 1968, he later admitted, six hundred thousand of his troops had been killed in battle since 1965. He had never scored a victory against American forces, and he never would.

But no matter the facts; by mid-year the war was psychologically lost on the home turf. Westmoreland never forgot his last meeting with Johnson in the presidency. The President took him on a helicopter ride in April over a Washington still smoking from fires set by rioters. "It looked considerably more distressing than Saigon during the Tet offensive," said the general.

President Johnson had one more act to play out before he left the scene. He went on national television at 8 P.M. Thursday, October 31.

"All air, naval, and artillery bombardment of North Vietnam will cease at 8 A.M. Washington time, Friday morning," he said. "I have reached this decision . . . in the belief that this action can lead to progress toward a peaceful settlement of the Vietnam war . . . What we now expect—what we have a right to expect—are prompt, productive, serious, and intensive negotiations in an atmosphere that is conducive to progress."

In the North Vietnamese prisons the American captives were stunned. Certainly no American President would abandon them without some concessions from the Communists? At the very peak of American power had he conceded all, for nothing in return? Had Korea been forgotten so quickly, where 12,700 Americans had died during two years of "truce negotiations"?

America had surrendered in Vietnam, lacking only a formal ceremony. Half a million Americans, still engaged in daily battle, were left in the field. For the troops, only one question remained: "How the hell do we get out of here alive?"

Part III

"PEACE WITH HONOR"

12

"About Face!"— Withdrawal Begins 1969

RICHARD Milhous Nixon brought the first new thinking to the Vietnam problem in the twenty-five years that it had existed. Johnson had been a follower,
sort of a committee chairman running a consensus machine, trying to please everyone. Nixon was a leader, a pragmatist with a shrewd understanding of world geo-
politics. He saw even before his election that the war was a liability, destroying the
nation from within. He also saw through the myth that world communism was a
monolith; cracks were already apparent in the Soviet Union/Red China wall.

Soon after his narrow win over Hubert H. Humphrey in November 1968, Presi-
dent-elect Nixon took a step that had historic consequences. He asked a forty-five-
year-old Harvard political scientist to meet him in New York. Henry Alfred Kissinger was puzzled by the invitation, and the first meeting went cautiously, on both
sides. At further meetings, Nixon offered Kissinger an unusual post carrying the
title of National Security Adviser. As it turned out, one of Kissinger's principal
tasks was to help Nixon formulate and execute a policy to solve the Vietnam
problem. This was a heady assignment for Kissinger, a Jewish intellectual of modest background who had escaped Hitler in 1938, had become an American citizen
in 1943, and since 1957 had been sheltered under the Cambridge trees of academe.

The Nixon/Kissinger policy did not spring to life full grown, but was gradually
defined in the early months following Nixon's inauguration. As Kissinger put it in
his memoirs: "It seemed to me important for America not to be humiliated, not to
be shattered, but to leave Vietnam in a manner that even the protesters might later
see as reflecting an American choice made with dignity and self-respect." The
alternatives, as Kissinger summed them up, were to withdraw at once, in any
fashion, heedless of world opinion, or to withdraw at an orderly pace, seeking
shelter under the slogan of "peace with honor."

President Nixon, the new commander in chief, confers early in 1969 with Henry Kissinger, his National Security Adviser. Their plan wrought critical changes in South Vietnam, and 1969 saw a drop in American casualties, the beginning of U.S. troop withdrawal, and stronger pressure on the enemy in both Cambodia and North Vietnam.

Nixon chose the latter. As he had put it in a major campaign address: "The precipitate withdrawal of all American forces from Vietnam would be a disaster, not only for South Vietnam but for the United States and the cause of peace." After twenty-five years in the Indochina morass, the United States had erased the word "victory" from its vocabulary and replaced it with the word "withdrawal." As in any other addiction, withdrawal would bring excruciating pains.

On the battlefront, the year 1969 started off on a low key, and for a time it seemed there would be no repeat of Tet '68. The enemy was only slow in starting, and on February 20 he launched an offensive against more than one hundred populated places. There were no major frontal attacks against the cities, as in the previous year. The Viet Cong and North Vietnamese had reverted to their earlier, more successful tactics of guerrilla warfare. They were not successful this time, but the cost in blood to American and South Vietnamese forces was high. The attacks usually opened with rocket and mortar shelling from the jungle, which provoked the old response of Allied patrols on search-and-destroy missions.

On February 23, the one-day cost was 208 Americans killed in action, the highest single day's toll since January 31, 1968, the opening day of that Tet offensive. For the first months of 1969, the war was costing four hundred American lives per week, as against some two hundred per week in the last six months of 1968. One week in March, 1969, American deaths totaled four hundred fifty-three.

Something had to be done, and was: Operation Menu was launched. This was the code name for a B-52 bombing campaign against enemy sanctuaries on the Cambodian side of the border. It became one of the most controversial campaigns of the war, but only in America. American military leaders had been pressing for such a campaign for over a year. President Johnson had refused to give permission, even though these bases were clearly costing American lives.

The North Vietnamese bases, brazenly set up on Cambodian territory just a few miles from the South Vietnamese border, gave the enemy a great advantage. He could build strength at these bases, stretching four hundred miles from the DMZ to the Gulf of Siam, and attack into South Vietnam at will, retreating across the border in safety when the fighting got too hot. Many efforts had been made to shake Johnson—through members of Congress, through powerful friends in his own party, even through such national figures as General Eisenhower.

It had been to no avail. Even when Cambodia's leader, Prince Norodom Sihanouk, had indicated he "would not object" to American "hot pursuit" across his eastern border, Johnson's answer had still been "No." In his last year in office, he drew even tighter rein on American air power.

Nixon changed that. On February 11, barely in office, he authorized Operation Menu. Even before inauguration, Nixon had asked Kissinger for "a precise report on what the enemy has in Cambodia and what, if anything, we are doing to destroy the build-up there. I think a very definite change of policy toward Cambodia probably should be one of the first orders of business when we get in."

General Creighton Abrams, Westmoreland's successor, was delighted, pointing out that no Cambodians lived in the target areas; the North Vietnamese had driven them from their homes and villages. In addition to enemy arms coming down the Ho Chi Minh trail, military intelligence estimated the Communists had brought in at least ten thousand tons of Russian arms in 1968 through the port of Sihanoukville. (Documents captured in 1970 showed the actual tonnage "far exceeded" the American military estimates.)

Plans for the B-52 offensive were started immediately. Elaborate secrecy was decreed, even to setting up a separate reporting system in the Department of Defense to conceal the raids. All sorties were to be flown at night, all bombing was to be under ground radar control at the site, and all targets were to be reported as being in South Vietnam. Only the date for launching the campaign was left open.

Nixon himself made that decision, on February 23, when he was en route to Brussels for a NATO meeting. In response to the Communist offensive launched two days earlier, the President radioed from Air Force One the command to begin Operation Menu at once. Cooler heads, including Kissinger's, prevailed; launching such a campaign just before the NATO meeting would not be wise. Nixon postponed Operation Menu, but planning went forward.

The first raids would be limited to five miles inside Cambodia and there would be no public announcements, but press stories were to be ready in case the enemy protested the raids. Part of the planning directed that "the State Department is to be notified [of the initial raid] only after the point of no return . . ."

223

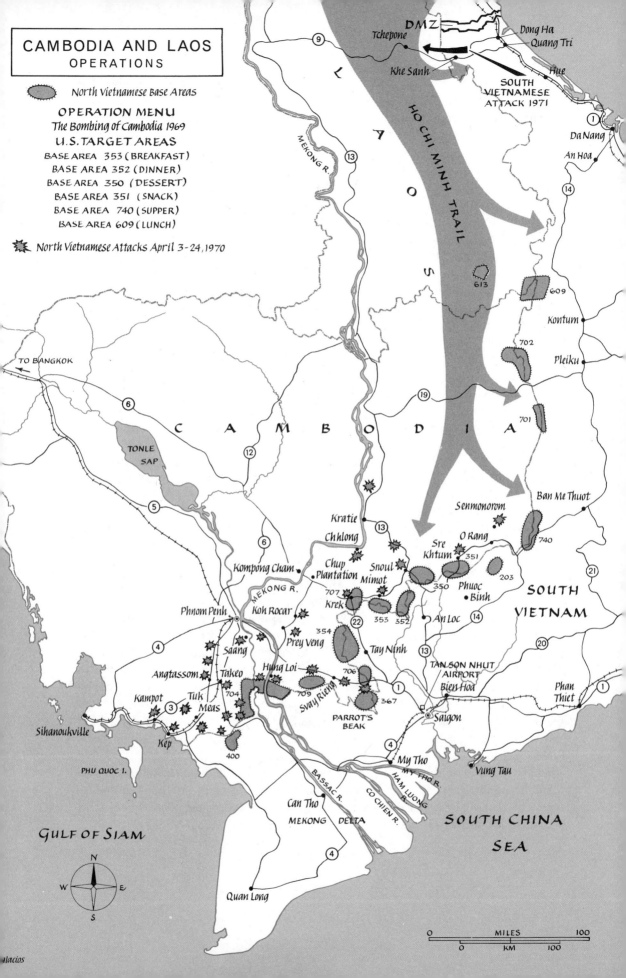

CAMBODIA AND LAOS
OPERATIONS

North Vietnamese Base Areas

OPERATION MENU
The Bombing of Cambodia 1969
U.S. TARGET AREAS

BASE AREA 353 (BREAKFAST)
BASE AREA 352 (DINNER)
BASE AREA 350 (DESSERT)
BASE AREA 351 (SNACK)
BASE AREA 740 (SUPPER)
BASE AREA 609 (LUNCH)

North Vietnamese Attacks April 3-24, 1970

DMZ
Tchepone
Dong Ha
Quang Tri
Khe Sanh
Hue
SOUTH
VIETNAMESE
ATTACK 1971
Da Nang
An Hoa

L A O S

HO CHI MINH TRAIL

9
13
14
613
609
Kontum
702
Pleiku
19
701

C A M B O D I A

TO BANGKOK

6
TONLE
SAP
5
12
6
Ban Me Thuot
Senmonorom
Kratie
Chhlong
13
O Rang
Sre
Khtum
351
203
740
Kompong Cham
Chup
Plantation
Snoul
Mimot
350
Phuoc
Binh
SOUTH
VIETNAM
21
707
Krek
An Loc
14
Phnom Penh
Koh Rocar
353 352
22
354
Prey Veng
Tay Ninh
13
20
Saang
Hung Loi
706
TAN SON NHUT
AIRPORT
Bien Hoa
Phan
Thiet
1
Angtassom
Takeo
709
Svay Rieng
367
1
Kampot
Tuk
Meas
704
PARROT'S
BEAK
Saigon
3
4
Sihanoukville
Kep
400
My Tho
MY THO R.
Vung Tau
PHU QUOC I.
HAM LUONG R.

MEKONG R.

BASSAC R.
CO CHIEN R.

GULF OF SIAM

Can Tho
MEKONG
DELTA

SOUTH CHINA
SEA

4

Quan Long

N
W E
S

0   MILES   100
0   KM   100

Palacios

The Marines' role in I Corps dropped in 1969 and Army forces gradually took over. First Division marines fight south of Da Nang in March (above left). Army artillery pours on the fire to protect 101st Airborne units near Phu Bai in June (above right). Seabee engineers build a new bridge near Dong Ha, close to the DMZ, in August (below left). Troops of the 101st Airborne move in to clean out a hot spot in the A Shau Valley in late September (below right).

The battleship returns to military life as the USS New Jersey *fires a full salvo of nine 16-inch projectiles into enemy shore positions in South Vietnam in early 1969.*

Kissinger said later, "We saw no sense in announcing what Cambodia encouraged and North Vietnam accepted." For, in fact, neither nation made any announcement of the raids or protested them. As far as Kissinger was concerned, North Vietnam was clearly violating international law by using a third country's territory for war bases without permission. The raids, in his view, were well within the scope of the Hague Convention of 1907, in that Cambodia was "unwilling or unable to defend its neutral status."

The closest Nixon came to revealing anything unusual being prepared was when he told a news conference on March 14 that "We have issued a warning [to North Vietnam]. I will not warn again." The next day, the North Vietnamese fired five giant rockets into Saigon, and Nixon gave the order for Operation Menu to begin.

The first raid, nicknamed Breakfast, took place on the night of March 18 against Base Area 353 (see map, p. 224). This was in the Fishhook, where Tay Ninh Province (21) joins Binh Long (22) in III Corps, only fifty miles north of Saigon, an area long controlled by the Viet Cong. Bomber crews reported spectacular results, with seventy-three secondary explosions, about five times the normal expectation. Base 353 was clearly a major enemy supply depot for ammunition, gasoline, vehicles, and arms.

Not a word leaked out of Hanoi about the raid; General Giap obviously did not wish to call attention to bases he never admitted having. Only the American media gradually leaked the bombing program, with overtones of outrage, but Menu went on full tilt until May 26, 1970. In that period, the B-52s flew 4,308 sorties, some up to thirty kilometers inside Cambodia, and dropped 120,578 tons of bombs. General Abrams said later, "Menu has been one of the most telling operations in the entire war." There is no question that it saved many American lives.

After the opening raid, Nixon personally approved five more Menu raids in May: Dessert, against Base 350, just north of the Fishhook; Snack, at the west end of Phuoc Long Province (III 18); Supper, against Base 740, west of Quang Duc Province (II 13); Lunch, against Base 609, bordering Kontum Province (II 6), and Dinner, against Base 352, at the very tip of the Fishhook.

After that, since results were so salutary and since the enemy was not protesting, control of Operation Menu was passed to General Abrams and the local commanders. The raids went on, with results so good that Cambodia ceased to be a threat until 1970, when Prince Sihanouk was overthrown and took refuge in China.

Throughout the rest of the spring, ground fighting continued heavy in all areas except in III Corps. The Saigon area was strangely silent. Operation Menu was hurting the enemy from the air, and American and South Vietnamese troops applied heavy pressure in both the Fishhook and the Parrot's Beak. These areas, once belonging to the Viet Cong, were now Allied territory, for the first time in the war.

One American ground offensive got heavy media attention in 1969: the cleaning out of the A Shau Valley in I Corps, west of Da Nang and Hue. The Americans had abandoned this area in 1966, lacking the forces to hold it, but from 1968 on it was largely under American control. American patrols swept the area regularly, without serious opposition, until early May 1969, when a battalion of the 101st Airborne Division ran into enemy opposition.

Clearing the enemy out, with the help of South Vietnamese troops, took nearly a month, and would normally have been routine. However, one of the area's features, Ap Bia Mountain, which General Abrams ordered taken for military reasons, quickly acquired the media nickname of Hamburger Hill, with semantic overtones of chopped meat. Together with TV photo footage (some unrelated to the fighting), Ap Bia soon came to rival the Battle of Stalingrad on American television sets.

At home, war opponents sounded off from all sectors. Senator Edward M. Kennedy of Massachusetts, the Democratic whip, put on his field marshal's cap and declared that such attacks were "senseless and irresponsible." Senator Mike Mansfield of Montana, another Democrat, said that instead of such fighting the United States should "apply pressure in Paris. That is where peace is going to be made, not on the battlefield." Ap Bia, or Hill 973 (in meters, or 3,075 feet), cost the Americans forty-six killed and three hundred eight wounded. The North Vietnamese lost five hundred ninety-seven men killed alone.

After Ap Bia, quiet did fall on the battlefields, and for good reason. President Nixon announced the first withdrawal of American troops from Vietnam. This was, of course, good news for Hanoi; Ho Chi Minh and General Giap had been calling for American withdrawal since 1965. For the Americans in the field, it was an epochal announcement that came about this way.

The bare outlines of Nixon's Vietnam strategy could be seen, by close readers, even before his inauguration. As the strategy evolved, it had two parts:

227

The Mekong Delta, once an enemy stronghold, now belongs to the Allies. American forces make their last patrols there in the spring of 1969 (top; center), but by summer the turnover to South Vietnamese forces was in full swing and the U.S. Navy and the Army's 9th Infantry Division pulled out, leaving behind such installations as this floating base off Nam Can, at the far southern tip of Vietnam (bottom).

At Ben Het in June 1969, an Army Caribou drops supplies, and 1,200 fresh troops move in to protect this base in Kontum Province, near the Cambodian border. The Communists threw in everything, including Russian tanks, but Ben Het was held in a two-month steady battle.

"Vietnamization," or turning the war over to the forces of South Vietnam, and withdrawal of American forces. By March, Nixon had begun to fill in the details. Withdrawal—the most emotional part for Americans—would begin shortly, and its speed and dimension would depend on three criteria:

1. The ability of South Vietnam to defend itself without American troops.
2. The rate of progress in the Paris peace talks.
3. The level of enemy activity.

From spring on, pressure began to mount at home. Most Americans, even the hawks, welcomed Nixon's determination to get American troops out; the main discussion related to the speed of withdrawal. Would it be at a seemly pace, or in unseemly haste? Even Nixon didn't know then; both he and Kissinger hoped it would be under circumstances that would not injure the United States in the eyes of the world.

But a start had to be made, and it came at an unlikely place: Midway Island, a tiny sand island in mid-Pacific, the locus of a famed naval battle in World War II, remote from any other land mass and now inhabited mainly by the infamous gooney birds. Why Midway? Just because it *was* remote.

President Thieu had been invited to meet President Nixon, but not in the United States. The administration feared Thieu's presence in America might cause disrup-

Fighting slowed during 1969 in the Saigon sector but patrols were constant, as these troops of the 1st Cavalry Division sweep the Quan Loi rubber plantation 65 miles north of the capital (top). Cam Ranh, a full-grown city (above left), is moving U.S. forces both in to fight the enemy, and out to go home, as the first big troop withdrawals get under way. Technicians service a switchboard at the II Field Force Headquarters, Long Binh, outside Saigon (above right).

tions, even riots. But Thieu could be shown off at Midway under controlled circumstances; the island had limited facilities for media housing and communications.

En route there, Nixon stopped at Honolulu on June 7 and that afternoon met the military leaders at the Kahala Hilton. There he broke the news: The first American withdrawal from Vietman—twenty-five thousand troops—would take place in August. Kissinger said he found it "painful" to watch General Abrams get the word.

230

"He knew then," said Kissinger, "that he was doomed to a rear-guard action, that the purpose of his command would increasingly become logistic re-deployment and not success in battle."

The next day the presidential entourage, numbering over five hundred people in all, descended on Midway and welcomed Thieu to the island. The two presidents met in the commandant's house while the lesser hordes repaired to the officers' club. Nixon and Thieu talked for ninety minutes and then it was deadline time for the American media. Nixon emerged from the house and, speaking from the steps, gave the news to the world. The first Americans would be out of Vietnam in sixty days. There was an air of jubilation in the Nixon party, and even Thieu was happy, or so he said; his country now had an opportunity to prove itself.

The elation began to evaporate almost immediately. In the United States the political magpies began pecking withdrawal to pieces. They wanted more withdrawal, they wanted it faster, they wanted this outfit home, this one out next, this one out now. They wanted the credit for whatever was done, and none of the blame for the things that couldn't be done.

The American military saw nothing but problems, but set about executing the Commander in Chief's policies, however unwelcome they might be. For the career military there is little glory or promotion in winding down a war, especially a losing one.

For the troops going home, it was sheer ecstasy; for the troops not going home, or not yet, anxiety and hope, or despair; for the troops still heading for Vietnam, or soon to be ticketed, utter gloom; and for the millions of parents and loved ones at home, there was happiness at an early return, hopes and fears for those left at the front, and despair and anger at those not yet called.

It didn't take long for the pressure to build and for Nixon to understand that withdrawal had a life of its own. For the next three years, the President would have to wrestle with the problems of extrication from Vietnam—daunting problems involving human emotions, national objectives, international honor. Johnson had tried to hide from Vietnam's problems and was destroyed; Nixon tried to face them and he, too, would be destroyed.

That war claimed another victim, the United States military. When allowed to fight, it had given an honorable account of itself. When the nation deserted its own forces in the field, the military lost the rewards that sustain any soldier—duty, honor, country. From March 31, 1968, the night of President Johnson's speech, the nation's sense of defeat was exported to South Vietnam with nearly every soldier sent there. The seeds were sown throughout the rest of 1968, and they began to sprout in 1969. Morale, discipline, élan, spirit, call it what you will, eroded steadily.

The Marines had seen it coming and the command was worried, right up to the commandant of the corps. It was no accident that the Marines, who had been the first into Vietnam, would also be the first out. The Marines had disliked Vietnam from the start; it was not their kind of war. From the day that Johnson became a lame duck, the Marine command began planning for withdrawal, and with Nixon's election the bargaining began. The final bargain struck was that all Marines would

WITHDRAWAL OF MAJOR U.S. ARMY AND MARINE UNITS
Total Withdrawn: by Increments
A — Army   M — Marines

Increment Number	Date	Number Withdrawn	Units Withdrawn
I	8/69	25,000	A – 1st and 2nd Brigades, 9th Inf. Div. M – 9th Reg., 3rd Div., plus aviation and service units, for 8,388 total
II	12/69	40,500	A – 3rd Brigade, 82nd Airborne Div. M – Remainder 3rd Div., plus aviation and service units, for 18,483 total
III	4/70	50,000	A – 1st Inf. Div. and 3rd Brigade, 4th Inf. Div. M – Various units, for 12,900 total
IV	7-10/70	50,000	A – 3rd Brigade, 9th Inf. Div. and 199th Inf. Brigade M – Various units, for 17,021 total
V	12/70	40,000	A – 1st and 2nd Brigades, 4th Inf. Div. 1st and 3rd Brigades, 25th Inf. Div.
VI	4/71	60,000	A – 1st and 2nd Brigades, 1st Cav. Div. 2nd Brigade, 25th Inf. Div. M – Various units for 10,600 total
VII	6/71	29,300	A – Various units M – Last Marines leave, 14,000 total
VIII	8/71	28,700	A – 173rd Airborne Brigade and 1st Brig., 5th Inf. Div. (mechanized)
IX	11/71	42,000	A – 23rd Inf. Div. (American); 11th Inf. Brigade and 198th Inf. Brigade
X	12/71 – 1/72	45,000	A – 101st Airborne Div.
XI	2-4/72	70,000	A – 5 infantry battalions, 6 air cavalry battalions, other units
XII	6/72	20,000	A – 196th Inf. Brigade (last Army combat brigade to leave). 3rd Brigade, 1st Cavalry Division. Other small units
XIII	8/72	10,000	A – Various small units
XIV	11/72	12,000	A – Final miscellaneous units

President and Mrs. Nixon and Henry Kissinger arrive in Saigon, July 30, 1969, in Air Force One and are greeted by General Abrams and Ambassador Bunker.

be out of Vietnam by July 1971, and they were. Of the 25,000 troops to be withdrawn in Increment I, 8,388 would be Marines. By the end of 1969, the entire 3rd Division was gone. As one officer said: "We fought to get our forces out of Vietnam and we did."

The Navy had begun to leave even earlier, favored by circumstances. Johnson slashed the role of the aircraft carriers with his 1968 bombing embargoes. Thereafter, the carriers and their support structure went on virtual standby duty. As the construction boom in Vietnam wound down, the Seabees began going home, three battalions in 1968 and nine more in 1969. The third, and final, aircraft carrier disaster struck on January 14. The nuclear-powered *Enterprise,* the world's largest warship, burst into flames from an accidental rocket explosion. Heroic work by the crew saved the ship, at a cost of twenty-eight lives and injury to hundreds of men.

In the Delta, turnover time began early in 1969, for the Navy, the Coast Guard, and the Army's 9th Division. The Navy's River Assault Division 91, with twenty-five boats, was turned over to the South Vietnamese Navy on February 1, and in June sixty-four more Navy assault craft went to the Vietnamese. In the same month, the 9th Division began pulling out. Said the commanding officer: "The Vietnamese were now ready to take over." On August 25 both the 9th Division and the Mobile Riverine Force were inactivated, and the Navy closed off its supply line at California; all construction equipment and materials were put on "hold." When the Seabees departed they took some equipment with them, but left behind asphalt plants, rock crushers, and other primary equipment useful in building roads, bridges, and buildings for Vietnam.

On July 30, Vietnam had an unexpected visitor, President Nixon. He flew in unannounced, on a world trip, to the consternation of his security force, and he landed in Saigon; no one-hour stops, like Johnson's at Cam Ranh Bay, for him. Nixon helicoptered from Tan Son Nhut to the downtown palace of President Thieu, then out to Di An Camp, twelve miles from the city, for small talk with troops of the Big Red One division, then on to the next stop, Bucharest. As he departed Saigon, he let fly one last remark: This great city will "never become Ho Chi Minh City."

There was a brief flare of fighting in August, as the North Vietnamese and Viet Cong forces attacked many towns and bases across Vietnam, including Cam Ranh Bay. These were mostly small forays or rocket and mortar attacks, and they were quickly suppressed. (So exotic was American electronic equipment by now that it could track incoming fire, target the source, and reply within minutes with devastating counterfire.)

But the scare traveled all the way to the summer White House at San Clemente and led President Nixon to announce a delay in Increment II of the withdrawal. He was quickly deluged with outrage by congressmen and media. Never again did the President try to delay an announced withdrawal, and never again did one withdrawal increment end without the next one being announced. Thus, in August, Nixon reconfirmed Increment II, the withdrawal of 40,500 more troops for December. Once again, a high proportion would be Marines, a total of 18,483 this time.

Racial trouble had already erupted in the Marine Corps, when blacks assaulted a group of whites at Camp Lejeune, North Carolina, in mid-July. One Marine, a nineteen-year-old, was mortally injured and died a week later. On August 11, at least sixteen Marines were injured in racial fights at the Kaneohe Marine Air Base in Hawaii. It was clearly time to act, and on September 2 the Marine Corps commandant issued ALMAR 65, an order to the entire Corps, designed to stamp out all vestiges of discrimination. This order also approved some special changes for blacks —the modified Afro haircut was now permitted, and Black Power salutes were to be accepted on informal occasions.

The Army had also acted to cool racial tensions. Early in 1969, General West-moreland, now U.S. Army Chief of Staff, appointed a special team headed by Lieutenant Colonel James S. White, a black. The team made a quick tour of Army installations around the world and discovered that the hour was already late. Its report led to "alleviating programs" that may have helped when real trouble came. The fact is that 1969 brought a very dangerous commodity—idle time—to all branches of the military in Vietnam. The races—white, black, and Hispanic—segregated themselves on base and off. Mix in the summer heat and cold beer, and an explosive mixture was formed. Sometimes it detonated, like the night someone threw a live hand grenade through the door of a crowded enlisted men's club on base in I Corps.

Add drugs, prostitution, the black market, desertion, and the general decline in Army quality, and real trouble was guaranteed. It erupted in 1968, at a place called My Lai, but it didn't come to light until 1969.

Early in April, reports began to surface that many inhabitants of the village of My Lai, in Quang Ngai Province (I 5), south of Chu Lai, had been wantonly murdered by American soldiers. It was said that at least a hundred, and perhaps up to six hundred villagers, including many women and children, had been butchered on March 16, 1968.

On September 5, 1969, First Lieutenant William C. Calley, Jr., twenty-six, was charged with slaying "at least" 109 Vietnamese civilians. On the day of the massacre, Calley had been commanding officer of the 1st Platoon, Company C, 1st Battalion, 11th Infantry Brigade, 23rd (American) Infantry Division. Staff Sergeant David Mitchell, twenty-nine, a squad leader in Calley's platoon, was charged on thirty counts of assault with intent to commit murder. At one time or another, dozens of

Lieutenant William Calley (center), charged with 102 counts of murder in the My Lai incident, shown here with his military attorney, Major Kenneth Raby (at Calley's right), arriving in Saigon.

Army officers were under investigation, either in the My Lai incident itself or in efforts to cover it up. Lieutenant Calley was the only person convicted in the My Lai case. He was first sentenced to hard labor for life, but after a series of appeals and reviews his conviction was overturned by a federal district court in 1974. In all, Calley served three years under house arrest at Fort Benning, Georgia.

My Lai was the worst instance of the breakdown in American military discipline in Vietnam, but there were others. The case of the Green Berets broke in the media on August 6, when the Army announced that Colonel Robert B. Rheault, former commanding officer of all three thousand Special Forces troops in Vietnam, and seven other officers and enlisted men "are being held pending investigation of charges growing out of the fatal shooting of a Vietnamese national." The victim was Thai Khac Chuyen, an agent assigned to watch enemy movements in Cambodia. The story was that the Green Berets suspected Chuyen was a double agent who worked for the North Vietnamese and consulted with the CIA. Chuyen was reportedly shot and his body put in a weighted sack and dropped in the South China Sea. In any event, Chuyen was never seen again.

The case quickly escalated into a scandal in the United States, especially after a lawyer said he had "evidence to prove that the CIA has ordered the killing and effectuated the killing of over a hundred people in South Vietnam in the past year." The CIA denied this and any connection with Chuyen's disappearance. Adherents on both sides, including congressmen, alternately praised and attacked the work of the CIA and the Green Berets. An attorney for one of the Special Forces officers, Major Thomas C. Middleton, Jr., complained that the accused were being held in solitary confinement under brutal conditions at the Army stockade at Long Binh, twelve miles north of Saigon.

In September, Secretary of Defense Melvin Laird ordered the defendants out of solitary, and at the end of the month the Army abruptly dropped the entire case. Secretary of the Army Stanley R. Resor said the CIA had refused to provide any witnesses "in the interests of national security" and thus the defendants could not receive a fair trial. They were being released immediately and "will be assigned to duties outside Vietnam." President Nixon's only involvement, according to the White House, was to approve the CIA's decision not to provide witnesses. Colonel Rheault retired from the Army within a month, and Chuyen's widow, who had threatened to kill herself and her two children, was given $6,472 as a "missing person gratuity."

Early in August, after five days of heavy fighting in the highlands west of Chu Lai, A Company, 3rd Battalion, 196th Infantry Brigade, had had enough. Ordered to make another try against a jungled hill, Lieutenant Eugene Shurtz, Jr., reported to the battalion commander by field phone that his men refused to move. Lieutenant Colonel Robert Bacon replied: "Repeat that phrase. Have you told them what it means to disobey orders under fire?" Shurtz said he had, but "some of them have simply had enough. There are boys here who have only ninety days left in Vietnam. They want to go home in one piece." A couple of old noncoms eventually talked the young draftees back into action, but the incident was typical of a changing war. The same theme, with variations, was being played out on all fronts. The 196th was a good outfit; Vietnam had ruined it. Nobody wanted to die for a nameless piece of real estate, and especially when other guys were going home. There were no brass bands waiting and no parades at home; alive was better than dead.

Just a month earlier, on July 8, General Abrams had bid farewell at Tan Son Nhut to the first GIs going home. To the 814 men of the 3rd Battalion, 60th Infantry, 9th Division, the "Old Reliables," he said: "You have fought well, under some of the most arduous and unusual combat conditions ever experienced by American soldiers. You are a credit to your generation." Someone yelled, "Okay, Aircraft No. 1, let's go," and the transports began taking off. After nearly a quarter century in Vietnam, America was cutting the cord.

At home, it was not another "long, hot summer" of burning cities, as in 1968, but unrest grew as fall came on. There were marches, rallies, even a "Moratorium," a national demonstration for an end to the war. On October 15, Martin Luther King's widow led 30,000 people past the White House in a candlelight procession. A month later, 250,000 people marched in the largest antiwar demonstration yet. Its slogan was: "Bring home the troops. All the troops. Now."

Henry Cabot Lodge quit the peace talks in Paris, saying "the other side has flatly refused to respond to all proposals in any meaningful way." President Nixon announced: "We have gone as far as we can or should go in opening the door to negotiations that will bring peace." In Saigon, Vice President Ky stated: "To make one more concession is nothing but surrender."

The demonstrations at home did not move Nixon. "To allow government policy to be made in the streets would destroy the democratic process," he said. In a nationwide television address in November, Nixon said of the Paris talks: "The effect of all the public, private, and secret negotiations can be summed up in one sentence: No progress whatever has been made except agreement on the shape of the bargaining table."

Withdrawal of troops would proceed, he said, but "if I conclude that increased enemy action jeopardizes our remaining forces in Vietnam, I shall not hesitate to take strong and effective measures to deal with that situation. This is not a threat. It is a statement of policy."

Appealing for patience at home, the President declared: "Once the enemy recognizes that it is not going to win its objectives by waiting us out, then the enemy will negotiate and we will end this war before the end of 1970."

Public response to the speech was strong and favorable. The Gallup Poll showed support of the President at 58 percent, and in fact during all of 1969 public support for Nixon's stand on the war had never gone below 44 percent.

For one small band of Americans, the prisoners of war, 1969 brought some relief. It came with the death of Ho Chi Minh, announced to the world on September 3 by Radio Hanoi. There was genuine sorrow in some circles at the passing of the seventy-nine-year-old Communist warrior. To some he was a national patriot and hero, a father figure of great warmth and compassion. To many people throughout the world he was an arch-murderer and terrorist. To the POWs, he had symbolized

Unrest bubbles at home, as marchers protest the war at the White House in April 1969 (top). In October the other side, protesting the protesters, burns the Viet Cong flag in Washington over coffins containing the names of American war dead (center). Meanwhile, near Chu Lai, troops of the Americal Division rush into a hot spot with nearly half the men wearing black armbands to show their sympathy with the anti-war protesters (bottom).

At his last rally in June 1969, Ho Chi Minh exhorts his people to carry on fighting. By September he is dead at 79. Ho is flanked in this picture by his ultimate successor, Premier Pham Van Dong, left, and two other officials, right.

the very worst in torture and bestiality. Many an American prisoner had died and disappeared under Ho Chi Minh's rule. What would his death bring?

To their joyous surprise, life for the POWs quickly improved. Cell walls were knocked out, so the Americans could be together, at least occasionally. The covers came off the cell windows and the eternal darkness ended. There was more and better food, more time for exercise, and the cigarette ration was doubled, to six per day. By October the men were getting three meals a day, instead of two, and there was even hot tea.

Obviously, there had been a big change in policy. Some guards confessed they had been wrong in torturing their prisoners. One of them, the Cat, recited as if by rote that the Vietnamese had been good to prisoners for thousands of years but that in the case of the Americans he and the other guards had "misinterpreted and misapplied this policy."

None of this was announced publicly, and the Red Cross was never allowed into the prisons. Under Ho Chi Minh, Hanoi had never furnished lists of prisoners, and the dead were never accounted for. In hundreds of American homes, thousands of loved ones lived lives of anguish, never knowing if their men were dead or alive.

President Nixon's first year in office had not brought peace, but it had brought hope. Within months of his inauguration, he had reversed the Vietnam tide of war, the first fundamental change since 1945. Instead of America's blood and resources flowing to a tiny spot on the map of Southeast Asia, the Americans were at last extricating themselves. Nixon topped off the year with a Christmas present for the nation. He announced Increment III in the withdrawal—fifty thousand more Americans would be coming home by April of the new year.

Hanoi saw the year differently. The Communists' year-end summary, widely published and distributed to the people in North Vietnam, saw only victory ahead. The Americans had been defeated, it said, and their withdrawal had already begun. According to the summary, "This is a new opportunity, which demands that we make greater efforts in all fields of operations in order to gain a great victory."

13

Winding Down
1970–71

THE VIETNAM war was a long time dying, and the pain was great for all concerned. On the military side, the United States continued its withdrawal of
troops. About 140,000 more came home in 1970, and another 160,000 in 1971.
Vietnamization began to take hold and American casualties declined sharply. The
last major combat role for United States ground forces did not take place in South
Vietnam, but in the Cambodian jungles just across the border.

This action was foreshadowed early in 1970 with the overthrow of Prince Sihanouk, Cambodia's chief of state. On March 18, while Sihanouk was in Moscow,
Premier Lon Nol seized power in an attempt to head off a Communist takeover of
his country; but in the following weeks the Communists strengthened their hold on
a large part of the country, particularly the areas near the South Vietnamese border, and closed in on the Cambodian capital, Phnom Penh. President Nixon felt the
Communist advance menaced Saigon itself, and decided the North Vietnamese
bases in Cambodia should be wiped out. An offensive into Cambodia would test the
effectiveness of Vietnamization, he believed, and he ordered General Abrams to
begin planning.

There would be two main thrusts into areas well known to the military, the
Parrot's Beak and the Fishhook, just northwest of Saigon. No Americans would
take part in the Parrot's Beak operation. The incursion into Cambodia was almost
entirely a South Vietnamese operation, and it had spectacular success. The United
States supplied advisors, medical aid teams, tactical air support, some troops, armor
and vehicles, and logistical backup.

The offensive was first announced in Saigon, by the Thieu government. Nixon
made his personal decision to go ahead on Sunday night, April 26; he was under no
illusion as to what the reaction would be at home, although even he could not have
imagined the civil upheaval to come. William P. Rogers and Melvin R. Laird,

241

Americal Division troops gas up an M 155 Sheridan tank at Tam Ky during a March 1970 sweep north of Chu Lai (top), while another Sheridan rolls north out of Tam Ky (bottom).

Some Marine units were going home, but for the air units there was still a busy war ahead. These shots at the fully developed Da Nang base show an A-6 Intruder taking on a bomb load (top), a pair of RF-4B reconnaissance planes poised in their concrete revetments (center), and an EA-6A electronic surveillance plane ready for takeoff (bottom).

Nixon's Secretaries of State and Defense, respectively, opposed American participation, but Nixon had the full backing of the military, of Kissinger, and of Ambassador Ellsworth Bunker.

The South Vietnamese Army, about twelve thousand strong, crossed the border into the Parrot's Beak on April 29, with the B-52s out in front. At almost the same time, the mixed U.S./ARVN group penetrated the Fishhook, and the battle was on. In Washington, Nixon went on national television on Thursday night, April 30. The Communists, he said, had responded to withdrawal of American troops by increasing the tempo of war throughout Indochina. "To protect our men who are in Vietnam and to guarantee the continued success of our withdrawal and Vietnamization programs, I have concluded that the time has come for action," he said. "If, when the chips are down, the world's most powerful nation, the United States of America, acts like a pitiful, helpless giant, the forces of totalitarianism and anarchy will threaten free nations and free institutions throughout the world."

The morning after his speech, Nixon was at the Pentagon early for a briefing. Looking at the huge situation map he noted that the Parrot's Beak and the Fishhook were marked as enemy strongholds, and that four other areas were also marked. Between the ARVN and American forces, he wanted to know, "could we take out *all* the sanctuaries?" The briefers seemed unhappy, fearful that the media and Congress would not approve. Nixon, nettled by this negativism, thought for a moment and then said, "I want to take out all of those sanctuaries! Make whatever plans are necessary, and then just do it! Knock them all out so that they can't be used against us again. Ever!" As a result, enemy bases all along the Cambodian border came under attack in the next three weeks, some by South Vietnamese forces, others in combined operations with United States troops.

The Cambodian operation lasted two months. According to intelligence sources, the North Vietnamese had about five thousand regulars in the sanctuaries and some forty thousand Viet Cong. They were routed, with over ten thousand known casualties, and in addition lost elaborate permanent bases and vast amounts of equipment.

One underground base, "the City," contained miles of tunnels, with over three hundred bunkers and eight hundred camouflaged huts. In thirteen major operations, the Allies captured enough individual weapons to arm fifty-five enemy battalions, along with 1.5 million rounds of ammunition, a basic load for fifty-two thousand troops. Enough crew-served weapons to equip ninety battalions were also seized, along with tons of food and enemy documents.

The long-term gains were even bigger. The Communists were knocked out in Cambodia for two years. In addition, Lon Nol's forces closed the port of Sihanoukville to the enemy until the spring of 1975, when Cambodia went down to the Communists along with South Vietnam.

By the end of June, all American troops were out of Cambodia, but nearly forty thousand South Vietnamese troops remained in the area to prevent the return of the enemy. The United States lost 339 killed in the Cambodian operations and 1,501 wounded. Forty-three American aircraft were lost. The South Vietnamese losses were 800 killed and 3,410 wounded. Sir Robert Thompson, the British expert on

Units of the U.S. 11th Armored Regiment roll through the Snuol rubber plantation inside Cambodia, rooting out the Communist forces who thought they could find refuge just outside Vietnam (top). A happy GI of the 4th Infantry Division reclaims a box of new American .45-caliber pistols at an enemy arms cache 50 miles west of Pleiku while his buddy inspects one of the weapons (above).

jungle warfare, declared the offensive had bought two years' time for the Allies. In fact, the North Vietnamese were impotent until their spring offensive of 1972, their final attempt at military victory, and their final defeat while the United States still had a part in that war.

But there was no winning at home. Cambodia had unleashed the full power of the media and the dissidents; a new element now entered the picture—the radicals' burning and bombing. On May 3, only days after Americans had gone into battle in Cambodia, two youths set fire to the Army ROTC building at Kent State University in Ohio and burned it to the ground. Governor John Rhodes, terming the radicals "worse than the brownshirts" of Hitler, sent the National Guard to the campus. The following day, around noon, a crowd of demonstrators, some students, and some outside agitators began throwing rocks and other missiles at guardsmen. Firing broke out, and soon four students lay dead on the domestic battlefield. That was not the first violence and anarchy and it was not the last; nor was it confined to the academic community, though many an administration had lost control of its student body.

In a rash of arson and murder across the country, banks, school buildings, public buildings, even libraries and research centers were attacked. Troops and police were called out to guard the President of the United States and his home, the White House. The President, concerned for the lives of his children, arranged special

Thousands of demonstrators in Washington turn out in fine May weather to protest against the Vietnam war.

protection for them. The tormentors gloated that the President was a prisoner in his home, so he deliberately made public appearances to prove he was not.

Through it all, Nixon's standing in the polls remained high. The group that he dubbed "the silent majority" was clearly supporting the administration. Nonetheless, the nation had its own combat casualties at home. More than ten persons were killed and hundreds of civilians were injured (including many on-duty police). Thousands of persons were arrested in nearly two thousand demonstrations coast to coast.

The incredible irony was that the nation suffered this bloodletting while its elected leaders were struggling to end the war. Americans were coming home by the thousands; the draft calls were dropping and soon would end entirely. On the diplomatic and political fronts Nixon and Kissinger fought to bring Hanoi to some reasonable terms.

In one of the most exciting chapters of the diplomatic war, Kissinger met in February 1970 with Le Duc Tho, a founder of the Vietnamese Communist party and trusted confidant of Ho Chi Minh. The first meeting was in Paris, and over the next months there was a series of meetings in that city and in secret hideouts in its suburbs. For a time, Kissinger flew secretly to Paris every Friday afternoon, met with Le Duc Tho, and was back at his Washington desk by Monday, trying to appear "rested" after a quiet weekend at home. It seemed, for a while, that Le Duc

Constantly traveling on secret missions for Nixon, Henry Kissinger spends many hours in flight reading up for his next stop, be it Paris, Peiping, Pakistan, or wherever.

Tho was really interested in an end to the warfare, but the mood passed, and the Paris initiative was broken off, for the time being.

But beyond Paris, Kissinger was playing out an even larger drama—the break in the Communist front. The monolith was crumbling, a matter of far greater import to the world than Vietnam.

It was a secret battle, but an exciting one in the historical perspective. As early as 1968, Nixon and Kissinger had perceived cracks in the Communist structure, and once in office they pursued every opportunity to widen the split. By early 1971, word was leaking out that the Chinese would welcome a visit from President Nixon. In the utmost secrecy, Kissinger visited the Chinese capital July 9–11, while the world thought he was ill in Islamabad, the capital of Pakistan. The Chinese leaders received Kissinger cordially, and made it clear that American support against the Soviet Union would be welcome. President Nixon would electrify the world the next year with his visit to Peiping.

The principal military action in Vietnam in 1971 was Lam Son 719, an attempt by the South Vietnamese to cut the Ho Chi Minh trail in Laos. It had a limited success, probably delaying the North Vietnamese invasion another year, into 1972. Once again, it caused an uproar at home, the media joining forces with dissidents to portray the campaign as a military disaster for the United States. Actually, no American ground forces crossed into Laos; the only American support across the border was air cover and transport.

Lam Son was a daring concept that suffered from faulty execution. As planned by General Abrams and his staff, the 101st Airborne Division would seal off the DMZ and attack westward through Khe Sanh to the Laotian border. The ARVN 1st Division would pass through and cross the border on Route 9, heading west for Tchepone (Muang Xepon), twenty-five miles inside Laos. Airborne ARVN troops would drop on Tchepone and move east to meet the invading armor on Route 9 from the west. The object: Destroy enemy installations and supplies and prevent invasion of I Corps by the North Vietnamese. American armor and artillery had to stop at the border; that was the law: Congress had cut off all funding for American forces in Cambodia as of July 1, 1970, under the so-called Cooper-Church Amendment.

Nixon approved Lam Son and the press was briefed in Washington, under embargo—and promptly leaked it. Lam Son got off on January 30, but soon stalled, and the media began predicting defeat. According to plan, Tchepone was to be occupied as soon as possible, and not later than February 22. The South Vietnamese, fighting without American troops, played the offensive too slowly and cautiously.

The air assault on Tchepone didn't come until March 3 and was never fully successful. To critics, it looked like the ARVN wanted to get to Tchepone only so it could retreat. By March 8 it was pulling back under orders to destroy Communist Base Area 611 on the retreat. Actually, the retreat was more like a rout. As the

ARVN troops, operating with their own helicopters, now control the Delta and are shown boarding with packs, water jugs, and rifles for a foray into the Mekong River country.

South Vietnamese got nearer the border they came under the umbrella of American artillery, but some troops had to be extricated by helicopter. In the evacuation, some soldiers mobbed the rescuing helicopters. There were dramatic pictures of the choppers taking off with South Vietnamese soldiers hanging from the landing skids, obviously panicked.

Officially, Operation Lam Son cost the enemy over 19,000 casualties, and there was no Communist offensive in 1971. The Laos operation was accompanied by several forays into Cambodia by South Vietnamese troops. One of these was against Chup, opposite Tay Ninh Province in III Corps, where the North Vietnamese were building a new base. This operation, led by General Do Cao Tri, went well until February 23, when the general was killed in a helicopter crash. The operation collapsed.

Lam Son ended early in April, at a cost of 176 Americans dead and 1,042 wounded. The ARVN paid a higher price: 1,146 dead, 4,245 wounded. Also among the casualties was a helicopter load of combat photographers, shot down on February 10 over Laos. Besides the plane crew, those killed were Larry Burrows of *Life*

The Lam Son operation, a push by native troops into Laos to cut the Ho Chi Minh trail, was a fiasco despite American backup. Cambodian troops, shown in training, volunteered to help the South Vietnamese (above), and Americal Division troops pushed to the Laos border but were ordered to stop there (left). In the rout that followed, Laotian refugees await flight into South Vietnam and safety (below).

magazine, Henry Huet of the Associated Press, Kent Foster of United Press International, and Keisaburo Shimamoto, representing *Newsweek*. In all, the Vietnam war took the lives of more than fifty journalists and cameramen. As the Laos operation closed out, so did Increment VI of the withdrawal—over 265,000 American troops had gone home since Nixon came to office.

The year 1970 brought the American military the worst internal problems it had ever known. Morale and discipline were falling; crime and drugs were rising; and even the Marines were not immune. On Thursday night, February 19, 1970 (by ironic chance the twenty-fifth anniversary of D Day at Iwo Jima), the commanding officer of Company B, 1st Battalion, 7th Regiment, sent out a five-man "killer patrol" in the Que Son valley south of Da Nang. Enlisted men said later their orders were to "get some damned gooks tonight." Sappers, guerrillas, and ambushes had been taking a heavy toll on Company B, and the men on patrol were tired, frustrated, and angry.

They moved into Son Thang, a hamlet populated by known Viet Cong families,

Where My Lai once stood is now just a potato field, surveyed by a nearby farmer, a survivor of the massacre, and his children.

and began calling people out of the huts. A woman ran for the tree line and the Marines opened fire. In minutes, sixteen Vietnamese were dead—five women and eleven children. It was My Lai on a small scale, even to the attempted cover-ups and the trials. The lance corporal leading the patrol was acquitted of all charges; two privates served one year; another was acquitted of all charges; and the fourth turned prosecution witness, escaping all charges.

Vietnam also added a new word to the military lexicon: *fragging*. It meant throwing or rolling live fragmentation grenades, or using other lethal weapons, against your own side, usually superiors you didn't like. In 1970, the Army had 271 cases of actual or suspected fragging, and in the same year the 1st Marine Division had 47 fraggings. In the worst case, the night of February 5, a Marine tossed a grenade into a crowded enlisted men's beer hall, killing one Marine and wounding 62 others.

Late in 1970 the Marines instituted Operation Freeze to combat fragging. Upon report of an incident, the unit involved was immediately isolated by special teams. Any Marine from another unit was immediately arrested, and roll was called to see if any unit members were missing. All leaves and rotations were cancelled, and individual interrogation began. The interrogators could promise protection, including transfer out of Vietnam, to anyone who gave information. These methods usually resulted in finding suspects and arresting them. Only then could the unit's normal privileges be restored.

Prevention was also stressed. Access to grenades and other explosives was tightened; surprise inspections were conducted; and officers were trained to watch for suspicious actions. All this, and the big troop reductions of 1971, put fragging back into proportion. In 1971, only two fraggings occurred before the Marines were gone from Vietnam.

Drugs, too, became a serious problem in 1970—both drug trafficking and drug using. Southern Asia had been the opium center of the world for centuries, and the war in Vietnam supplied not only plenty of money but also thousands of pushers and users. Almost any drug desired was available, from hashish to heroin, and there was no shutting off the supply; it was an important part of the economy of Southern Asia, from the poppy farms of Thailand and China down to the pushers in Da Nang, Saigon, and the villages.

The U.S. Army first treated drugs as a criminal problem, with a program based on prosecution and dishonorable discharge. But by 1970 drugs had become a social and medical problem, so an amnesty program was begun in the 4th Division during the summer. Drug users who turned themselves in were promised treatment and a chance at honorable discharge. The Marines stayed tough until the fall, but then moved to an amnesty program and a special campaign, the administrative discharge. The dishonorable discharge route took too long and involved too much red tape. Using the administrative discharge, commanders could get rid of Marines with a record of "substandard performance of duty, numerous minor discipline infractions, or diagnosed character behavior disorders." The 1st Marine Division used this rule to get rid of 121 cases in 1969, and a booming 809 bad Marines in

1970. The real "solution," however, was to go home, and as withdrawal went steadily on, all the military's problems—drugs, alcoholism, violence, crime—were simply exported back to the United States, where they turned into a civilian problem that lasted a generation.

One particular aspect of the war that caused extreme anguish in the United States was the case of Americans classified as missing in action (MIA) or prisoners of war (POW). Throughout the war the North Vietnamese demonstrated a barbarous attitude toward American prisoners, both in personal treatment and in the release of information. Thousands of Americans suffered physical torture in the prisons while their loved ones at home suffered psychological tortures of uncertainty. North Vietnam released only the information it wanted to, and inflicted

Homeward bound, salvaged American military equipment awaits shipment at Da Nang. In military parlance, this was a "retrograde operation."

further pain by inviting to Hanoi only those Americans it knew would aid their side.

The United States at one time or another listed 4,705 Americans as either POWs or MIAs and used every avenue it could conceive of to bring pressure on Hanoi. It was to no avail, and the POWs became one of the most wrenching issues of the war. In all the bargaining to end the conflict, the United States never compromised on the POWs. Their safe return was a prerequisite to any settlement.

Many schemes were considered for relief of the POWs; one was executed—the raid on a prison camp at Son Tay. In the summer of 1970, a photo interpretation expert in Washington, examining reconnaissance photos, discovered that one of them showed stones and other objects arranged in a North Vietnamese compound in such a way as to carry a message: "55 Americans are in prison here, 6 need immediate rescue." The site was Son Tay, twenty-five miles west of Hanoi. With the

On a shattered Vietnam hillside, a lone American still stands guard in this Pulitzer prize–winning photo of 1971, made by David Kennerly.

approval of President Nixon, a special rescue team began training at Eglin Air Force Base in the Florida panhandle.

On Friday night, November 20, a party of 56 commandos took off in three HH-53 helicopters from the U.S. air base at Udorn, in northern Thailand, on a 300-mile sortie into the heart of North Vietnam. The helicopters were refueled over Laos, found the target in the dark, and at 2:18 A.M. on Saturday went into action.

Two of the choppers, "Redwine" and "Greenleaf," blasted the guard towers, landed outside the prison, and began blowing holes in the walls. The chopper "Blue-Boy," with a fourteen-man assault squad, landed inside the compound. Dick Meadows leaped out with a bullhorn, crouched in the compound and roared out his message: "We're Americans. Keep your heads down. We're Americans. This is a rescue. We're here to get you out. We'll be in your cells in a minute."

Within minutes the commandos burst into the cell blocks and the messages began coming back to Blue-Boy—"negative items," "negative items." And finally on the command net: "Search complete; negative items." The prison was empty! The enemy had disappeared into the countryside.

Searchlights came on; rockets and grenades and even SAMs were fired, lighting up the night. It was time for the commandos to go. Blue-Boy, disabled in landing, was blown up in the compound by its crew, who ran for the other two helicopters. Exactly twenty-seven minutes into the raid, all Americans were safe on board their helicopters and headed for Laos. Everything had gone perfectly except for one detail: No Americans had been rescued.

Was the Son Tay raid a failure? Not in all ways. It was a great psychological boost, both at home and in the prisons, where the Americans quickly heard about it. Now they knew they had not been forgotten! The North Vietnamese closed outlying prisons and brought all POWs to Hanoi, which gave them more companionship and more consistent (if not better) treatment. President Nixon said he considered the try worthwhile. The final relief of the POWs would have to wait.

By the end of 1971, South Vietnam had been stripped of all the big American units. The last of the Marines, once a force of 85,000 troops, pulled out in June, and of the seven Army divisions that had served in Vietnam, only the 101st Airborne was left. Even that outfit was packing up in December and would be out in a matter of weeks. The main brigades were gone too, the 173rd, the 198th, and the 199th. The only large combat units left were the 196th Infantry Brigade and the 3rd Brigade of the 1st Cavalry Division; they would be out by June of 1972.

What once had been a roaring military machine of half a million American men belonged now to the Vietnamese and to history. Nearly all the grunts were gone, and Vietnamization was taking over some of the American installations and weapons. The monsoons, the heat, and the blowing sand began to take over the rest, and the ruins were picked clean by thousands of Vietnamese human maggots, appalled at a society so rich it could throw away precious wood and metal. The Vietnamese were going back to a way of life centuries old, but they too, like the Americans, would never be the same.

14

The Last Campaign
1972

GENERAL GIAP was convinced that 1972 was his year to strike. His forces had never been stronger, nor the Americans weaker. Thanks to the Americans' gift—four years free from U.S. aerial bombing—North Vietnam had had time to arm and train. The weapons of war from the Soviet Union had come in a flood—trucks, tanks, artillery, antiaircraft guns, SAMs, ammunition, pipe, petroleum, more MIGs. Construction had been booming in North Vietnam—roads and pipelines were pushing south, toward the DMZ; the trails down through Laos and into Cambodia were now an efficient, well-developed supply network.

Even the political signs seemed favorable. The Americans were sick of the war and no one, not even President Nixon, would dare to reverse the pullout from South Vietnam. It was an election year, and if Nixon wanted a second term he would have to offer the voters peace—peace at almost any price—and certainly not an escalated war. The United States Army would never be sent back to South Vietnam. As soon as the winter monsoons subsided, the North would strike!

Rarely had a look into the future been more befogged. Giap had been blind—militarily and politically. The United States had withdrawn most of its army but still had, on his very border, the world's most powerful air force and navy. In addition, the South Vietnamese army had swollen to over a million men. But Giap's supreme error was in his misreading of Nixon the man.

He underestimated Nixon's courage—the courage to make the hard decisions—and he did not understand that Nixon was never more dangerous than when he appeared to be cornered. Giap thought he had Nixon cornered. He thought Nixon was on the defensive. Actually the President was on the offensive; his own stars had told him that 1972 would be his greatest year.

Nixon wasted no time. In mid-January he announced Increment XI of the withdrawal—70,000 more American troops would be coming home by the end of April.

256

That was more than half the American troops left in South Vietnam. Giap exulted, but on January 25 Nixon warned him. In a television speech from the Oval Office, the President declared: "If the enemy's answer to our peace offer is to step up their military attacks, I shall fully meet my responsibility as Commander in Chief of our armed forces to protect our remaining troops."

Nixon was mildly surprised that Giap did not open his offensive at Tet, but he took no chances. Early in February the President secretly ordered another aircraft carrier to Vietnam, along with more B-52s and all-weather fighter bombers. Then he launched his offensive on the political front.

On Thursday morning, February 17, Air Force One (now renamed "The Spirit of '76" by Nixon) lifted off the runway at Andrews Air Force Base outside Washington. Nixon was off to Peking, opening a new era in history. When the plane door opened in China, Chou En-lai stood hatless in the winter cold at the bottom of the stairway. Nixon descended with a smile on his face and his right hand thrust forward. The two world leaders shook hands, and Nixon wiped out John Foster Dulles' insult to China at the Geneva conference in 1954. Said Chou: "Your handshake came over the vastest ocean in the world—twenty-five years of no communication." He referred to 1947, the beginning of the Communist campaign for power in China.

The Nixon visit to China, lasting a week, did not bring instant friendship, but it opened a door. The parting was friendly on both sides, and in his final toast Nixon

In Peiping in 1972, during "the week that changed the world," President Nixon and Chinese Premier Chou En-lai raise their glasses in a toast to Sino-American friendship, creating a wide breach in the Communist world front.

declared, "This was the week that changed the world." Hanoi was discomfited; Moscow was alarmed. The Russian countermove was to invite Nixon to visit Moscow in May; if he went, he would be the first American President ever to visit the Soviet capital.

General Giap's military offensive, the largest ever, finally got off the mark on March 30, nearly two months late. It was a powerful assault—at least eight North Vietnamese divisions—but the South Vietnamese and the Americans were ready. General Abrams had been sounding the alarm since January, and the stakes were high. This was the decisive test of Vietnamization; if Thieu's forces could win, with American air power but without American troops, American money and weapons might just assure him of eventual victory. If North Vietnam failed, the enemy would be forced back to the bargaining table.

Early on March 30, the dawn of Good Friday, three North Vietnamese divisions crossed the DMZ near the eastern end, heading down Route 1 toward Quang Tri City. Other fresh units struck in through Khe Sanh and drove down the A Shau Valley toward Hue and Da Nang.

On the same day, two more North Vietnamese divisions drove into the Central Highlands, quickly captured Dak To, and headed south on Route 14, in the direction of Kontum and Pleiku. Giap's third front opened at 5:30 A.M. on April 2, when two North Vietnamese divisions crossed the border from Cambodia and began pushing down Route 13 toward Saigon, only 60 miles away. This time there was no pretense that the attacks were peasant uprisings, or "patriot" cadres of the Viet Cong. This was an all-out invasion by North Vietnam, and it came armed with the best new Russian weapons. More than 200 Soviet tanks churned across the DMZ spearheading troops armed with Russian 130-mm recoilless artillery.

The word came to Nixon on Good Friday morning as he and Kissinger were talking in the Oval Office. One of Kissinger's aides sent in a note. Kissinger read it and turned to Nixon: "The North Vietnamese have attacked across the DMZ," he said. "This is probably the beginning of the offensive we have been expecting." It was, and Nixon welcomed it. If he won this battle, the United States could negoti-

Nixon and Kissinger plan the 1972 American spring campaign; this time it's Linebacker I, all-out American air support but no American ground forces. Bomb the north, the President said, then added, "defeat is not an option."

ate from strength; if he lost . . . "I don't give a damn about the domestic reaction if that happens," the President said. "The foreign policy of the United States will have been destroyed, and the Soviets will have established that they can accomplish what they are after by using the force of arms in third countries. Defeat is not an option."

Within hours, Nixon gave the Navy authority to attack up the North Vietnamese

President Nixon ordered in more airpower, both Air Force and Navy. Here the supply ship USS Sacramento *feeds the carrier USS* Hancock *in the South China Sea (above), and American planes bomb the warehouse area of Haiphong (below).*

coast 25 miles above the DMZ, a permission never before granted. He approved immediate tactical air support to the 18th parallel, including the B-52s. He ordered more carriers, cruisers, and destroyers to the South China Sea. When General Abrams showed signs of opposition to this escalation and fell back on claiming rank, Kissinger reminded Admiral Moorer that "the Commander in Chief has some prerogatives too." The military got the message.

Only two aircraft carriers were on station at the outbreak, the *Coral Sea* and the *Hancock.* The *Constellation* was quickly called in from Hong Kong, the *Enterprise* from the Indian Ocean, the *Midway* and the *Kitty Hawk* from Hawaii. For good measure, the *Saratoga* was ordered out from Mayport, Florida—the only Atlantic fleet carrier to see duty against North Vietnam.

April was an exciting month for American air power. The B-52s were moving back into those magnificent air bases in Thailand. Tactical squadrons, both Air Force and Marine, reopened the South Vietnamese bases, and the Navy carriers cleared the decks. After four years of frustration, the air weapon was coming into its own. No longer would every shot be called from a querulous White House. This Commander in Chief not only gave the field commanders their head, he goaded them on. They had a powerful weapon, and he wanted it used.

The U.S. Air Force still had 20,000 men in the Vietnam theater, and swung into action worldwide to strengthen those forces. The 35th Tactical Fighter Squadron got orders in Korea on April 1, staged through the Philippines, and the next day arrived at Da Nang and at Ubon, in Thailand, ready for action. On April 7 two Marine F-4 squadrons (twenty-two planes and crews) flew into Da Nang from Japan. A third Marine squadron arrived April 13 from Hawaii. The carriers *Kitty Hawk* and *Constellation* were on station by the first days of April, and at the same time USAF forces were moving west from a half dozen bases in the United States. Seymour Johnson Air Force Base in North Carolina was processing over a thousand men in the first week of April, and the Military Airlift Command was geared up to move men and materials ten thousand miles at a clip. President Nixon was determined not to lose Vietnam before he could fashion some kind of a peace settlement.

General John W. Vogt, Jr., commander of the Seventh Air Force, now had almost full authority to set priorities, choose the targets, and determine the forces and the ordnance to execute them. There was another vital difference from previous crises—Air Force and Navy coordination was stronger now, the equipment was ready and so were the bases, and the objectives were urgent. There was no more Rolling Thunder, with its gradual acceleration, its limited objectives, its constant checks by Washington. This operation was tagged Linebacker I; it was urgent, and the air boys were ready and eager.

This time the newest weapons were used—the "smart bombs," destined to revolutionize aerial bombing. These were the Electro-Optical Guided Bomb (EOGB) and the Laser Guided Bomb (LGB), two-thousand-pound and three-thousand-pound bombs able to home in on any targets sighted by the pilot or crewman.

The EOGB used a small TV camera in its nose. The Weapons Systems Operator

(WSO), in the rear seat of the F-4, could find the target on his television scope, select a high-contrast aiming point, and release the bomb. The EOGB guided itself to the target, impacting with a high degree of accuracy, and was a great advance over the Walleye Glide Bomb, first used in 1967 by the Navy.

With the LGB system, the WSO sighted the target and illuminated it with a low-power laser beam emitted from a pod under the plane. The target had to be continuously illuminated by the laser or the bomb would stray off course. But if the EOGB could see the target when it left the plane, it usually hit the bull's eye. A great advantage of both bombs was that they could be released farther from the target, with less enemy interference, and the plane could then quickly leave the area.

At first the offensive went well for Giap. In the north, he drew up his strength around Quang Tri City and opened an attack on April 27 with tanks and artillery. The South Vietnamese defenders panicked and retreated in bad order as their officers deserted. The city fell on May 1, and thousands of civilian refugees headed down the road toward Hue. Giap's troops slaughtered thousands of civilians, including many women and children. In the Central Highlands, Pleiku was threatened, and on the southern front An Loc, only fifty miles from Saigon, was besieged. On May 2, Kissinger met Le Duc Tho again in Paris, but "Ducky" was insolent. His forces were winning everywhere, why should he negotiate? It was a dark hour for the United States.

Nixon was grim, but in no mood for surrender. He would never bow to the North Vietnamese, nor would he go to the Moscow summit as a loser. Over the first few days of May he came face to face with his crisis and made his decision, alone and in

Kissinger meets North Vietnam's chief negotiator Le Duc Tho (center, with interpreter) in Paris in May, but the Communist is insolent; he believes General Giap's great 1972 offensive will crush South Vietnam.

secrecy. On Thursday afternoon, May 4, he decided to mine the harbors of North Vietnam. It was the only way he could win; cut off the Russian supplies and bomb the north—to oblivion, if necessary. Few stood with him on that day, but to Kissinger it was "one of the finest hours of Nixon's presidency."

The President called in Admiral Moorer and asked him how soon he could be ready. Moorer, overjoyed, said the plans to mine the harbors had been ready for years; they could be executed quickly and cheaply. At one stroke, the North Vietnamese harbors could be closed and the enemy's main supply line severed. Nixon ordered it done on May 8, and set his TV announcement for that night, Monday, when the deed would already have been accomplished.

The A-6s, flying from three carriers, did the job against heavy flak, and the results were spectacular. The main ports—Haiphong, Hon Gai, and Cam Pha—were quickly closed, and the lesser ports to the south—Thanh Hoa, Vinh, Quang Khe, and Dong Hoi—followed shortly. The mines simply paralyzed shipping. Merchant ships en route to North Vietnam scattered for other ports. The ships already in harbor—twenty-seven of them in Haiphong alone—dared not move; they sat out the war there.

One hour before his speech, Nixon briefed Congressional leaders in his office. An aide told the Chinese at United Nations headquarters in New York. Kissinger called Soviet Ambassador Anatoly Dobrynin to his office and broke the news; the Russian seemed stunned. At 9 P.M., Nixon told the world:

"There is only one way to stop the killing. That is to keep the weapons of war out of the hands of the international outlaws of North Vietnam.

"I have ordered the following measures, which are being implemented as I am speaking to you. All entrances to North Vietnamese ports will be mined to prevent access to these ports and North Vietnamese naval operations from these ports. United States forces have been directed to take appropriate measures within the internal and claimed territorial waters of North Vietnam to interdict the delivery of any supplies. Rail and all other communications will be cut off to the maximum extent possible. Air and naval strikes against military targets in North Vietnam will continue."

Then he outlined his terms for peace:

"First, all American prisoners of war must be returned.

"Second, there must be an internationally supervised cease-fire throughout Indochina."

After this, "We will stop all acts of force throughout Indochina, and at that time will proceed with a complete withdrawal of all American forces from Vietnam within four months."

The day after the speech, Nixon wrote one of his characteristic memos to himself:

"We have the power to destroy [North Vietnamese] war-making capacity. The only question is whether we have the will to use that power. *What distinguishes me from Johnson is that I have the will, in spades.*"

In the United States, Congress and the media were hostile, as had been expected, but Nixon was ebullient. He went right after the Pentagon; he was tired of its "timid" attitude, and sick of those "dreary 'milk run'" bombings that the Johnson administration so favored. He wanted new ideas, and new actions, now!

On the diplomatic front, Nixon scored a heady victory. Dobrynin was back in Kissinger's office in a few days with a mild protest about one Soviet seaman being killed in Haiphong, but there was no mention of the summit or of canceling it. When the Russian had left, Kissinger went in to see the President, smiling broadly. "I think we've passed the crisis," he said. "I think we'll be able to have our mining and bombing and have our summit too." The Moscow summit, starting May 22, came off well. Nixon had achieved his dream: to be the first American President in history to be invited to the capital of Russia. The summit meeting took place while American air power was assaulting North Vietnam as never before.

The Navy and the Air Force divided up their targets and went to work with the "smart bombs" fully integrated. In four days, May 10–13, the Laser Guided Bombs dropped seven important bridges, including the Paul Doumer bridge at Hanoi and, finally, the Devil's Jaw at Thanh Hoa. The latter, "the bridge which would never go down," had withstood thousands of sorties and bombs since 1964. On May 13 a few F-4s with LGBs simply destroyed this bridge.

The other targets included rail bridges in the far north, on both the northeast and northwest railroads leading down from China. Before the 1968 bombing halt these bridges had been off limits—for fear that conventional bombs might fall too near the People's Republic of China. Now, with the accuracy of the LGBs, these bridges were promptly destroyed.

For the carrier pilots, May 1972 was the biggest month of the war. They swarmed over the enemy, from the DMZ north, and the USAF threw in everything it had, including the B-52s, from Thailand. The carrier pilots had bagged the Navy's tenth MIG-21 in January and added a MIG-17 in March, but in May they killed sixteen MIGs, including seven on one day alone, May 10. For good measure, the USS *Chicago* brought down an unidentified plane with a Talos missile when the plane came too close for comfort. This was the only surface-to-air missile kill by any U.S. force during the entire war.

For the Navy, the May 10 battle was extra special because it produced the first aces of the war (five enemy planes), and those aces were Navy. The Air Force had to wait until August 28, when Captain Steve Ritchie got his fifth MIG and became USAF's first ace. (USAF Captain Charles DeBellevue topped them all on September 9 when he bagged two MIGs in one day to bring his total to six.)

Most of the May 10 action came in a big raid on the rail yards at Hai Duong, halfway between Hanoi and Haiphong. For the carrier *Constellation* it was an "Alpha" strike, meaning every resource the carrier had was laid on that day. The ship's A-6s and A-7s went after the target, and F-4s flew cover and AAA suppression. No less than twenty-two MIGs met them over Hai Duong. The F-4s dropped their ordnance first (one ton each) and then piled into the MIGs, running up the record one-day score of seven MIGs.

In the North as well as in South Vietnam, where the ARVN was fighting for its life, American air power saved the day. During the 1968–72 bombing halt, the

North Vietnamese had built their air force to some two hundred fifty MIGs, about one third of them the new MIG-21s. They also now had about three hundred SAM sites and more than fifteen hundred antiaircraft guns, up to 100-mm artillery. The answer to this had to be better weapons and better tactics, and the U.S. Air Force/ Navy had them.

Part of the answer was computer-controlled operations, from "Invert," the Air Force computer at Nakhon Phanom in Thailand, to the Navy's "Red Crown" station in the Gulf of Tonkin. To the fly-boys, Nakhon Phanom became known as "Naked Fanny." With so many American aircraft over North Vietnam, it was vital that none fire without positive identification or clearance from Red Crown or land base. Identification of MIGs was now electronic, faster than visual, and positive in accuracy. Electronic identification thus meant quicker use of missiles for standoff shooting. The newest Sparrows and Sidewinders had greater range, power, and maneuverability. These missiles, guided by their own radar, could be locked onto the enemy plane. A good fix meant almost certain death for a MIG. As heat-seekers, these missiles frequently went right up the MIG's tail pipe.

For hunting SAMs, the F-4s now had the same capabilities as the F-105 Wild Weasels. In addition, the F-4 was more maneuverable against MIGs. The new ECM (electronic countermeasure) pods could jam enemy radar over a wider range of frequencies, and were now assisted by chaff. This World War II tactic, revived and improved, was of great value against enemy ground radar. Chaff planes now were included in all major raids, strewing out millions of strips of foil to confuse and neutralize the enemy's radar. When Linebacker I ended, the North Vietnamese had lost 185 planes in air-to-air combat; the United States had lost 90.

By the end of 1972 almost all U.S. ground forces are out of Vietnam and the fighting is done by South Vietnamese troops. They found this bunker empty, because U.S. B-52s had bombed out the Communists.

On the ground, inside South Vietnam, American air strength was crucial. The United States put seven aircraft carriers on the line, and sent in seven Marine fighter squadrons for air duty on fields from Da Nang to Bien Hoa. The Air Force, by the end of May, had over two hundred B-52s at work over both South and North Vietnam, and tactical squadrons sortieing night and day from airfields in South Vietnam and Thailand.

By mid-June, Giap's offensive was stopped in its tracks. The Navy reported that, for the first time in the war, it was drawing no shore fire on its vessels. SAM launches in the North dropped sharply. The enemy was running out of ammunition. The same was true for the ground forces. Supply lines had been torn apart in North Vietnam, and more than a thousand rail cars were backed up in China. Nixon went ahead with American withdrawal; implementing Increment XII, he pulled out 20,000 more troops in June, including the 196th Infantry Brigade, the last Army combat unit to leave.

By mid-1972 the once powerful U.S. Army force in Vietnam was already fading into memory. Less than a division-equivalent of combat troops remained in the country. All major American commands had been deactivated, or had sharply shrunk. All major harbors and American-built bases had been turned over to the South Vietnamese and were already rusting back into the jungle, or being systematically looted and dismembered by South Vietnamese civilians.

In June, General Abrams, who in 1968 had taken over the fighting command in South Vietnam from General Westmoreland, went back to Washington, this time to succeed "Westy" as Army chief of staff. On July 3, 1972, General Westmoreland retired from active Army duty in a warm and emotional ceremony. The last of the

In July 1972, General Westmoreland retires from the Army and makes a last report to his Commander in Chief at the White House. Secretary of Defense Melvin Laird is at left.

265

Army's old Vietnam team was gone. Only American air power now stood between the South Vietnamese and the Communist hordes pressing down from the north.

The bombing of the Hanoi area stopped briefly in June, at Russian request. The Russians said Nikolai Podgorny, the Soviet Union's chief of state, would be visiting Hanoi, and his hosts, the North Vietnamese, would appreciate a halt in the bombing during his visit. The United States agreed; as Kissinger put it, "our bombing and mining had greatly improved Hanoi's manners." However, after the visit the bombing was quickly resumed; Nixon wanted no misunderstanding in Hanoi. He would keep the pressure on, and even tighten the screws, until the North Vietnam-

Jane Fonda (left) visits the Communist enemy near Hanoi and urges the North Vietnamese gunners to shoot down "American imperialist air raiders," according to Hanoi reports. A few weeks later Kissinger talks with South Vietnam's President Thieu in Saigon (below).

ese showed signs of reason. Kissinger turned his own screws; he went to Peking in June to tell the Chinese what had happened at the Moscow summit. This in turn worried the Russians and made Hanoi feel even more alone in the Communist world.

By September, the pendulum had begun to swing. The South Vietnamese armed forces rallied on all fronts. In the south, An Loc was relieved and the besiegers were driven back into Cambodia. Giap's forces were also routed in the Central Highlands, and the Kontum/Pleiku axis was neutralized. In the north, the ARVN retook Quang Tri City. General Giap still held some territory within South Vietnam, but he had lost his gamble. His force had been shattered, with over a hundred thousand casualties, and most of his Russian equipment had been destroyed. This time North Vietnam could not be replenished—the mining had closed their harbors, the aerial bombing had destroyed their rail lines. General Giap did not fully realize it yet, but he was also losing his allies; both Moscow and Peking were tired of this little war, almost as tired as was Washington.

Saigon had its own worries. President Thieu's forces had made a respectable showing, and Vietnamization had survived a major crisis, but everyone knew it could not have been done without American air power, and no one knew this better than Thieu. Kissinger stopped in at Saigon and was amazed to find Thieu talking about American forces staying at least through 1973. In the most forceful way he could, Kissinger tried to make Thieu understand that, as far as the Americans were concerned, the war must end, and the sooner the better. Nixon had just implemented Increment XIV of the withdrawal plan, removing 12,000 more Americans from South Vietnam by November. This was the final phase of the formal withdrawal plan. Some 25,000 American military would be left in South Vietnam, a rear guard of indeterminate size and duration.

The stage was set for a climax in three capitals: Saigon, Hanoi, and Washington. Saigon faced a fight for its own life. Hanoi must decide how much bombing punishment it wished to take. Washington, in the person of President Nixon, contemplated no less than the annihilation of Hanoi, if that became necessary. It was showdown time.

15

The Showdown
1972–73

HENRY KISSINGER went back into session with the North Vietnamese on September 26, 1972, at a new site—a house in Gif-sur-Yvette, a suburb southwest of Paris. He listened patiently for two days to the enemy's "new" ten-point program for settlement of the war. The plan would not be acceptable to the United States, but it was the nuances of the Communist proposal that set Kissinger tingling. North Vietnam was ready to settle! The more they talked, the clearer it became. Their entire attitude had swung around. For their own reasons, whatever those might be, the North Vietnamese, after more than four years of charades, now wanted a quick end to the war.

The next meeting was set for October 8, and Kissinger was sure it would be crucial. After he reported to the President, Nixon immediately sent General Alexander Haig to Saigon to prepare President Thieu for a breakthrough. Thieu was so badly shaken he burst into tears. Nixon, at the same time, sent a message to Hanoi, via the Soviet foreign minister, Andrei Gromyko, who was in Washington to sign the SALT agreement. Nixon invited Gromyko to Camp David and sketched out his thinking—when Kissinger returned to Paris he would carry America's final offer. If Hanoi refused it, the United States would turn to "other methods" *after the election.* The last three words of that sentence carried a heavy weight. It was quite clear by now to both Moscow and Hanoi that Nixon would be reelected, and that he would defeat George McGovern by a far bigger margin than he had gotten for his first term in 1968. It would be to Hanoi's advantage to settle before the election, not after.

It was a new Le Duc Tho—smiling, affable, reasonable—who sat across the table from Kissinger on Sunday, October 8. Without the usual polemics, "Ducky" (the Americans used that appellation among themselves, but only in private) quickly outlined a simple plan for cease-fire, and settlement later of all political questions.

Kissinger was incredulous. This was better than the United States had been asking for three years, better than Congress had demanded, better than the media and Nixon's enemies required.

The negotiators went to work smoothing out the details, and at 2 A.M. on October 12, after a sixteen-hour session, came to agreement. Hanoi was adamant on one point—the agreement must be initialed by October 26 and signed October 30, the cease-fire to be effective that day. Kissinger left Paris immediately. As he put it later, "In blissful ignorance of the future, we landed in Washington, near joyous that we had brought home both peace and dignity."

As Kissinger saw it in his dreams, this was the possibility: Saigon would survive, generously supported by the United States; Hanoi would come around, tempted by American aid for reconstruction of the north, and pressed to settle by Peking and Moscow. No one, not even Kissinger, could foresee a Watergate and the crumbling of a presidency. Kissinger and Haig went immediately to the White House to celebrate and to talk of final details.

As agreed at Paris, Nixon ordered the bombing of North Vietnam reduced to two hundred sorties daily, with no bombing north of the twentieth parallel. He also cabled the North Vietnamese within forty-eight hours, as required: "The President accepts the basic draft for an 'Agreement on Ending the War and Restoring Peace in Vietnam,' except for"—and he outlined a few details to be ironed out in Paris. Kissinger would go to Saigon after the October 17 Paris meeting, then on to Hanoi, where the agreement would be initialed on October 22, and back to Washington for the great day, October 26, when the cease-fire in Vietnam would be simultaneously announced in Hanoi and Washington. Nixon also approved plans to rush war materials to South Vietnam before the standstill of October 26, when military levels must be frozen. Someone gave this the title Operation Enhance Plus.

Because of last-minute details, the final Paris meeting was eliminated, and the cease-fire day was moved from October 26 to October 31. Kissinger arrived in Saigon October 18 and found Thieu very nearly undone. He was no longer quibbling about this clause or that; he was simply unable to accept that the United States was about to pull out of Indochina. He said the United States was obviously conniving with the Soviets and the Chinese to sell out South Vietnam. Thieu collected himself well enough to put together his final demands: twenty-three changes in the Paris agreement. The next day, Sunday, October 22, Kissinger cabled Nixon: "Thieu has just rejected the entire plan or any modification of it and refuses to discuss any further negotiations on the basis of it." Kissinger started home.

On October 26, Kissinger was awakened at his Washington home at 5:30 A.M. with the news that Hanoi Radio was spilling out all the details of the Paris plan, concluding with the statement that the government of North Vietnam "strongly denounces the Nixon administration's lack of good will and seriousness." There was bitter disappointment in Washington, centered more on Saigon than on Hanoi, but within hours Kissinger, facing the TV cameras, was proclaiming to the world, "Peace is at hand." Those were his opening words, and, whatever they were intended to mean, they entered history. The final part of his statement was: "We will not be stampeded into an agreement until its provisions are right. We will not be deflected from an agreement when its provisions are right. And with this attitude, and with some cooperation from the other side, we believe that we can restore both peace and unity to America very soon."

Richard Nixon was reelected President of the United States on November 7, carrying every state in the union except Massachusetts. He defeated McGovern in the popular vote, 47 million to 29 million, the largest popular vote ever given a Republican. McGovern could not carry even his home state (South Dakota) and lost in the electoral vote, 520 to 117. McGovern had clearly misread the national temper on Vietnam. His central theme was simply to walk away from Vietnam, letting come what may. Nixon emerged with what could only be called a mandate on the war—stop it in some way with some "honor," and *then* get out. The President immediately began to consider how the Paris humpty-dumpty could be put together again. Nixon understood his home problem clearly; the Democrats had gained strength in Congress and would soon back him into a corner. It would vote, probably early in January, to cut off all funds for Vietnam. He had 60 days to end the war.

Two days after election, Nixon's emissary was on the way to Saigon. It was General Haig this time, because Thieu liked Haig; perhaps the general could succeed where Kissinger could not. Haig carried with him a letter from Nixon to Thieu: "You have my absolute assurance that if Hanoi fails to abide by the terms of

Kissinger makes his famed "peace is at hand" announcement in Washington in October 1972. When the Communists then balked, President Nixon laid on Linebacker II, the "Christmas bombing" of Hanoi that made the Communists agree to a cease-fire.

this agreement it is my intention to take swift and severe retaliatory action." Thieu was not greatly reassured; thousands of North Vietnamese troops were still in his country. He finally rallied enough to consider accepting the Paris agreement, but only with sixty-nine changes!

Kissinger sat down in Gif-sur-Yvette with these changes on November 20, but the mood was gone. Le Duc Tho stood firm on the Paris agreement, and five days of talk could not budge him. Kissinger was back in Washington by November 25, and he and Nixon called in Thieu's Washington representative, Nguyen Phu Duc. They spoke in the Oval Office, and Nixon's message to Thieu was: If we do not get agreement at Paris, Congress will end the war. To Kissinger, the meeting yielded an even deeper insight: Nixon alone is now in charge; Nixon believes his enemies are closing in on him; Nixon will not accept defeat.

Negotiations resumed in Paris on December 6, but it was soon clear that Hanoi believed it had the upper hand. The North Vietnamese were now greedy, arrogant. On December 13 the talks came to an end; "Ducky" had made it plain he intended no agreement. It was, as Kissinger put it, "a cardinal error in dealing with Nixon; they cornered him."

Nixon had already reached his decision; resume the bombing. He did not do this lightly, but he did it resolutely. Nixon talked with Haig and Kissinger in the Oval Office on December 14, and the final American military campaign gradually evolved. The North Vietnamese harbors would be reseeded with mines, and the full panoply of American air power would be turned loose—B-52s and fighter bombers, everything the Air Force and the Navy could muster.

Sixteen major targets were designated for Hanoi—transportation, power, industry, and communications, including the Radio Hanoi towers. For Haiphong, thirteen major targets were designated, including full treatment of the docks and shipping. Nixon, Kissinger, and Haig discussed the consequences—heavy air losses, civilian casualties, more American POWs. They talked it all out, and Nixon said: "I know, but if we're convinced that this is the right thing to do, then we will have to do it right."

On the same day, December 14, 1972, Nixon ordered the full program executed, "effective three days hence." When Nixon saw the first bombing plans, he was appalled at the red tape within the military over control of planes, logistics, and minor matters. He called Admiral Moorer and told him, "I don't want any more of this crap about the fact that we couldn't hit this target or that one. This is your chance to use military power effectively to win this war, and if you don't I'll consider you responsible."

Nixon said later that his December 14 decision "was the most difficult decision I made during the entire war; at the same time, however, it was also one of the most clear-cut and necessary ones." He made one other decision: to keep silent and let the actions speak for themselves. Explanations would do no good at home, and any ultimatum to Hanoi might rouse the Communist world to full war rather than lose face. "So I did it with the minimum amount of rhetoric and publicity, and it succeeded exactly as I had intended," Nixon wrote later. At the same time he sent a message to North Vietnam via Paris: The United States would be prepared to meet again at any time after December 26 to conclude an agreement.

In the early hours of Sunday, December 17, the Navy's carrier planes went back to work, reseeding the mines in Haiphong harbor and its two main satellite ports, Hon Gai and Cam Pha. It was certain now that North Vietnam would receive no further supplies by sea for at least the next four months. The next day, the American B-52s and hundreds of fighter bombers launched Linebacker II, one of the most concentrated, most humane, and most successful aerial bombing campaigns in history.

On the night of Monday/Tuesday, December 18–19, a fleet of 121 B-52s attacked the Hanoi area in three waves. The fighter bombers went in first—F-111s and F-4s sowing chaff. Then came the first of the big boys, barreling down the Red River valley from the northwest with a tail wind of over a hundred knots. The first B-52s hit Hanoi's main airfields—at Hoa Lac, Kep, and Phuc Yen—and then went after the Kinh Ho/Yen Vien industrial areas north of Hanoi. The bombers came in three waves that night—the first one early Monday evening, a second wave at midnight, and the third just before dawn on Tuesday.

Besides the airfields and industrial targets, the Gia Lam railroad shops were hit and the Hanoi radio towers were taken out, with the loss of one B-52 over the target; "Charcoal I" was hit by two SAMs and destroyed, the first bomber lost in Linebacker II and only the second B-52 downed during the entire war to that date.

The big bombers were back the next night, hitting many targets a second time and also raiding a large power plant at Thai Nguyen, fifty miles north of Hanoi, and a rail-highway junction at Bac Giang, thirty miles northeast of Hanoi. The tactics were the same as those used on the first night—attacks from the northwest, in waves spaced about five hours apart. On each night, the enemy had expended about two hundred SAMs, from an inventory estimated at a thousand missiles.

The North Vietnamese bagged no B-52s on the second night, but on Wednesday night the tables were turned. The enemy fired some two hundred twenty SAMs and brought down six B-52s in nine hours. It was time to change tactics. Starting Thursday night, December 21, the bombers went out in smaller groups, attacking at no set times, approaching from a variety of directions, and departing from the targets more quickly. Both the pilots and planners had spotted the flaws in the early bombing plans, and corrections were already in progress when Nixon noted in his diary: "I raised holy hell about the fact that they kept going over the same targets at the same time." It was the loss of planes and crews that bothered him, he said, not the hot waves of criticism, national and international. He had expected that, and paid no attention to it.

Besides the bomber raids, the enemy was being punished by the daylight attacks of the fighter bombers, using the smart bombs. The B-52s bombed only at night, from above 30,000 feet, and only against large, well-defined military targets.

Linebacker II was nothing like the carpet bombing or firebombing of World War II, which obliterated whole cities in Europe and Japan. The smart bomb sorties were precision attacks, which took out high-priority targets with great accuracy

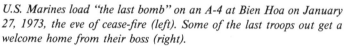

U.S. Marines load "the last bomb" on an A-4 at Bien Hoa on January 27, 1973, the eve of cease-fire (left). Some of the last troops out get a welcome home from their boss (right).

and relatively little loss of civilian life. Nonetheless, the media reported outrage in expected places and, through malice or ignorance, conjured up shades of the Dresden and Tokyo bombings of World War II. Nixon received support in messages of encouragement from Nelson Rockefeller, Ronald Reagan, Senators Howard Baker and Robert Taft, and others.

On the first three nights of heavy raids, most of the B-52s had come from Guam, a long haul for the big planes. The smaller raids, starting on Thursday night, December 21, were staged from Thailand, mostly from U Tapao, south of Bangkok, and the new tactics paid off. The Haiphong area came in for its first attacks on Friday, December 22, and on the same day President Nixon sent a message to the North Vietnamese, asking them to resume peace talks on January 3, 1973. If they agreed, the President said, he would suspend bombing north of the twentieth parallel on December 31.

Nixon had decided he would suspend Linebacker II for one day—Christmas, December 25—and then resume it, with more force than ever, if necessary. He wanted Hanoi to understand that this was not Lyndon Johnson talking, but Richard Nixon. Hanoi got the message.

For December 26, Nixon ordered the biggest raid yet, sending the B-52s against both the Hanoi and Haiphong military complexes. That same afternoon, Hanoi sent up its first signal; it suggested resuming the Paris talks on January 8. The President countered that the United States would want technical talks on January 2, to prepare for Kissinger's return to the bargaining table on January 8. But the bombing

The last act at Paris: the North Vietnamese sign the cease-fire (above) and the Americans, headed by Kissinger, also sign (below). Neither side looks happy.

went right on, refined now to a pattern of small, staggered attacks that threw the enemy off balance and damaged him severely, at small cost to the attackers. About sixty B-52s, plus many fighter bomber sorties, were hitting the enemy each day and night until December 29, when Hanoi decided it had had enough. On that day, North Vietnam agreed to both the January 2 and January 8 meetings in Paris.

Effective 7 A.M. Saturday, December 30, the United States ceased bombing above the twentieth parallel. Linebacker II was over. In eleven days it had proved once again that the Communists understood one thing—force. It also seemed to prove what many had been saying for years: precision air power, properly used, could punish the enemy so severely he would have to seek terms.

What had Linebacker cost? It had cost the United States fifteen B-52s and eleven fighter bombers lost, four B-52 crewmen killed, twenty-nine missing, and thirty-three captured. Altogether, the B-52s had flown 740 sorties; the fighter bombers, over one thousand. The enemy had lost eight MIGs and fired his whole bag of one thousand SAM missiles. North Vietnam claimed it lost 2,000 civilians killed in Hanoi.

In the United States, the antiwar factions screamed of "annihilation" raids and brought in Dresden and Tokyo. Actually, there was no comparison. The World War II aerial bombings had been saturation raids. The British/American air raids on

Some American POWs came home within weeks of the cease-fire, to scenes like this one at Travis AF Base in California, as Lieutenant Colonel Robert L. Stirm, USAF, meets his family again.

None will forget Hoa Lo, or "Hanoi Hilton" to bitter Americans. North Vietnamese guards peer in at Americans still behind enemy bars in March 1973 (above), and, finally, guards are left with empty cells (below). Thousands of Americans never came home.

Dresden killed thirty-five thousand civilians in one blow in February 1945; the Tokyo fire raids by B-29s on the night of March 8–9, 1945, killed more than eighty thousand civilians in the greatest single blaze in the history of mankind. But Linebacker II was precision bombing, aimed at military targets only, and it was picking the North Vietnamese economy to pieces. The Communists were now closed in,

276

shut off from outside help. The Hanoi government now had only one option: Accept a cease-fire or face destruction.

Le Duc Tho stalled a little at the January 8 meeting, but Kissinger had expected that. The next day "Ducky" was ready to settle, and Kissinger was able to cable Nixon: "We celebrated the President's birthday today by making a major breakthrough in the negotiations. In sum, we settled all outstanding questions in the text of the agreement." On January 15, the fateful announcement came from both Hanoi and Washington—at 10 A.M. the United States would stop all mining and bombing of North Vietnam for an indefinite time.

The following day General Haig was in Saigon with Nixon's final word for President Thieu: The United States would initial the agreement with Hanoi on January 23. "I will do so, if necessary, alone," Nixon said. "In that case I shall have to explain publicly that your government obstructs peace." Thieu at last capitulated. "I have done all that I can for my country," he told Ambassador Bunker.

The cease-fire, initialed on January 23, 1973, became effective on January 27. At his news conference on January 31, Nixon officially announced "peace with honor." He could not resist adding to the media: "I know it gags some of you to write that phrase, but it is true, and most Americans realize it is true." The polls supported him on that; the January Gallup poll gave Nixon an approval rating of 68 percent, while the respect for Congress rating fell to an all-time low of 26 percent. Kissinger wrapped up the Paris experience, unofficially, with a luncheon for both delegations —the first time they had eaten together in three years of frustration. "Tho and I,"

AMERICAN POWS RELEASED IN FEBRUARY, MARCH 1973

Year Captured	USAF	USN	USA	USMC	Civilians	Total
1964	0	1	1	0	0	2
1965	35	23	0	2	1	61
1966	61	23	0	2	1	87
1967	94	50	10	5	0	159
1968	28	16	34	11	16 (all at Tet)	105
1969	1	1	8	1	2	13
1970	0	0	10	1	1	12
1971	7	1	6	0	1	15
1972	99	21	7	4	1	132
1973	0	1	0	0	0	1
Total	325	137	76	26	23	587

Kissinger wrote later, "made toasts to a lasting peace and friendship between our peoples." There was little of that to come, on either side.

The war in Indochina did not end, nor has it ended yet; it simply moved on to another phase. For the Americans, one paramount interest remained: bringing home the prisoners. As an organizational move, it was quickly and smartly done, surcharged with emotion yet somehow incomplete, unsatisfying. For America, it seemed, Vietnam was destined to bring nothing but rage and sorrow.

Operation Homecoming, the return of the POWs, was planned as carefully as any military offensive. At a meeting in August 1972, in Honolulu, the Air Force's 9th Aeromedical Evacuation Group had been designated to coordinate all aspects of the recovery, aided by an advisory group of physicians, chaplains, lawyers, and consular and public affairs experts. All American prisoners, no matter where released, would be flown first to the Joint Homecoming Reception Center at Clark Air Force Base, near Manila. Some 600 Americans would be coming out of captivity, and this would be the first chance to help them. A majority had been prisoners for at least four years, and a few had suffered more than eight years under barbaric conditions.

On January 27, 1973, as prescribed by the Paris agreement, North Vietnam produced a list of the prisoners it said it held. There were 588 names on it—566 military and 22 civilians. This included nine Americans held in Laos. In addition, three Americans held in China—two pilots and a CIA agent—would be released through Hong Kong. In all, that accounted for 591 Americans. But where were the other Americans, the hundreds, perhaps thousands, still classified by the United States as MIA—missing in action? The Communists stood mute; human life means little to them. Another wound was left to fester—another Vietnam sore that would not heal.

The first bus loads of American prisoners arrived at Gia Lam airport on February 12, 1973, and drove out across the bomb-pocked runway toward the big Air Force C-141. Inside the buses, the Americans held back their feelings—grim, wary, waiting. As they filed off the buses, North Vietnam guards stood ready to herd them toward the plane. But in the first group a senior American prisoner set the tone.

He ordered his men into formation and they marched to the plane in good order —Americans now, prisoners no longer. Only when the C-141 lifted off did they let go. They were the first 108 POWs going home, most of them to joy, some to sorrow, and all to a world that had left them behind. Other plane loads followed this first one, and the enemy finally completed the release of the POWs on March 29. The war was over, but it was not over.

In the weeks and months that followed, the remaining American troops came home, some twenty thousand in all. The Air Force stayed on a little longer, making bomb runs over Laos until April 17 and over Cambodia until August 15, when Congress decreed their end. Six more Americans were killed in Vietnam in 1973— three Army men and three civilians. They were all on "noncombat" duty, looking for American bodies or other grim tasks in cleaning up the field of battle. More than thirteen hundred Americans were still unaccounted for, lost forever perhaps in the jungles and jails of a suffering land that knows no peace.

The Vietnam Memorial in Washington, a stunning architectural conception by Maya Ying Lin, records on a long wall of polished black granite the names of more than 58,000 Americans who gave their lives in the Indochina war (top; above left). The statue of three servicemen, sculpted by Frederick Hart, was added several years later and placed near the wall (above right).

APPENDICES

Abbreviations

AAA	Antiaircraft artillery
AFB	U.S. Air Force Base
AID	U.S. Agency for International Development
ARVN	Army of the Republic of Vietnam, the South Vietnamese army (pronounced "arvin")
BLT	Battalion landing team
CIA	U.S. Central Intelligence Agency
CIDG	Civilian Irregular Defense Groups, paramilitary groups made up of aboriginal tribesmen in the interior of South Vietnam, organized, trained, and usually led by the Green Berets
CINCPAC	Commander in Chief, Pacific, of the U.S. Navy and titular commander of all U.S. military forces in the Pacific Ocean area
CINCPACAF	Commander in Chief, Pacific Air Forces
CINCPACFLT	Commander in Chief, Pacific Fleet
COMUSMACV	Commander, U.S. Military Assistance Command, Vietnam
DMZ	The demilitarized zone set up by the Geneva Accords of 1954; a zone 10 kilometers wide along the seventeenth parallel that was to be kept free of all military forces and equipment
DRV	Democratic Republic of Vietnam, or North Vietnam, a Communist government
ECM	Electronic countermeasure
EOGB	Electro-optical guided bomb
FC	Forward controller, the air or land officer who has tactical command of all planes and artillery at the scene of attack against enemy ground forces
HMM	Helicopter, Marine, Medium
ICC	International Control Commission, established by the Geneva Accords of 1954 and made up of representatives from Canada, India, and Poland
JCS	U.S. Joint Chiefs of Staff, a formal agency of government consisting of the heads of the U.S. military services, who are the principal military advisers to the President, the National Security Council, and the Secretary of Defense
JGS	Joint General Staff (South Vietnamese)
KIA	Killed in action
LGB	Laser-guided bomb
LZ	Landing zone for helicopters

281

ABBREVIATIONS

MAAG	Commonly used acronym for the U.S. Military Assistance Advisory Group, activated in Saigon in 1950 to assist French reoccupation of Indochina
MACV	The U.S. Military Assistance Command, Vietnam, the unified American command set up in Saigon in 1962 with authority over all U.S. military activities in South Vietnam
MAF	Marine Amphibious Force, the overall U.S. Marine command in South Vietnam
MEB	Marine Expeditionary Brigade, the first name of the Marine force sent to South Vietnam in March 1965, soon changed to MAF
MIA	Missing in action
MIG	The Soviet Union's principal fighter aircraft
MRF	Mobile Riverine Force, a combined U.S. Navy/Army command put together in 1968 to combat the Viet Cong forces in the Mekong Delta
NATO	North Atlantic Treaty Organization, a post–World War II alliance of the United States, Canada, and most of the free countries of Western Europe against the threat of aggression by the Soviet Union
NLF	National Liberation Front, formal name for the Viet Cong
NMCB	U.S. Navy Mobile Construction Battalions, or Seabees
NSC	National Security Council, a U.S. agency and staff responsible for planning, coordinating, and evaluating the nation's defense policies. Members include the President, Vice-President, Secretaries of State and Defense, and the Director of the Office of Emergency Preparedness
NVA	North Vietnamese Army
NVAF	North Vietnamese Air Force
OJT	On-the-job training
OSS	Office of Strategic Services, a worldwide American intelligence service during World War II, forerunner of the CIA
POL	Petroleum-oil lubricants, used to designate targets for U.S. air attack
PRC	People's Republic of China
R & R	Rest and recuperation program for U.S. troops
ROK	Republic of Korea troops, referred to as "rocks"
RSSZ	Rung Sat Special Zone, a forty-mile stretch of rivers and marshes between Saigon and the sea, especially the main shipping channel, Long Tau (Rung Sat means "Forest of Assassins")
SAM	Surface-to-air missile
SEAL	U.S. Navy commando teams trained to operate on sea, air, and land
SEATO	The Southeast Asia Treaty Organization, formed in 1954 by the United States, Australia, France, Great Britain, New Zealand, Pakistan, the Philippines, and Thailand to oppose further Communist gains in Southeast Asia
SF	The Green Berets, or, formally, the U.S. Army Special Forces
TAOR	Tactical area of responsibility
USA	U.S. Army
USAF	U.S. Air Force
USNA	U.S. Naval Academy
VC	Viet Cong, the Communist guerrilla forces in South Vietnam, under direct control of North Vietnam
WIA	Wounded in action
WSO	Weapons system operator, who rode the rear seat of the F-4 to operate the aerial "smart bombs"

Bibliography

ANDERSON, CHARLES R., *Vietnam: The Other War.* Presidio Press, San Rafael, California, 1982.

BERGER, CARL, ed., *The United States Air Force in Southeast Asia, 1961–1973.* Office of Air Force History, Washington, 1977.

BONDS, RAY, ed., *The Vietnam War.* Crown, New York, 1979.

BRAESTRUP, PETER, *Big Story.* Westview Press, Denver, Colo., 1977.

BUCKINGHAM, WILLIAM A., JR., *Operation Ranch Hand: The Air Force and Herbicides in Southeast Asia, 1961–1971.* Office of Air Force History, Washington, 1982.

DICKSON, PAUL, *The Electronic Battlefield.* Indiana University Press, Bloomington, Ind., 1976.

DUNG, GEN. VAN TIEN, NVA, *Our Great Spring Victory.* Monthly Review Press, London, 1977.

DUNN, LT. GEN. CARROLL H., USA, *Vietnam Studies: Base Development in South Vietnam, 1965–1970.* Department of the Army, Washington, 1972.

ESPER, GEORGE, and THE ASSOCIATED PRESS, *The Eyewitness History of the Vietnam War.* Villard Books, New York, 1983.

FOX, ROGER P., *Air Base Defense in the Republic of Vietnam, 1961–1973.* Office of Air Force History, Washington, 1979.

FULTON, MAJ. GEN. WILLIAM B., USA, *Vietnam Studies: Riverine Operations 1966–1969.* Department of the Army, Washington, 1973.

FUTRELL, ROBERT F., *The United States Air Force in Southeast Asia: The Advisory Years to 1965.* Office of Air Force History, Washington, 1981.

HALBERSTAM, DAVID, *The Best and the Brightest.* Random House, New York, 1972.

HANAK, WALTER, ed., *Aces and Aerial Victories, The United States Air Force in Southeast Asia 1965–1973.* Office of Air Force History, Washington, 1976.

History of U.S. Decision-Making Process on Vietnam Policy, also known as "The Pentagon Papers" (Gravel Edition, 5 vols.). Beacon Press, Boston, 1972. See also Porter, Gareth, "Vietnam, A History in Documents," and "The Pentagon Papers as Published by the New York *Times.*" Quadrangle Books, New York, 1971.

HOOPER, VICE-ADMIRAL EDWIN B., USN, *Mobility, Support, Endurance: A Story of Naval Operational Logistics in the Vietnam War, 1965–1968.* USN, Naval History Division, Washington, 1972.

HOSMER, STEPHEN T., Konrad Kellen, and Brian M. Jenkins, *The Fall of South Vietnam: Statements by Vietnamese Military and Civilian Leaders.* Crane Russak, New York, 1980.

HUBBELL, JOHN G., *POW, A Definitive History of the American Prisoner-of-War Experience in Vietnam, 1964–1973.* Reader's Digest Press, Pleasantville, N.Y., 1976.

JOHNSON, LYNDON B., *The Vantage Point: Perspectives of the Presidency, 1963–1969.* Holt, Rinehart & Winston, New York, 1971.

KARNOW, STANLEY, *Vietnam: A History. The First Complete Account of Vietnam at War.* Viking Press, New York, 1983.

KEARNS, DORIS, *Lyndon Johnson and the American Dream.* Harper & Row, New York, 1976.

KELLY, COLONEL FRANCIS J., USA, *Vietnam Studies: U.S. Army Special Forces, 1961–1971.* Department of the Army, Washington, 1973.

KISSINGER, HENRY, *The White House Years.* Little, Brown, Boston, 1975.

LAVALLE, LT. COL. A. J. C., USAF, ed., *Last Flight from Saigon,* USAF Southeast Asia Monograph Series, vol. IV, Monograph 6. Office of Air Force History, Washington, 1981.

283

BIBLIOGRAPHY

LAVALLE, MAJ. A. J. C., USAF, ed., *The Tale of Two Bridges and The Battle for the Skies Over North Vietnam,* vol. I, USAF Southeast Asia Monograph Series. GPO, Washington, 1976.

LEWY, GUENTER, *America in Vietnam.* Oxford University Press, New York, 1978.

MERSKY, PETER B., and NORMAN POLMAR, *The Naval Air War in Vietnam.* Nautical & Aviation Publishing Co., Annapolis, Md., 1981.

MILLER, MERLE, *Lyndon, An Oral Biography.* Putnam, New York, 1980.

MOMYER, GEN. WILLIAM W., USAF, *Air Power in Three Wars.* Office of Air Force History, Washington, 1978.

NALTY, BERNARD C., *Air Power and the Fight for Khe Sanh.* Office of Air Force History, Washington, 1973.

NIXON, RICHARD M., *RN: The Memoirs of Richard Nixon.* Grosset & Dunlap, New York, 1978.

PALMER, GEN. BRUCE, JR., USA, *The 25-Year War; America's Military Role in Vietnam.* University Press of Kentucky, Lexington, Ky., 1984.

PATTI, ARCHIMEDES L. A., *Why Vietnam? Prelude to America's Albatross.* University of California Press, Berkeley, Cal., 1980.

Pentagon Papers. See "History of U.S. Decision-Making Process on Vietnam Policy."

PIMLOT, JOHN, ed., *Vietnam, The History and the Tactics.* Crown, New York, 1982.

PLOGER, MAJ. GEN. ROBERT R., USA, *Vietnam Studies. U.S. Army Engineers, 1965–1970.* Department of the Army, Washington, 1974.

PORTER, GARETH, ed., *Vietnam, A History in Documents.* New American Library, New York, 1981.

SCHEMMER, BENJAMIN F., *The Raid* (on Son Tay). Harper & Row, New York, 1976.

SCHLESINGER, ARTHUR M., JR., *A Thousand Days; John F. Kennedy in the White House.* Houghton Mifflin, Boston, 1965.

SHARP, ADM. U. S. GRANT, USN, *Strategy for Defeat, Vietnam in Retrospect.* Presidio Press, San Rafael, Cal., 1978.

SHARP, ADM. U. S. GRANT, USN, and GEN. WILLIAM C. WESTMORELAND, USA, *Report on the War in Vietnam, As of 30 June 1968.* GPO, Washington, 1969.

SHORE, CAPT. MOYERS S., II, USMC, *The Battle for Khe Sanh.* USMC, History Division, Washington, 1969.

SHULIMSON, JACK, *U.S. Marines in Vietnam, An Expanding War, 1966.* USMC, History Division, Washington, 1982.

SHULIMSON, JACK, and MAJ. CHARLES M. JOHNSON, USMC, *U.S. Marines in Vietnam, the Landing and the Build-up, 1965.* USMC, History Division, Washington, 1978.

SPECTOR, RONALD H., *United States Army in Vietnam, Advice and Support: The Early Years, 1941–1960.* USA, Center of Military History, Washington, 1983.

STANTON, SHELBY L., *Vietnam Order of Battle.* U.S. News Books, Washington, 1981.

STARRY, GEN. DONN A., USA, *Armored Combat in Vietnam.* The Ayer Company, Salem, N.H., 1982.

STOCKDALE, JIM AND SIBYL, *In Love and War: The Story of a Family's Ordeal and Sacrifice During the Vietnam Years.* Harper & Row, New York, 1984.

SUMMERS, COL. HARRY G., JR., USA, *On Strategy, A Critical Analysis of The Vietnam War.* Presidio Press, San Rafael, Cal., 1982.

TAYLOR, GEN. MAXWELL D., USA, *Swords and Plowshares.* Norton, New York, 1972.

The Marines in Vietnam, 1954–1973: An Anthology and Annotated Bibliography. USMC, History Division, Washington, 1974.

The World This Year, vols. 1964–1974. The Associated Press, New York.

TOLSON, LT. GEN. JOHN J., USA, *Airmobility in Vietnam, Helicopter Warfare in Southeast Asia.* Arno Press, New York, 1981.

TREGASKIS, RICHARD, *Southeast Asia: Building the Bases: the History of Construction in Southeast Asia.* USN, History Department, Washington, 1975.

TULICH, EUGENE N., *The United States Coast Guard in Southeast Asia During the Vietnam Conflict.* USCG, Washington, 1975.

WELSH, DOUGLAS, *The Vietnam War.* Galahad Books, New York, 1982.

WESTMORELAND, GEN. WILLIAM C., USA, *A Soldier Reports.* Doubleday, New York, 1976.

WHITLOW, CAPT. ROBERT H., USMCR, *U.S. Marines in Vietnam, The Advisory and Combat Assistance Era 1954–1964.* USMC, History Division, Washington, 1977.

WOLFE, TOM, *Mauve Gloves and Madmen, Clutter and Vine.* Farrar, Straus & Giroux, New York, 1976.

ZUMWALT, ADM. ELMO R., JR., USN, *On Watch, A Memoir.* Quadrangle Press, New York, 1976.

Index

287

INDEX

288

INDEX

Missionaries, 204
Mitchell, S. Sgt. David, 235
Montagnards, 45, *96*, 204
Moorer, Adm. Thomas H., 260, 262, 271
Morse, Wayne, 101
Morton, USS, 101
MRF (Mobile Riverine Force), 181–84, *186*, 234
Mu Gia Pass, 162
Mutual Defense Assistance Program, 12–13
My Lai, 235–36, *251*

Nam Dong, 90–93, 95
Napalm, 13
National Front for the Liberation of South Vietnam, 35. *See also* Viet Cong
NATO (North Atlantic Treaty Organization), 10
Navarre, Gen. Henri, 13, 15, 17, 20, *20*
Nehru, Jawaharlal, 20
New Jersey, USS, *226*
New York *Times,* 65, 171
New Zealand troops, 133
Nghiem, Brig. Gen. Le Van, 58
Nha Trang, 14, 33, 68, 122
Nhu, Ngo Dinh, 26, 51, 68–70, *70*, 73, 74
  death of, 76–79, *78*
Nhu, Madame Ngo Dinh, 35, 51, 68, *70*, 71, 73, *78*
Nitze, Paul, 144
Nixon, Richard M., 13, *17*, 21, 36, *38*, *222*, 236, 255, *265*
  Communist China recognized by, 248, 257–58, *257*
  reelection of, 268–70
  Vietnam policy of, 221–31
    bombing, 147, 223, 226, 227, 263, 266, 269, 271–76
    Cambodia invasion, 241–46, *245*
    peace talks, 237, 247–48, 258–59, *261*, 262–63, 268–70, 273, *274*,
    U.S. withdrawal, 221, 227–34, 237, 240, 256–57, 265, 267, 278
  Vietnam visit by, *233*, 234
Nolan, Capt. John, *170*
Nolting, Frederick, 46, *48*, 68
North Vietnam, 25
  Chinese aid to, 31, 87, 109
  formation of, 3–4, 10
  land reform in, 31
  map of, 163
  Soviet aid to, 31, 87, 109, 176
  U.S. agents in, 27, 31
  U.S. air attacks on, 98–100, 108–14, 141–47, 161–66, *165*, 168–69, 187, 189, 191–93, 211, 217, *259*, 263, 266, 269, 271–76

U.S. visitors in, 171–72, *266*
  See also Haiphong; Hanoi
North Vietnamese army, 86, 105
  1972 offensive by, 256–65, *264*
North Vietnamese army units
  divisions
    304th, 205
    325th, 118
    325C, 205
  regiments
    18th, 128
    19th, 152
    32nd, 136
    33rd, 136
    66th, 136
    98th, 152
North Vietnamese navy, 97–98

O'Daniel, Lt. Gen. John W., 15
Olsen, Betty Ann, 204
O'Neill, Maj. James E., 68
O'Malley, Corp. Robert E., 129
Oriskany, USS, 110, 166, 167, 168
OSS (Office of Strategic Services), 6–8
Ovnand, M. Sgt. Chester M., 33

Paris agreement (1973), *274*, 277–78
Pate, M. Sgt. Johnie, *62*
Pathet Lao, 40
Patti, Maj. Archimedes L. A., 6–8
Paul, Lance Corp. Joe E., 129
Peace movement. *See* Anti-Vietnam war protests
"Pentagon Papers," *161*
Phu Bai, 122, 126–27
Phuc Yen, 101, 164
Plain of Reeds, 149
Pleiku, 69, 108–9, 112, 119, 122
Plei Me, 136
Podgorny, Nikolai, 266
Potsdam Conference, 6
Princeton, USS, 58, 116, 125
Prisoners of war
  U.S., 86–87, 100, 101, 144, 166–68, *167*, 194, 204, 211–13, *213*, 217, 237–40, 253–55, *275*, *276*, 277–78
  Viet Cong, *57*, *88*

Quang, Tri, 160–61
Quang Khe, 99, 113
Quang Tri, 128, 261, 267
Qui Nhon, 68, 109–11, *109*, 122, 128, 131, 136
Qui Vinh, *113*
Quong Trang, *178*

Racial tensions, 234–35
Radar
  North Vietnamese, 144, 264
  U.S., in B-52 attacks, 162
Railway Security Agency, 59
R & R (Rest and Recuperation), 156

Ranger, USS, 110, 167
Reagan, Ronald, 273
Resor, Stanley R., 236
Rheault, Col. Robert B., 236
Rhodes, John, 246
Richardson, Lt. Gen. John L., 54
Ridgway, Gen. Matthew B., 22
Ritchie, Capt. Steve, 263
Robbins, Barbara A., 116
Rockefeller, Nelson, 273
Rogers, William P., 241
Roosevelt, Franklin D., 3–4
Rostow, Walt Whitman, 39, 43–44, 211
Rotation, 156
Rusk, Dean, 45, 47, 67, 68, *79*, 80, 114, 116, 119, 161, 191

Sacramento, USS, *259*
Saigon, 4, 226
  "Black Sunday" (1945) in, 6
  Buddhists of, 71–73
  Chinese in, 25
  French-Viet Minh conflict in, 8
  map of area of, 103
  1955 struggle in, *29*, 30–31
  U.S. settlement in, 83–84
  Viet Cong attacks in, 106, *107*, 116
  Tet offensive, *197*, 199–201, *199*, *200*
Saigon Military Mission (SMM), 27
Sainteny, Maj. Jean R., 7–8
Salisbury, Harrison E., 171–72, 194
SAM missiles in North Vietnam, 144–46, *145*, 189, 264, 265, 272
Sam Son, 184
Saratoga, USS, 260
Sarit, Thanarat, 40
Sather, Lt. (JG) Richard, 100
SATS (Short Airfield for Tactical Support), 126
Schlesinger, Arthur, Jr., 37, 217
Schmidt, Maj. Norman, 194
Schweers, Capt. Carl A., Jr., *96*
Seabees, 54, 119, 126, 133, 233, 234
SEAL teams, 90
SEATO (Southeast Asia Treaty Organization), 27–28
Shangri-La, USS, 110
Shank, Capt. Edwin G., Jr., 89, 93
Sharp, Adm. Ulysses S., Jr., 90, 98, 101, 118, 128, *186*, 192, 193, 196
Shaughnessy, Capt. John F. Jr., 68
Shimamoto, Keisaburo, 251
Shumaker, Capt. Robert H., 110
Shurtz, Lt. Eugene, Jr., 236
Sihanouk, Prince Norodom, 223, 227, 241
Silver Bayonet, 136–37
Soc Trang, 58, 62
SOG (Studies and Observation Group), 90

290

INDEX

withdrawal of, 231–33, 255
See also Helicopters—Marine
United States Marine Corps units
  brigade, 9th Expeditionary, 125,
    126
  divisions
    1st, 125, 153, 176, *225,* 252
    3rd, 43, 125, 153, 176, 232, 233
    5th, 125
  regiments
    3rd, 124
    7th, 128, 251–52
    9th, 114, 123–24, 205
    26th, 205
  wing, 1st Marine Aircraft, 58, 176
United States Navy, 27, 32, 119, *151*
  attacks on North Vietnam by, 144–
    45, 162–64, 166, 171, 259–60,
    263
  carriers of, in Vietnam service, 110,
    146, 168, 189, 233–34, 260,
    265
  in Mekong Delta, 181, 184, *186,*
    228
  mining by, 187, 262, 272
  in secret warfare, 90
  in Tonkin Gulf incident, 95–102
  withdrawal of, 233–34. *See also*
    Seabees; *specific ships*
United States strength in Vietnam
  1960–1973 table, 35
  1963 withdrawal, 80
  1965 reinforcement, 118–25
  Nixon's withdrawal, 221, 227–34,
    237, 240, 256–57, 265, 267,
    278

Valeriano, Col. Napoleon, 31
Vance, Cyrus, 106

Vanocur, Stanley, 139
VC. *See* Viet Cong
Veth, Rear Adm. Kenneth L., *186*
Viet Cong, 25, 33–35, *34,* 54
  captured documents of, *191,* 196
  desertions from, 176
  after Diem's overthrowal, 79–80
  headquarters of, 111, 149, 173, 244
  prisoners from, *57, 88*
  strength of, 43, 46, 86
  terrorism of, 194, 204
  Tet offensive of, 108
  weapons of, *57,* 87, *88, 151, 183,*
    209, 244
  See also North Vietnam
Viet Cong units
  battalions
    60th, 131
    80th, 131
    90th, 131
    267th, 149
    506th, 149
  division, 9th, 105, 106
  regiments
    1st, 129–31, 152
    2nd, 152
Viet Minh, 4, 25
Vietnam
  early history of, 4
  first U.S. casualties in, 8, 33, 49
  Great Migration in, 26, 31
  reunification of, in Geneva Accords,
    24
  three divisions of, 4
  See also North Vietnam; South
    Vietnam
Vietnamese Air Force, 33, 45, 46, 59,
    61, 67–68, 89, 93–95
  in Da Nang factional fight, 160

Diem's palace bombed by, 51
Vietnamese Communist party (Lao
    Dong), 4, 34
Vietnamization, 229, 255, 258, 267
Vietnam Memorial, 33, *279*
Vinh, 99, *113*
Vogt, Gen. John W., Jr., 260
Vung Tau, *85,* 119, 131, 156, 182

Waldie, Lt. Col. Thomas E., *68*
Walleye Glide Bomb, 184–87
Walt, Maj. Gen. Lewis W., 128, 131,
    151, 160
Wells, Capt. Wade C., *186*
Wells, Col. Joseph B., 11
Wenzel, Capt. James E., *68*
Weschler, Rear Adm. Thomas R., *151*
Westmoreland, Gen. William C., 83–
    85, *84,* 89, *192, 210*
  as Chief of Staff, 211, 235, 265, *265*
  as commander in Vietnam, 90, 93,
    106, *106,* 107, *109,* 111–12,
    114–15, 119, 122, 128, 137–38,
    146, 161, 169, 184
    Honolulu conferences, 118, 131,
      156–57, 168
    1967 recommendations, 190–94
  Tet offensive and, 198, 199
Wheeler, Gen. Earle G., 65–67, *67,*
    68, 115, 118, 191, 192, 209–10,
    210
White, Lt. Col. James S., 235
Whitesides, Capt. Richard, 86
Williams, Second Lt. Charles Q., 119
Williamson, Brig. Gen. Ellis W., 134
Wilson, Charles E., 26
World War II, 3, 6, 8

Xuyen Moc, *117*